Career Ladders for Challenged Youths in
Transition from School to Adult Life

Career Ladders for Challenged Youths in Transition from School to Adult Life

■ ■ ■

Shepherd Siegel,
Matt Robert, Karen Greener, Gary Meyer,
William Halloran, and Robert Gaylord-Ross

Foreword by
Gene Edgar

pro·ed
8700 Shoal Creek Boulevard
Austin, Texas 78758

Printed in the United States of America

Library of Congress Cataloging-in-Publication Data

Career ladders for challenged youths in transition from school to
   adult life / Shepherd Siegel ... [et al.] ; foreword by Eugene
Edgar.
      p.   cm.
   Includes bibliographical references (p.).
   ISBN 0-89079-546-0
   1. Mentally handicapped youth—Vocational education—United
States. 2. Education, Cooperative—United States. 3. Career
education—United States. I. Siegel, Shepherd.
LC4631.C37 1992 993
371.92'82—dc20   91-48273
                                                      CIP

.1679946   1-27-94

pro·ed

8700 Shoal Creek Boulevard
Austin, Texas 78758

1 2 3 4 5 6 7 8 9 10   97 96 95 94 93

To San Francisco

Contents

Foreword

"When you do something, you should burn yourself completely, like a good bonfire, leaving no trace of yourself."

Shunryu Suzuki

"This element of poetry, the delight in exploring the medium for its own sake, is an essential ingredient in the creative process."

Jacob Bronowski

I met Robert Gaylord-Ross in September 1989 at a transition conference in Charlotte, North Carolina. It was one of those immediate chemical connections—we both instantaneously liked each other. We talked of transition, basketball, social justice, rap music, experimental design, family, classical music, and metaphysics. We spent four hours together. We exchanged a few working papers over the next few months and chatted two or three times by telephone. There was one other face-to-face meeting at a large group dinner in Washington, D.C., and then Robert tragically died in December 1990.

Shep Siegel cornered me at a juvenile corrections conference in Lexington, Kentucky, in April 1988. Bright-eyed, bushy-tailed, gung ho, he was full of energy and questions. He was (and is) impossible to put off—he is simply too deeply committed to his work to not take seriously. We have remained in close contact over the years and Shep has not lost his enthusiasm for life.

These two colleagues have conducted their work with passion, insight, and strong, straightforward activity, leaving no trace. They have worked with delight in exploring the task. They are models for us all and this text is a fine example of such work.

My personal journey in special education has taken me through a classic work-study program for mildly mentally retarded students. As a student teacher in 1965, I worked in such a program developed by Jack Dinger in Altoona, Pennsylvania. The participating high school students received half-day instruction in a "watered-down" version of the regular curriculum (I taught *Julius Caesar* and *Ivanhoe* to the students, papier-mâché castles and all) and spent the other half-day in community work-study placements. The program was successful; 42% had annual incomes greater than a starting teacher's salary in Pennsylvania (Dinger, 1961).

But times have changed. Educational philosophy has changed to a focus on mainstreaming. Mildly mentally retarded students are now labeled as individuals with mild disabilities. The IQ cutoff for such students has been set in the low 70s as compared to 85 (Iowa continues to use the old cutoff of 85). Special education seems to be consumed with concerns about access rather than outcomes. And, to be sure, our economy has changed and there are fewer jobs that pay livable wages.

Somewhere along the line the profession has come to ignore work-study options for students with mild disabilities. One of the reasons is that "tracking" is in great disfavor. The current Zeitgeist equates sameness with equity. To take students out of the mainstream curriculum is equated with segregating them, decreasing their opportunities for adult adjustment, and unfairly forcing them to give up their chance to attend college—the ultimate goal of U.S. education. Even data from countless follow-up studies indicating poor outcomes for special education graduates have not stemmed our reluctance to explore alternative secondary options for students with mild disabilities.

To be sure, some voices are calling for serious modifications in secondary programs, but the overwhelming sentiment of the profession is to keep students with mild disabilities in mainstream programs. My personal inclination is to recommend alternative curricular options for these students, but I have been stymied by not having a "ready model" to suggest as a viable alternative. The Career Ladder Program (CLP) now provides such an example.

In the introduction to the CLP model, the authors clearly state their philosophical position that the overall goals of education should be to facilitate more caring relationships between people and to lead to happiness and positive self-esteem. They acknowledge, rightly so, that in our society the only path to such a lofty goal is through employment. The authors also acknowledge the issue of structural unemployment inherent in a capitalistic society and the need for societal change in order to address equity issues for all citizens. These topics cut across disability issues and are deep-seated in the political and economic structure of our society. Thus the problems (and proposed solutions) addressed by this model relate to all disenfranchised youth, not only those with disabilities. But rather than simply commenting on the ills of our society, Shep, Robert, and their colleagues have developed an action-based response to the problems. The CLP offers all of us a way to "do something" rather than to simply sit back and complain.

As with all workable models, the CLP has been based on several underlying principles that serve as benchmarks for the development of specific components and guide the developers in making decisions. While others who plan to replicate this model will have to adapt its procedures, they will need to follow these basic principles.

Individualized response to personality and learning styles is such a cliché that many of us fail to take it seriously. However, one reason notions become clichés is that they are often true! Many of us, certainly myself, fall into the trap of believing that one method or procedure is the best. Even though we give lip service to individualization, we practice standardized approaches. Direct instruction versus whole language, behaviorism versus humanism, modality learning versus skill instruction, field dependent versus field independent—all tend to be viewed as dichotomies rather than continua. To really individualize, we need to expand our professional repertoires and give up our parochial beliefs. This is not a plea for sloppy thinking or a call to "do whatever you want," but rather a recommendation that we all keep a "beginner's mind" about appropriate instructional approaches for individual students.

Employment skills are a complex mix of temperament, attitude, human relationship skills, and specific job skills. Focusing on any subcomponent of this overall mix will not result in a "good worker." Task analysis of these subcomponents is necessary, but instruction probably needs to be directed toward wholeness rather than focused on one bit of the skill.

Family involvement, like individualization, is almost always recommended but seldom seriously implemented. Including family members in decision making is easy when we work with "compliant" families. Working with families who are disagreeable, cantankerous, or consumed with interpersonal problems, or whose values conflict with those of the professional staff, is less satisfying. Far too often we view these families as resistant, dysfunctional, or not helpful. But these are the families who need to be most involved. To do this often requires providing support services (e.g., access to health care, employment opportunities, counseling, or assistance with housing). Providing total wraparound services for families is often the most pressing need in order to ensure students' success.

Possibly the single most important principle of this program is to give students ongoing services after their placement and graduation. In education, we view our treatment as a "cure" for an acute disorder. We attempt to "fix" our students so that they can function in life, unaided by support services. In reality, many of our students have chronic disorders (Kazdin, 1987); to be successful, they require ongoing support services after graduation, perhaps for long periods, perhaps only sporadically. The availability of ongoing support must become an integral part of our service delivery system.

Benefactors are people who care about us, provide us with emotional and tangible support when we need it, allow us to flounder when we need to flounder, and, most important, hold us in unconditional, positive regard. Everyone needs a benefactor. It may be a parent, a significant other, or a friend. Many of our students have no one who fills this role. Facilitating benefactor relationships is as important as teaching reading, providing career awareness, addressing social skills, and making job placements. Is this a role for educators? Of course it is.

Membership in a legitimate group provides people with a sense of well-being, the feeling of belonging, the comfort of social support, and norms for behavior. Many of us drift into such groups, become connected, and experience social acceptance. Others remain isolated, lonely, and disenfranchised. This may lead us to join an antisocial, dysfunctional group or simply to pass through life unconnected and isolated. Our personal quality of life is directly affected by our social relationships, our friends, our group membership. Helping students to find their niche in such groups is a responsibility of our intervention programs.

The CLP has developed specific, detailed procedures based on these principles. Professionals interested in replicating the model will find many examples of each component in this text. Problems in implementation are not glossed over; rather, they are confronted with clarity and specific recommendations. Details are provided for implementing the community classroom and the cohort service delivery model, all of which will undoubtedly need to be modified for local situations. But if we follow the basic principles and are creative in making local adaptations, we will find the gist of the model within the pages of this text. We can no longer lament the lack of a blueprint for developing a modern version of the old work-study model.

Achieving the goal of providing challenged students with a satisfying quality of life is, and will continue to be, a very difficult task. This text and the CLP model go a long way in helping us attain this goal, but without individual energy, passion, belief, and hard work by all of us, our students will continue to experience despair. Without major changes in our political and economic systems, the most innovative programs will struggle to be even marginally successful. But to not try, to not become engaged in the struggle, to not burn ourselves in selflessness in an attempt to make things better, would be a far greater injustice *to each of us* than are the inequities of our society. Robert Gaylord-Ross's efforts will be rewarded if we at least try our best.

Gene Edgar
Seattle, Washington
August 8, 1991

References

Bronowski, J. (1956). *Science and human values*. New York: Harper & Row.

Dinger, J. (1961). Post school adjustment of former educable retarded pupils. *Exceptional Children, 27*, 353–360.

Kazdin, A. E. (1987). Treatment of antisocial behavior in children: Current status and future directions. *Psychological Bulletin, 102*, 187–203.

Suzuki, S. (1970). *Zen mind, beginner's mind*. New York: Weatherhill.

Acknowledgments

The Career Ladder Program was a small program, serving only 127 youths and their families. To them we offer our thanks, for their belief in the program was the key ingredient to its success.

The Career Ladder Program was a large program, bringing together the resources of over one hundred local, state, and national organizations. To them we offer thanks, for the program worked only to the extent that these organizations respected and collaborated with each other:

- To the transition staff of the San Francisco Unified School District, especially the special education counselors of San Francisco's public high schools, Kofi Avoke, Jeff Bruno, Igen Chan, Will Cole, Yvette Fang, Eric Gidal, Mark Johnson, Susan Kwock, Dorian Laird, Mary Magee, Vic Milhoan, Susanna Praetzel, Joanne Prieur, Josephine Richau, Bill Schwalb, David States, Michelle Wagner, and Michele Waxman

- To the California State Department of Rehabilitation, especially Harry Brown, Lisa Eng, Keith Foster, Linda Gamble, Jim Kay, Phillip Magalong, Kate Moran, Susan Muñoz, Rei Nishimura, and Kathy Shields

- To the employers of San Francisco, especially the California State Auto Association and its personnel department, the Marriott Corporation, the Photo & Sound Company, Saint Luke's Hospital, and the University of California Medical Center

- To San Francisco State University and the University of California at Berkeley, especially Ron Morrisette, Adriana Schuler, and John Sullivan

- To the other youth-serving agencies of San Francisco, especially Natalie Lopes and Beth Garvey of Arriba Juntos, Louise Nakamura of the City College of San Francisco, Coleman Advocates for Youth, Sherry Tennyson of the Department of Social Services, New Ways Workers, the Youth Employment Coalition, and Fred Hanson and Gary Fong of Youth for Service's Auto Tech Program

- To Eunice Elton of the Private Industry Council

- To Mark Donovan of the Bridges from School to Work program

- To Patrick Campbell, Pat Dougan, Lisa Hartman-Stie, Judy Hegenauer, and Bob Snowden of the California State Department of Education

- To Edward T. Wilson, Sr., of the Office of Special Education and Rehabilitative Services, U.S. Department of Education

Personal thanks go out to Sherman Anderson, Kristen Bachler, Linda Bourgaize, Deborah Brians, Bob Cipriano, Lyle Engeldinger, Desiree French, Cory Gaylord-Ross, John Greener, Beth Iannazzi, Sandy Johnson, Sam Kaner, Tom Long, Debbie Meyer, Cathy O'Connor, Pat Paul, Susan Portugal, Blair Roger, Suzanne Shaw, George Tilson, Steve Warren, Christine West, Pamela Wolfberg, Steve Zivolich, and all the friends who helped to make the Career Ladder Program a positive force in the community.

Introduction

This book develops one domain of the concept that all aspects of life in our society will be enhanced by a fuller integration of the nation's diverse groups. Along with methods and policies for achieving that integration must come opportunities for enhancing the human relationships found at school, at work, and in our public places. Though the reader will find an emphasis on the efficient management and documentation of a work experience program, the commitment to more caring relationships between all citizens is the underlying theme and purpose of the instructional program. The trend toward two-career families and the subsequent neglect of caring relationships with children drives this point home. We are so busy managing our fiscal survival that our spirits and the emotional nourishment of our children have suffered.

Ironically, the way to a more complete society is a more complete integration of marginalized youth into that very work life. The overemployed, on the other hand, probably have something to learn from the cultures and experiences of those who have been excluded from work. Although these two themes—the costs of two-career families and the role of cultural identity and its contribution in the workplace—are relevant and need to be addressed, this book is about a third necessary piece of the puzzle, vocational integration.

Much has been written and said about the value of work and employment. Those who have failed to achieve a gainful career are also missing out on the richness of having an economic life, the self-respect that comes from being able to earn a decent wage, and the sense of community and personal growth that comes from being part of a work culture—the human relationships that can in fact be nourished in a work, service, or retail setting.

We believe that, for all the virtues of the current market system, it is one that does not naturally support meaningful relationships between people. In fact, it prospers through advertising and the promotion of false needs that substitute commodities for community—that quality of life and intimacy we viscerally know to be frequently lacking.

We believe that through the fulfillment of the potential of social services and by the responsible sponsorship of a democratic government, community can be created. The government can and should sponsor the growth of the intimate and ongoing relationships that constitute true community—first with those in greatest need, and eventually with all its citizenry. We propose that this include but not be limited to the realization of gainful careers, an end to welfare dependency, and full participation as citizens for the disabled, disenfranchised, and disenchanted young people of this nation.

We propose revamping the social service delivery system so that it attends first to the nature of the deliverer-citizen relationship, and then to the meeting of social and economic goals. We believe that these reforms will turn the tide of the economic imperatives that demean us as human beings and subsequently impoverish authentic community and culture.

We have chosen the underemployment of youth as the issue that will give this point of view a concrete focus. Fewer and fewer Americans are able to ignore the underemployment of our young people. Some of the symptoms are so tragic that they are themselves considered problems: substance abuse, crime, welfare dependency, homelessness, and suicide. These horrors would not completely disappear if our young people were more fully employed, but they would begin to. When we speak of employment, we know which indicators must be measured—percentage of time employed, wages, benefits, educational level, and so on—but in our value system *employment* is also a code word for a meaningful life and a fuller sense of citizenship. In our hearts, we all know that meaningfulness, with work as one critical element, is the only real solution to the so-called social problems that afflict us.

There are serious issues surrounding the relationship of meaningfulness to work, but these issues are not the immediate subject of this book. We write this manual under the assumption that competitively paid employment, postsecondary education and training, and ascension up the career ladder are all a part of citizenship, an insufficient but critically necessary aspect of a legitimate, meaningful, and self-respecting life.

There is a serious mismatch between the needs and behaviors of the employment community and the groups who find themselves excluded from it. This is an issue not only of employment skills, but of values. Again, this conflict of values is not the main topic, but it is the subtext that underlies every word. We seek to mollify and resolve that conflict through the teacher's and the service provider's commitment to a higher purpose and by proposing methods for bringing people who have been marginalized into the work world. In other words, rather than directly attacking a negative-outcome ''social problem'' like substance abuse or teen pregnancy, we propose the differential replacement of this type of behavior with another one—an effective and cost-effective work experience and career development service that can function as a vehicle of empowerment and hope. So-called social problems are addressed, but always in the context of serving a positive vocational outcome. Graduates of the Career Ladder Program (CLP) commit themselves to legitimate life-styles and make progress in the search for meaningfulness in their lives. We believe that the only solution to the most debilitating of our problems is through the enlargement of legitimate career opportunities. This means

the inclusion of learning styles, abilities, skill levels, and cultures that are more diverse than those generally accommodated in the work world.

Flattening of organizational hierarchies and cooperative work groups are touted as a necessary path to the economic recovery of the United States. They are also a fantastic opportunity for the integration of people with fewer or different skills.

But the employment of marginalized youth is not simply a matter of creating job slots, nor does it just mean selling the work world and having youth buy into the work aspect of our society. Even if every young person exiting the educational system were to make an inviolable resolve to get and keep a decent job, even if every employer in the nation could afford to offer a decent job to every applicant who came to the door, we would still be faced with the problems of helping these new workers to succeed.

Underemployed youths bring diverse learning, emotional, social, and cultural styles with them to the workplace. The workplace itself presents a social ecology, work demands, and a culture of its own. Discord is inevitable. A model for reducing that discord makes up the subject of this book. When recognition of the true nature of our problems is translated into programs that create real and meaningful career opportunities for underemployed people, when it is translated into counseling services and popular movements that inspire in underemployed people a passion to take responsibility and to venture into the risk of a career, we will still have to deal with job situations where mismatches between the worker and the task occur. In these pages, the reader will find a service delivery model—a technology, if you will—that enables professionals to effectively address these difficulties. The spirit of the Americans with Disabilities Act will become a reality only when students exit school ready to take advantage of the accommodations employers are willing to provide.

Certainly, the activities that go on in the classroom are vital to the career prospects of youths and their development as good citizens. We have no quarrel with the value of the academic learning and social development that occur in school. But the subject matter in this book is the learning that takes place in the community, specifically in the workplace. It is an approach of career exploration, training, placement, and ongoing development. Career-oriented activities for the presenior years can be coordinated with classroom activities to mutual benefit. In fact, we offer a substantial classroom curriculum designed to complement the work experience. However, we have chosen to focus on community-based experiences. This book is a ''how-to'' volume—how to break down the barriers between the school and the community so that youths will feel a part of it and be empowered to participate in it by the time they graduate.

The CLP was a special education program. But the critical strength of special education lies not in its designation of particular individuals as handicapped or disabled, but in the opportunities it affords educators to attend to student variance more intensively. The social implications of Public Law 94-142 spawned a movement that brought a new respect for diversity, and an energetic quest to understand the wide array of behaviors we humans manifest. Even more importantly, special educators brought new levels of competence to systematic methods of instruction and accountability. The implications for improving the education of all children are obvious. Regardless of the future of special education, these advances are part of a contribution that should not be wasted. Consequently, this book dispenses with the language of disability whenever possible. We hope that the model will be viable with many special needs groups such as adjudicated, foster home, immigrant, teen parent, homeless, drug-involved, low-achieving, sexual minority, transient, and dropout populations.

The first chapter is an exposition of six principles that were key to the CLP's success. In many ways, this chapter contains all the reader really needs to know, for consensus on these principles can generate a successful program formatted quite differently from the CLP. These principles form the heart of the matter. We hope that they are convincing enough so that the reader will continue to read and take advantage of the materials that follow.

The rest of the volume speaks to what educators can offer to young people as they approach their graduation from high school. Chapter 2 is the central chapter addressing this endeavor. In it, the mechanics of managing a community classroom are elaborated. The community classroom is the core experience and the crux of the program, but using it is a calculated risk, for if it is not properly managed, interns will actually damage their employability, and none of the other components of the program will be able to function properly. When it is well planned and executed, the community classroom is a powerful introduction to the work world that truly gives the transition from school to work a tangible and meaningful expression.

Chapter 3 presents the curriculum that accompanies the community classroom experience. The beginning of the chapter outlines the posture that the teacher of the Employment Skills Workshop must assume; this is followed by a series of lesson plans that cover an entire semester. The curriculum is designed to accompany a community-based work experience. In a self-contained classroom, these lessons will lose their effectiveness.

Our next chapter stakes out a lot of territory. In it, we describe the postsecondary services that fulfill the commitment first made to the CLP interns during their community classroom experience: ongoing availability of service. As with the other components, we build these services from young people outward, attending to their needs as they arise. The services described are thus a considerable expansion of what vocational rehabilitation professionals usually provide. However, they are always services that enhance and relate to vocational outcomes. In this chapter, the reader will also find our arguments for a reform of day-to-day service delivery, which we call *continuous cyclical triage*, and a dramatic challenge to the overall format of social service delivery, which we have dubbed the *cohort service delivery model*.

In chapter 5 we begin to describe the activities that will enable a staff to develop a community-based vocational training program. Though plans for the previously described components must be in place, this chapter addresses their catalyst: the development of host sites where a community classroom will be allowed to establish itself and offer on-site training to a small group of interns. The techniques for developing working relationships with employers are detailed here. This chapter tries to answer the often-asked question: "Sounds like a great program, but how do you get the employer to agree to participate?"

The volume concludes with a review of the legislative background of the transition initiative and a return to the issues of administration, but this time with an eye toward legislation and social change that would enable the efforts begun by programs like the CLP to expand and flourish. The administrators who wisely commit to an innovative and effective program delegate the decision making to their frontline staff. Consistent with this approach, we voice a call for legislators and policy makers to allow special dispensations to these administrators, so that the seeds sown by such a new service delivery model may take hold. We are proposing nothing less than a more intimate merger of educational, social service, and private-sector concerns with the community they serve.

Six Principles of Effective Transition Programming

CHAPTER

Shepherd Siegel ■

When we visit different cities and towns and school and rehabilitation districts, the consensus on school-to-work transitions for youths who face risky circumstances is clear. Frontline practitioners want explicit and well-structured program components that they can immediately put to use. They will listen to esoteric theories, social rhetoric, and conceptual models, but they know the problems of the front line and the lack of adequate resources to deal with them. They may be tired of outsiders trying to give them the inside story, but if a good plan presents itself, they are ready and extremely eager to put it into action.

This is both good and bad news. The bad news is that the need is so dire. The employability of youths with mild disabilities[1] is still on a decreasing trend. True, America is witnessing a new commitment to education, and American business is making statements of enthusiastic participation. But the "crack" transitioning students fall into only widens as youths leave decaying home lives and pass through schools that are displaced both from those home-life realities and from the work world into which the youths are supposed to be graduating. And every five years, the educational field seems ready to scrap itself and start all over.

Which is also the good news, for it is a misnomer to call education a social "science." In certain domains of learning and cognitive functioning, educational research does accumulate truths in a scientific manner, though at a grievously slow pace. But the field as a whole is a unique cultural activity. It is grouped with other scholarly fields, but perhaps inappropriately so. The harsh and bumpy rides created by the economy, immigration, the sexual and cultural habits of youth, and the myriad of unresolved social tensions create an immense demand on the educational system, which is somehow supposed to be a grounding and enabling force in this maelstrom. No mere science has ever been expected to accomplish so much.

Thus when educators[2] regularly recommit to the renewal of their approaches and demonstrate zest for restarting educational programs, they are behaving with propriety and responsibility. Education is a field

---

[1]Throughout this volume, the population of interest will be identified as youths with mild disabilities, for it is in the context of special education that the model was developed. As the principles of this chapter unfold, the program's applicability to many other overlapping groups of youths facing risky circumstances will be apparent.

[2]The broader term *educator* is used instead of *teacher*, with the intent to include all professionals engaged in the educational process with youths, that is, the process of increasing citizenship. Thus, counselors, job coaches, the CLP personnel described herein, and even adult service providers in the rehabilitation and other adult service fields may fit this definition of the educator. Our deliberate intent is to emphasize the similarities among the endeavors of these various professionals.

in constant flux. It realigns itself with rapidly changing economic and cultural norms and deviances. It nobly aims to serve the mainstream by actuating it to include society's outliers without destroying them. This is not the immediate task of science but rather the task of citizenship.

Could it be done better? Certainly. There are many issues of training, financing, and positioning that cannot be addressed here. But when the failures and weaknesses of education are put up for public display, its urge to reinvent itself should not be counted among them. Only as new programs demonstrate success and the ability to revise themselves in response to changing conditions should they be more permanently installed.

This is why the program described in these pages cannot be limited to a simple manual. Make no mistake, this book will not disappoint the reader's clear request for a structured program. There are lesson plans, forms that can be duplicated, and step-by-step procedures, all of which can increase the employability and the career outcomes of youths with mild disabilities. But the program ''works'' only if the implementation of procedures occurs with a clear understanding of the principles that brought them into being.

In this first chapter, we will define transition, and also answer the question of why it is an important activity. Following will be an explanation of the one overarching and six underlying principles that drive the CLP. We believe these principles to be key to the CLP's success. As practitioners review the other ''nuts and bolts'' components of the program in the subsequent chapters, they will find some parts useful and others superfluous; some activities compatible with their styles and others foreign; some procedures easy to implement and others impossible; and some practices that can be initiated without cost along with others that are prohibitively expensive.

If the replication of this program was defined as the use of only those aspects that were deemed useful, compatible, easy to implement, and inexpensive, no communities would benefit from the same success that the CLP experienced in San Francisco. By the same token, the rigid replication of the model without regard to expense or ease would carry no guarantee of success. But with a deeper understanding of the principles, application of the structured methods explained herein will in fact result in their cost-effective, compatible, and within-the-system regeneration. Every community is unique, but we believe that there are universal qualities to these principles, and that, armed with them, practitioners can successfully adapt the CLP model to most American communities. With their activation in a community-based educational program, the educator can become an involved participant who is effective in the world of adolescents and in the world of work and adult life.

What Is Transition and Why Should Educators Provide Transition Services?

Life is full of transitions, and in this book we are dealing with only one, albeit a crucial one: the transition from secondary school to adult life. However, a program is doomed to either fail or oppress if it restricts itself to the chore of moving young citizens from one box (school) into another (employment). Granted, employment is a critical aspect of citizenship, but by itself it is insufficient. The relationship formed between the transition specialist (see chapter 4) and the participating youth is often a positive one even when it is confined to support for job success; however, we believe that too to be insufficient.

The transition from school to adult life is the transition from less participation in mainstream society to more. Restructured schools may someday change that fact by increasing participation throughout the school-age years. When they do, transition programs will become less critical and unstable. But in the present moment, we support this definition of increased participation. A transition that does not increase the participation and citizenship of the youth involved may still qualify as a transition by some, but it is not the one we committed to when we became educators.

In this broader context, then, the transition specialist engages the youth in a meaningful relationship and develops common goals with that youth to bring more power, meaning, participation, and responsibility into her or his life. When a trusting relationship is developed on that basis, higher employment rates and greater participation in postsecondary training and college will result, but as a byproduct of the communal mission and contract entered into between the youth and the service provider. Work and college in and of themselves are insufficient motivators; they are representations of greater yearnings. It is the variously expressed desires for independence, belonging, self-sufficiency, enjoyment, meaning, and control of destiny that drive youths to succeed. To the extent that our programs can resonate with and respond to those desires, they will engender measurable successes with those youths. This, then, is the overarching principle at work in the CLP: *Services provided by the Career Ladder Program are shaped by the needs of the youths served.*

For the present purposes, those services are directed toward enabling a successful vocational adjustment. The principles may apply to other types of success as well: educational, emotional, cultural, and social. They may apply to other groups of special needs youths besides those in special education—group home, substance abusing, newcomer, adjudicated, dropout, low-achieving, parenting, sexual minority, transient, and homeless.

This means that when the transition specialist enters into a relationship with a youth, there must be a readiness to at least listen and at most deliver services that attend to (seemingly) nonvocational issues. The above listing of other groups of youths with special needs infers the issues beyond learning disability that so many special educators face. Thus, without losing focus on the vocational nature of the program, the transition specialist must be prepared and enthusiastic about opening the window on the relationship so that other issues that are in fact impeding a successful transition into adulthood can be addressed. Two features of the program exemplify this perspective: the affective curriculum that is integrated into the Employment Skills Workshop (see chapter 3) and the overall practice of the transition specialist (see chapter 4).

The needs of youths must be understood and expressed by them. We cannot tell them that a job is their need; they have other needs that must be respected. If we limit what we provide to job placement and support, the success of the program will likewise be limited. Multiservice centers and restructured schools may be able to bring a more compre-

hensive array of services under one roof. This will make the work of the transition specialist a little more convenient and efficient, but it will not diminish the necessity of seeking an understanding of the whole person when engaging a youth (hereafter referred to as an *intern*) in the program. With all these qualifiers expressed, then, let's get to the business of delivering vocational services.

The Six Principles of the CLP

The six principles below are presented as two sets, each with a context, a service, and a tool. A context is the setting that must be engineered to best deliver the service. The service is the practice of the educator, which is always aimed at providing tools. The tool is activity that enables the interns to own the program for themselves, and to continue its principles without the aid or cost of the program providers (see Figure 1.1). The first three principles tend to apply to school-sponsored services during the last year or two of secondary school, and the last three principles emphasize services to youths who have most recently exited the public school system, but all six principles have application throughout the transitional years.

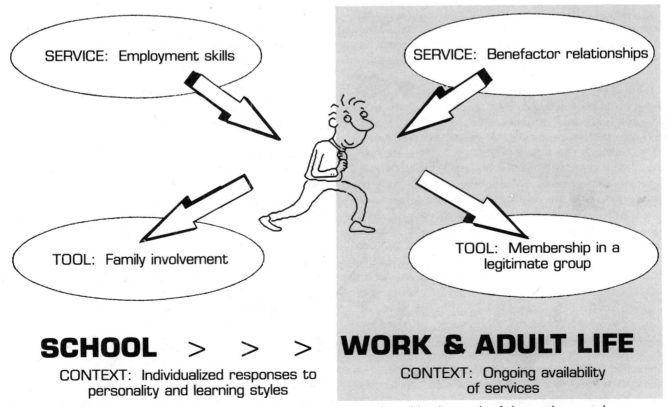

SERVICE: Employment skills

SERVICE: Benefactor relationships

TOOL: Family involvement

TOOL: Membership in a legitimate group

SCHOOL >   >   > WORK & ADULT LIFE

CONTEXT: Individualized responses to personality and learning styles

CONTEXT: Ongoing availability of services

FIGURE 1.1 Services provided by the Career Ladder Program are shaped by the needs of the youths served.

Principle 1
Context: Individualized Responses to Personality and Learning Styles

To successfully negotiate a career, adolescents need the best possible vocational education, including but not restricted to supervised work experiences. Each individual presents a different profile of social, vocational, and emotional needs that must be assessed and addressed. Settling for a standardized approach would result in little more than the success of those who were going to succeed anyway, leaving behind those who have truly special needs. Such a program is actually a waste of taxpayers' money. Only by respecting special needs and offering an individualized program that addresses them can a service make a significant impact on rates of success.

Inherent in this principle is the ability to challenge and not underrate the potential of the intern. Interns feel useful and gain meaningfulness, self-esteem, competence, and employability when the program makes reasonable demands of them. In a vocational context, this means that job placement requires more than job development and occasional monitoring. Supported employment techniques must be utilized to analyze the job and the intern, and to ensure that challenge, learning, efficiency, and competency are part of the experience. In the actual delivery of on-the-job support, interns will perform better when we use systematic and data-based instructional methods to communicate objectively with them, and when we devise means for improving job performance. The tried-and-true special education techniques of objective writing—arrays of behavioral interventions, self-monitoring, and social skills training—are all good examples of this approach. Vocational programming can be further individualized through the development of counseling techniques, life space interviews, team building, and other approaches to an affective rapport with the youth's human environment. (See chapters 2 and 3 for a full development of this approach.)

One young man, John, serves as an example. He was an intern at an insurance company and processed policies 3 hours a day. He was capable of doing the job, but would wander off the task and engage in "doodling" behaviors on scraps of paper. His instructor began measuring John's productivity rate and trained John's supervisor to do the same (after reassuring all nearby co-workers that he was not conducting time studies on them). John was intrigued by the process and by the direction in which the data were moving. Soon he learned how to measure his own rate. Within 2 weeks, all "doodling" ceased, and John's rate approached that of his co-workers.

Principle 2
Service: Employment Skills

The skills most critical to developing an employment record are attendance, social skills, employer-pleasing behaviors, job skills, and job search skills. These can be taught through the systematic address of objectives, social skills training, counseling, job skills training, and job search skills training. Youths need employment skills to develop careers.

In the CLP model, employment skills are taught in an effort that is coordinated between the workplace and a weekly Employment Skills Workshop (chapter 3). Interns learn sophisticated generalization skills that will enable them to hold jobs, engage in lifelong learning, and have successful careers when lessons taught in the Employment Skills Workshop are prompted on the job. Employers can "own" the program too, by sharing responsibility for the careers of CLP interns when they participate in their selection, training, and evaluation.

But when these skills are translated into curriculum goals, we run the risk of losing students the same way we lose them to academic curriculum goals. To avoid this, the interns must own the curriculum goals. They will own them and strive to become better and more independent job seekers and job holders when the curriculum utilizes a process approach and integrates self-monitoring, cooperative learning, and peer counseling methods and principles. The educator's role is to be able to effectively and objectively communicate the quality of the interns' performance.

Maria is a young woman whose experience illustrates this principle. Near the beginning of her internship, she insisted on being transferred to another department at the same insurance company. Her supervisor was racist, so she said, and "had it in for her." During the weekly Employment Skills Workshop, she had a chance to vent her anger and to work on the problems in a group. With the whole group of about 15 youths and 3 adults supporting her, she moved through her feelings to an understanding of the issues. She and the group generated many actions she could take, and from these a strategy was devised: With her on-site instructor acting as facilitator, she would try to engage in this same problem-solving process with the supervisor who so troubled her. The two made peace. In fact, a robust friendship grew, and the next serious problem Maria faced was her reluctance to move to another department when she was promoted.

Principle 3
Tool: Family Involvement

Family involvement is needed because people do not live in isolation. A family that does not support success for its members can easily sabotage and waste the efforts of a service provider. By the same token, it can offer support that critically empowers a troubled youth to mature and succeed.

Families share in the responsibility for the careers of our interns and can be key players in their development when they participate in the mandatory preprogram meeting and go on to sustain an ongoing relationship with program staff, emphasizing positive aspects and confronting areas in need of improvement (see chapters 2 and 4). The CLP finds consistency with a Re-ED approach that views a troubled and troubling youth as only the defining member of an intolerant system (Hobbs, 1982; Siegel, 1988). Transition specialists put this principle to work and bring the key players, usually in the family, onto the team that is developing vocational success.

In instances where a family is not available, other key players, even in the workplace, must be engaged. Sometimes a school counselor can fulfill this function. Sometimes a spouse, boyfriend, or girlfriend will rise to the challenge. Certainly, group home or probation personnel must be involved along with the CLP staff. Ultimately, peer support can take over this "natural support" function (see Principle 6).

One young man, Enrique, though successful at work, had to leave his home when his mother moved out of the area. Only through the extra efforts of his school counselor was he able to maintain a roof over his head. Vo, a newcomer from Vietnam, was forbidden from participating in the program for fear of hurting his chances at college. The transition specialist went to the home, drank tea with the family, and was able to convince them that Vo could work and go to school. With his father's blessings, Vo has gone on to be successful at both. Edgar is a young man who has held jobs successfully, but who, when he lost a job, would fall into drinking and despair. The consistent support of his parents helped to reconnect Edgar to the CLP staff as he struggled through this period of floundering.

Principle 4
Context: Ongoing Availability of Services

Many special needs youths take a longer time to develop trust. When services are always available, they make possible an open-ended commitment, allowing the youths to take the needed amount of time to develop the attachments that will ultimately benefit their career development. Some youths may only need to use the service once, but that one time could occur at any time after their high school graduation. Other youths have ambitions to ascend a career ladder, which means that even though they may be counted as a "success" now, they may want more education and a better job later on and not know how to develop it; thus they have an *intermittent* need for service. A few have special needs so profound that they will actually need lifelong services in order to experience success in the work world. But any youth who knows that some support is never more than a phone call away—even if that phone call is never made—gains the confidence and calmness necessary to venture forth into a career. Continuous availability of services significantly alters the emotional tenor of the typical service provider–client relationship. The alternative is that youths will continue to "fall between the cracks," or will be constantly "passed off" from one organization to another, failing to find the right service in time. Thus there must be some constancy in the resources they are likely to seek.

One young man, Bill, worked for a "mom and pop" store on and off for 3 years after high school. His relationship with the owners was such that he would be fired or quit every few months and would be rehired after a 2-week layoff, which was really a cooling-off period for whichever party had terminated the employment during their regular squabbles. For this young man, the process had a certain stability. His transition specialist realized that the relationship had its own life and dedicated his time to simply making regular visits, building trust by listening, and encouraging the young man to enter a training program where he could learn to change and balance tires and tune up cars, since he had expressed just such an interest. After about 2½ years of counseling, the young man finally enrolled in the course, quit the store job for good, and has been working for a national-brand tire outlet successfully for 2 years. His case, which required prolonged effort but never more than a few hours a month, demonstrates that the ongoing availability of services truly shaped to the lives and circumstances of the people served can make a significant difference to them. Chapter 4 offers a full discussion of practical ways to implement this principle.

Principle 5
Service: Benefactor Relationships

Youths need to be believed in by a benefactor (Edgerton, 1967) whom they trust. This benefactor must understand and be able to marshal the technical resources for engineering vocational opportunity and development, but must also be a counselor who can develop long-term, authentic, and committed adult relationships—alliances and friendships—with our graduates.

The benefactor never disqualifies a youth and fulfills the promise of continuous availability of service. This is the best way to develop the trust and reliability that allows the benefactor to participate in the empowering process. During their floundering period, youths need to know that someone else is watching over them. Graduates will keep their jobs and have the best chance to ascend a career ladder when they have the benefit of long-term follow-up services offered by one or two individuals with whom they can have an authentic adult peer relationship.

Karinn is a CLP graduate who has moved in and out of several jobs since she graduated high school in 1986. She maintained contact with her CLP transition specialist, sometimes calling on him for a new job lead, but sometimes calling just to talk about boyfriends or the difficulty of still living at home with her parents. As she floundered about, the transition specialist was able to help her stabilize, counseling her away from bad decisions regarding the men in her life, enrolling her in a vocational program that would place her in a higher-paying and more satisfying job, and helping her with plans to ultimately move out of the area. Her reliance on him as a benefactor has helped her to steer a relatively safe course through her late adolescence and make a successful start of her adulthood.

Principle 6
Tool: Membership in a Legitimate Group

Youths and young adults need the reassurance of being members of a group of people who are engaged in a similar struggle to assume legitimate adulthood. They are no longer part of a school and often are not able to easily assume a new role as a working adult. Assuming competitive employment does not only consist of applying learned skills; it is also an emotional and developmental process whose success can depend on a melding of affective and vocational education. Members of a peer group where that happens are more likely to actually act on socially beneficial decisions made in the group, and subsequently to reduce their reliance on a social delivery system.

This is the ultimate "natural support" system, comprising not only co-workers and family, but peers. It is not beyond the reach of our educational system to teach the tools of building true peer support among the youths we serve. There need be no fear that continuous availability of services will result in a costly safety net analogous to welfare dependency because the service itself is conscientiously defined as the empowerment of the interns by creating self-reliance and peer reliance. All of the other curricular and vocational goals of the program will be met more satisfactorily when the program is managed with time for the interns to develop meaningful relationships among themselves.

For example, Bill was able to develop a job at the tire outlet for his buddy Jerome, another CLP graduate. Karinn also found a job for another graduate. CLP graduates have been used as guest speakers for in-school interns. A CLP transition specialist formed a support group for CLP graduates who had become parents, generally young mothers. Ultimately, many CLP graduates become integrated with the social groups at their workplace. But the surface has barely been scratched. The potential for support groups among transitioning students is untapped. That potential includes the possibility of peer group resistance to drugs and illicit careers, job networking, empowerment, and collective advocacy.

Conclusion

The beginning of this chapter may have skimmed over the critical second question, "Why should we provide transition services?" but posing that question is by no means a flip gesture. In fact, parts of that question must remain unanswered. If we substitute this chapter's definition of transition and ask, "Why should we provide services to increase the participation of youths in our society?" the answer begins to unfold. Our role as educators is to endow our students with citizenship, and in a democracy, citizenship can be measured by the level of participation people exercise. A career is a fairly dependable indicator of participation. Thus, youths need careers because that is how people develop a legitimate identity and gain economic power, and because to truly assume citizenship at this point in history depends in part upon having economic power. Services at the critical juncture between secondary and postsecondary school life will undoubtedly have a significant effect on the client-citizens' adult life. This is why we must provide transition services.

How intensively and for how long we provide them are more difficult questions that this book will only begin to answer. When are the supports removed and the so-called "fated" forces of our economy and society allowed to play themselves out? It is our contention that the principle of ongoing availability of services dispensed in a manner that empowers the young adult to survive and prosper and to develop "natural" supports is a true one. By this we mean that in a society actively working to accommodate diversity, a great majority of participants in a CLP-type program will have no need—or only intermittent need—of services 5 years after graduation.[3] The remaining 10% to 25% are more challenging individuals, and their progress will depend more on externally related factors in our society, such as the future of the workplace, the family and child rearing, how drug use is modulated, and how powerful the peer support of those who are more enabled may be.

Perhaps the idea of community itself—in a complex urban environment—can be developed and enhanced by cohorts of up to a hundred otherwise marginalized citizens who have one or two career managers working to sustain pockets of cohesion among the group and to provide the kind of liaison, counseling, and support services the CLP has begun to develop.

Whether or not a CLP model is precisely replicated is not the important question. The critical need is for our course to be steered by shaping services to the needs of the youths served, and for us to remember that education's mission is not employability, nor is it academic excellence per se. The purpose of education is to give students the tools of citizenship, those skills that will preserve and develop democracy. When educators have learned how to perform that duty, full employment and intellectual excellence will follow from a youth population that cares about the future of its own society.

This means that we have a lot of work ahead of us. It means that the need is still dire. But it also means that the solutions are within our reach.

---

[3]With a population of youths identified as having mild disabilities, the success rate after 5 years was greater than 90% (Siegel, Avoke, Paul, Robert, & Gaylord-Ross, 1991). The model has not yet been tested in the same way on youths with more severe disabilities or youths who are clearly defined as adjudicated, teen parenting, and so on, though all manner of risky circumstances entered the lives of the CLP graduates.

The Community Classroom

CHAPTER

Shepherd Siegel ■

The core experience of the Career Ladder Program is the community classroom. It is a 3-hour, semester-long, daily work experience. A group of 5 to 15 interns work throughout the business operations at a single work site, under the incrementally faded supervision of an on-site instructor (this position correlates well with what many programs call a job coach). In other words, employers have agreed to open their doors and provide work experiences—paid, stipended, or unpaid—to a defined group of youths who will be dispersed and integrated throughout the work site. In most cases, a regular employee is paired with each intern. Ultimately, the CLP had six community classrooms. (To learn how to convince an employer to commit to this kind of program, see chapter 5.) Implementation of the postsecondary services that follow (described in chapter 4), will result in a significant level of success only when graduates have had the background of the community classroom experience. The Employment Skills Workshop, described in the next chapter, will seem irrelevant and lack import if students are not participating in a community classroom experience that gives the course a real-life context. In other words, the essence of the CLP lies in the monitored work experience we call the community classroom. All the other aspects of the program originate from this experience. It provides the basis, training, context, and human bond that nourish vocational growth.

This chapter will describe many areas of concern and eventualities that must be anticipated and planned for by either an on-site instructor or a head teacher (we call this position the CLP manager) who manages and supervises several sites. This is unlike any other job in that the behaviors of players in a wide-ranging mesosystem (Bronfenbrenner, 1979)—the workplace (managers and co-workers), the school, the home, the transition offices, the payroll system, and so on—must be coordinated so that the intern has a positive experience and so that all the key players also participate and perceive the program positively.

The community classroom experience is composed of three phases: recruitment, orientation, and program. (See Appendix 2.1 for a delineation of these phases.) This chapter describes one approach that reconciled the best practices advocated by the CLP staff with the realities of the community that hosted it. Programs' features will vary by their interaction with the environments in which a user chooses to implement them. The intent of this chapter is to communicate the principles that underlie CLP so that future program developers will apply their wisdom in devising solutions to implementation problems in a way that always orders excellence above expediency.

The guiding principles can be summarized by two questions. Before, during, and after the community classroom experience is designed, the educator needs to face each critical decision by asking: How can I make this experience most closely resemble the expectations and values that prevail in the workplace? How can this event or the program's response to this behavior bring the intern closer to vocational independence?

Often, the creative and clever educator can design a response that is both efficient and educationally excellent. But the professional who truly effects change will frequently have to "go the extra mile" to devise an educationally excellent intervention. Usually, working extra hours to establish and teach the policy of the program in the beginning of the semester is ultimately less work and more effective. By the end of the semester, all interns either are able to meet the demands of the program or have been terminated earlier by testing the limits of what the program can deliver and tolerate.

For example, in the beginning of the semester, an on-site instructor may have to make an extra effort to consistently make wake-up calls to an intern with a punctuality problem. After a couple of weeks, the intern will either start coming to work on time, quit the program, or begin a probationary period. While this seems like more work, the problem will drag on if it is not dealt with assertively in the beginning of the semester; in addition:

1. The intern will not have learned an important lesson in attendance and will be less employable.

2. The policy will have been flaunted and will have lost credibility with all interns.

3. The program will have lost credibility with the employer.

4. The problem will have resulted in more work and aggravation over the long haul.

5. The relationship between the instructor and intern will have become based on an unsatisfying tolerance of a vocationally unacceptable behavior and will have lost its potential for quality.

Recruitment

Outreach and Referral

The CLP recruits interns from nine different high schools and five different alternative public schools. In this situation, the foreknowledge of referring teachers and counselors is critical. They must be aware of the nature of the service offered and must be able to make the best referrals and give the staff useful information. Appendix 2.2 features an initial referral form that asks for information we have found to be critical, such as expected date of graduation, reading and math levels, and availability (time of day). Word of mouth can be a powerful advertiser, and over the years, siblings and younger friends of interns have sought out CLP services. One teacher at each participating school is designated as a liaison and attends an orientation training. These teachers take responsibility for coordinating referrals from their schools and disseminating information to all the counselors.

A program for younger students offers a scaled-down version of the CLP and facilitates referral from within the vocational staff—these are youths we already know. They and others are invited to visit the sites where they can choose to work as seniors; this field trip activity serves to generate enthusiasm, help candidates make better choices, and further advertise the programs. In an ideal situation, middle school youths will have job shadowing experiences, where they spend intensive half-days in groups of three or less on various work sites. Freshmen and sophomores will have introductory "mini-internships" in community classrooms. The community classrooms described in this chapter are intended to serve high school juniors or seniors.

That is the way it worked out in San Francisco: generic referral from all schools to a centralized site, where youths were interviewed and assigned to work sites around the city based upon interest and ability. Site development is taken up in detail in chapter 5, but some perspective must be offered here. This model was developed in the context of an urban setting. Participating employers were necessarily large companies that could provide work opportunities for 5 to 15 youths without creating a segregated or enclave situation. A question arises as to how this model could be adapted to a less urban or rural setting, and one of our experiences suggests an answer. We were fortunate to develop work experience sites in the cafeterias of office buildings that all subcontracted with the same provider, Marriott. Since each cafeteria could only offer one to three internship assignments, we worked with five different office buildings, all within a few blocks of each other. In this way, the original model was adapted, and one on-site instructor traveled from building to building, monitoring interns throughout the day. The principle of never being more than 10 minutes away from each intern remained intact. Similarly, in a less metropolitan area, the community classroom could be adapted by restricting the supervisorial area of each on-site instructor to a manageable radius (less than 10 minutes to each intern). This is a critical feature of the program. Programs that deploy job coaches over larger regions frequently reduce the teaching task to one of "putting out fires" instead of the more proactive and efficient approach of being available to instruct and train. In a nonmetropolitan setting, this efficiency can be achieved by assigning frontline personnel to regions or neighborhoods that they can easily manage.

Still other configurations are feasible. Conceivably, a city could develop a community classroom program at each school, or form partnerships of two or three schools, rather than mixing all schools together as we did in San Francisco. The advantage of complete mixing is that it increases the types of work that can be offered to participating youths.

Interviews

To build credibility with employers and develop a structure that will be able to accommodate higher-risk youths over time, certain requirements and screens have been set up, beginning with the referral phase. Like all phases, it is critical that this one be implemented in a manner consistent with the posture adopted throughout the rest of the program. That is, reasonable demands are made of the student, and policies begin to resemble the work world more and the school environment less. Also, making certain demands right from the first interview does not indicate a desire to exclude any students. Instead, it is set up as an incentive to referring teachers to make sure that all candidates can meet the minimum requirements we set:

1. A good attendance record
2. A demonstrated desire to go to work
3. Family support for the youth to work
4. Previous vocationally oriented experiences
5. At least one job skill (e.g., the ability to alphabetize)

It is not unreasonable to expect that within the near future virtually every high school senior in the United States will be able to meet four of these five criteria. We usually demand that a candidate meet three of them and recommend the setting of this criterion as one (but only one) way to communicate work world demands to the teachers of the 9th- and 10th-grade classes. By the same token, the challenge of planning employment beyond high school is large; by making demands of teachers, we have been able to, for example, increase the number of candidates who come to us with social security cards and motor vehicle department identification, which are necessary for being hired. Assisting in the documentation process is a distraction from the already significant

task of quality vocational training. Candidates must have those certifications taken care of, but this will only happen when the requirement comes in the earlier grades. At the same time, an initial referral checklist (see Appendix 2.3) communicates the special needs of an intern candidate.

There is one initial interview of all students at their high school in order to establish the pool of seniors to select from for both the fall and spring semesters. Students are screened and recommended to the various community classroom site supervisors. The students are offered a choice of sites for which they may interview. Counselors and interviewers can also assist students in making appropriate choices based on their assessed abilities.

Students are then scheduled to interview with the site supervisor at specific times at the Transition Center (see Appendix 2.4). As part of the interview, alphabetizing and typing skills may be checked, and each student is given an application form to complete from the sponsoring employer. Interview questions focus on previous work experience and motivation to work. The job site, job duties, and Employment Skills Workshop are explained in general terms. Virtually all students who arrive at their interview reasonably on time are accepted. Students who are extremely withdrawn, aggressive, or immature may be screened out at this time; they can be referred to a more intensive program if one is available or are deferred until they can make appropriate behavior changes.

A second interview is scheduled at this time with the sponsoring manager at the job site (see Appendix 2.5). The employers have the final say in the hiring process. Up to twice as many candidates are sent as the employer has openings for. This is a critical feature of the program. It more realistically simulates the competition of the job market, and it begins the process of the employer taking responsibility by having participated in the selection of candidates. Job programs that simply place youths in employment settings miss out on this crucial opportunity to teach the realities of the job market, and to have the employer become more involved and committed to the success of the interns.

Enough sites exist so that a youth who is rejected from one site can interview again at another, and we have always been able to find a placement for any youth who is ready and eager to participate in the program. Teachers and referring counselors are notified of selected interns through the mail. Acceptance and notification to the families comes through the mail as well a few days after the interview (see Appendix 2.6). The employer's relationship with the intern at the interview should model procedures outlined by the Americans with Disabilities Act (and respect the confidentiality required by the Individuals with Disabilities Education Act). For example, a disability should be discussed when it might interfere with "essential job functions," and reasonable accommodations should be collaboratively planned between program personnel and employers. Issues of safety to others concerning, for example, intern candidates with arrest records, should be reconciled during the initial interview and screening process, so that these behaviors are not an issue at the employer interview. When the CLP model is used for a population with disabilities, it can become a safe and harmonious "training ground" for the employer and program personnel. Even when the CLP model is used with youths who do not have disabilities, the individualized procedures and respect for individual differences can and should transfer.

Orientation

The Family Meeting

The family meeting is one of the most critical events of the semester. It is during this meeting that the students, who are now referred to as *interns*, and one significant other person in their life will be deciding whether or not to take the program seriously. If the leader of this meeting can make the connection between what the program offers and what the interns and their families want from adult life, then an important alliance will be initiated, and the team that will enable and empower the youths to be successful will begin to function.

A letter has gone out to the homes of the selected interns, congratulating them on acceptance into the program and telling them that this evening meeting must be attended by them and at least one other person, whoever cares the most about their success after graduation. Attendance is mandatory.

Any person who fits the basic criterion of caring qualifies for attendance at this meeting. It should be someone who is of majority age, but siblings, spouses, steady boyfriends or girlfriends, parents, aunts, uncles, friends, and so forth are all acceptable as a significant other, as long as they are stepping forward to assume responsibility. It is the intern's choice.

The main purpose of the meeting is to obtain this demonstration of a commitment by one other person. At this point, the program transcends the school context; it becomes a team effort of the school and the community. CLP's staff now knows that there is at least one other person deserving of credit and praise for helping an intern to make her or his transition.

Now, if there is a problem during the semester, at least one other person can be counted on to help out. These are the people who really make the program work.

The second purpose is to explain how the program operates. There are three main components, which can be explained and summarized: (a) the community classroom, a supervised work experience where interns will work and meet objectives; (b) a weekly Employment Skills Workshop, where a teacher will teach the curriculum that is summarized by the CLP Pyramid (Figure 2.1); and (c) an ongoing commitment to interns who can successfully graduate from the community classroom phase, through the services of the transition specialist.

As the program is being explained, the staff members who fulfill each of the functions are introduced: on-site instructors for work sites; a vocational teacher/manager for work sites and the Employment Skills Workshop; transition specialists for postsecondary services; a coordinator as ombudsman; and advocates (see Appendix 2.7 for job descriptions).

Now that the team has been established and the program summary has provided a context in which the team will operate, the leader can talk about ways in which the family member can help the intern to succeed: by emphasizing at home, school, and work the absolute importance of good attendance and punctuality; by getting the right clothes; by reprioritizing medical and dental appointments and so on, so that they do not interfere with work; by helping with attendance and punctuality problems; and most importantly, by giving emotional support at home—no one has a good day at work every day, and now is the best time to face and accept that reality. Of course, family members must be encouraged to praise and be proud of the efforts of the interns.

The program's staff will continue and develop this relationship with the significant others through phone calls to them a minimum of once every 2 weeks, usually to report on the successes and progress of the intern. The staff are trained to maintain a 7:3 ratio of positive-to-negative messages in phone calls home. When these calls are perceived as primarily a source of praise, the instructor can build authentic relationships with the family and enlist their support if there ever is a problem.

The manager and other staff members explain in very clear terms, and repeat several times, the length of the unpaid trial period (6 weeks), and say that it is followed by pay only if the intern meets assigned objectives (in California, a State Department of Education project, WorkAbility, provided funds for a stipended minimum wage). These are individually developed objectives, job practices, and procedures that interns must follow and criterion levels that they

CLP Pyramid
of
Transition to
Permanent Employment

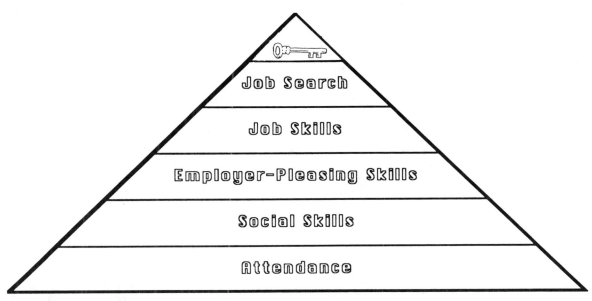

FIGURE 2.1 CLP Pyramid of transition to permanent employment.

must meet. One of the objectives for all interns is the processing of necessary paperwork, without which paychecks cannot be issued. Staff members question the group repeatedly, until understanding and ownership of the trial period occurs: Are they paid at the beginning of the semester? Will just filling out the paperwork get them paid? What else do they have to do? If they meet all the on-the-job requirements will they be paid? What else do they have to do, and so on.

The nature of Vocational Rehabilitation services is explained and the intake process begun. Jobs, tools, clothing, schooling, training, and college services are all part of what Vocational Rehabilitation can do for a person. It's best to clearly lay out and begin the intake and certifying process at this point. Interns should understand that they must, under current regulations, submit to physical and psychological examinations, unless they have a disability that is otherwise medically certifiable. At this point, having a case opened with Vocational Rehabilitation is a required part of the program. If other at-risk groups are being worked with, the criteria of cooperating adult service agencies (for example, income level) should be explained at this time.

On-site instructors repeat for everyone the time and date when they should report to work (the first day of school), and remind them to arrive a bit early. They take questions and comments from the group. They reassure people that they have entered a top-notch program, but remind them that success hinges on their determination to achieve it. They then use the remaining time to let the groups from each work site meet with their on-site instructor informally and begin filling out paperwork (work permits, employment and social security forms, Vocational Rehabilitation intake, etc.).

First Day on the Job

Interns take a tour of the job site. They are introduced to the supervisors at the various work stations. The employee break rooms are pointed out, and interns are encouraged to take their breaks and lunches with other employees. The company's function and history are explained. Interns are asked to look up the phone numbers for their host company and the number for the Transition Center where the Employment Skills Workshops are taught. The interns write down these numbers and are told the importance of calling in if they are going to be late, miss work, or miss the workshop. The rules of the program (see Appendix 2.8) are discussed and questions are answered. Interns may also be given some work tasks to assess their abilities in areas such as filing, data entry, and measuring.

Depending upon the nature of the work site and the new interns' class schedules, their first day on the job may be staggered over a period of 1 to 2 weeks. This can assist in the management of the community classroom and in assignment to different departments.

Interns are finally introduced to their own supervisor and assigned to a department or station where they will report to work each day. The on-site instructor has made these decisions based on the interviews so far and the instructor's knowledge of the work ecology. For example, CLP staff developed some special relationships with sponsoring employees over time, and interns were sometimes assigned to those employees known to be reliable benefactors. Some of our hosts are especially talented in dealing with certain attitude problems, or they may offer a cultural or ethnic identification opportunity that can maximize an intern's vocational growth on the job.

First Workshop

The Employment Skills Workshop is described in the next chapter, but it should be mentioned briefly here. Since the community classroom is in fact the core experience, the first workshop is held after the interns have been going to work for at least 3 or 4 days and have a real work experience to digest. Thus they are oriented to the no-nonsense work nature of the program, and the first workshop has a context. The trade-off, of course, is dependence upon the on-site instructor, the family meeting, and previous vocational training to have sufficiently prompted acceptable behaviors on the job.

Workshops almost always begin with a job-related individual task activity that interns can begin as much as 10 minutes early. The first workshop also emphasizes peer counseling activities that enable the group to begin to form and gain a sense of common purpose and camaraderie, and it offers exercises that build self-esteem. Then, first impressions of the workplace are discussed, and that discussion leads to lessons on how to make a good first impression on others. It is a time for the interns to reflect on the kind of impression they may have made their first days on the job. Finally, the exercise of Welcoming a Stranger can help the interns gain insight into the dynamics that are likely to occur at the job site, and can give them tools for making the interns who will be new the next week more comfortable (see chapter 3, Week 1, for a detailed lesson plan of the first workshop).

Anticipating Common Problems

Attendance is the most important requirement for getting an intern on the path to employability. On-site instructors need to be near-perfect role models, always arriving before the interns. The instructors must move aggressively and quickly when interns are late or absent without calling first. For example, if an intern claims that he or she cannot arrive on time due to the bus service, the instructor should take the bus route to check this out; if it is true, the instructor should work with the school counselor or employer to make a reasonable accommodation. Usually, an earlier dismissal from class can be arranged when transportation problems truly exist. If an intern is not there in a morning program, the on-site instructor should be on the phone within the first half-hour of work. A problem that persists can be solved by calling the home every morning when the intern should be waking up. This is usually annoying enough to other family members so that the intern will begin coming to work on time within 2 weeks. If the same problem occurs in an afternoon program, the solution must be similarly negotiated with the school counselor.

The attendance policy laid out in the CLP Rules (see Appendix 2.8) should be implemented with consistency. In a worst-case scenario, one or perhaps two interns will be terminated for failing to meet the attendance policy; this has a deterrent effect on other interns who are flirting with an attendance problem, causing them to comply with the policy. If staff members do not adhere to the policy, the quality of the training eventually declines to the point where interns will not be able to maintain employment after graduation (they have learned the wrong behavior) and/or the sponsoring employer will terminate participation in the program (the program has lost credibility).

As on-site instructors are making assignments to stations, some errors are bound to occur, and instructors should be alert to a bad match (of either personalities or person-to-task) and not hesitate to make an early change. However, this should not be confused with the situation of a youth who may be experiencing the "growing pains" most people undergo as they enter the workforce. An intern who is "acting out" in such a situation may need counseling and participation in a problem-solving process, rather than a transfer (see the "Personal Growth" section in the Week 4 lesson plan, chapter 3), to address this situation. Appendix 2.9 is a Counseling Checklist that can help the on-site instructor develop a counseling approach.

Sometimes a school or family problem is related to one on the job, and the on-site instructor needs to make a quick investigation and offer appropriate counseling to the intern to help the intern to develop and maintain some separation between her or his work and personal life. On-site instructors can offer assistance, referral, or counseling to other members of the intern's ecosystem so that all will work to reduce discord and encourage vocational success.

For many interns, early problems can arise from a misunderstanding of the rules, nature, or concept of the CLP, and they merely need to have the pay, attendance, or behavior policy repeated for them until they can articulate it themselves and begin to own it.

Referring counselors from the interns' home school generally provide all the necessary cooperation, but sometimes they need to have the program explained to them. Common issues include early dismissal from classes and independent arrival at work. A balanced arrangement might involve school support to obtain accommodating release from the school site, while stopping short of any overprotectiveness that maintains helpless behaviors (e.g., giving interns bus fare or a ride when they need to negotiate their transportation to work independently).

The Program

Working with Employers and Families

On-site instructors have the delicate and complex task of understanding and supporting the social and work needs of the employers. They teach the performance of tasks and respect for the performance of tasks to their interns, many of whom may be getting their first serious exposure to the work world. In some instances, the intern is the first member of the family in two or three generations to have a training and employment experience. Thus the on-site instructors must have a chameleon-like ability to speak the languages of the families, the interns, the school personnel, and above all the employer. Within one workplace, many different employer personalities must sometimes be accommodated. Power in the workplace is not always awarded to people who are themselves well adjusted, and unless the situation is clearly intolerable, the existence of unfairness must be taught and adapted to if that learning is within the intern's reach. The more philosophical explanations, and a process for dealing with the sacrifices we all make in order to sustain employment, are taken up in the Employment Skills Workshop.

The overriding objective is to develop an adult relationship with interns in which the instructor can give them and they will accept feedback that enables them to meet the criteria of behavior—social and vocational—established in the ecology of the workplace. Co-workers may perceive that the on-site instructor is there to accommodate, but she or he must continually emphasize that interns are to be treated like any other employee, and that they are not there to do make-work, or to perform tasks that are not marketable. While CLP's offer of accommodation is maximal—to the point of doing the work for the intern if necessary—the goal is to make every intern independent of school-sponsored supervision by the end of the semester. Employers are encouraged to take over the supervision as soon as possible.

Usually, the on-site instructor has been able to go to the work site a few days before the interns arrive and learn the tasks that they will be assigned. Also, the instructor can make arrangements with the sponsoring co-workers and managers, and can brief them on the interns who are soon to arrive. This preparation phase is especially crucial when the on-site instructor is new to the site; we have developed site-specific mini-manuals to brief new instructors on the idiosyncrasies of each job site (see Appendix 2.10).

The on-site instructor is there to serve the intern, but does so by representing the employer's needs in such a way that the intern can meet them. The instructor provides additional support and guidance if the intern needs it. Interns may have a variety of needs: instructions repeated many times, a task broken down into smaller steps, directions written down, an accommodating device designed or purchased. The on-site instructor is there to be alert to these needs and to meet them. In the beginning of the semester, this means doing whatever is necessary. *The instructor's job for the semester is then to incrementally fade out or transfer that support to the natural supervision of the work site.* The instructor teaches interns to identify and articulate their own needs in a mature fashion, for example, by asking co-workers for help on a task. If there is a serious gap between the intern's behavior and the employer's expectations, the on-site instructor makes an attempt to bridge that gap immediately and then creates interventions that will close it without external support. Often, a situation calls for a task analysis and a systematic approach to instructing the intern on a task. In other situations, a focused and intensive social skills training program is indicated, in which the intern has modeled and then rehearses the appropriate social behavior.

On-site instructors represent the interns' needs by developing challenging job tasks for them throughout the company, recognizing and eliciting their competence in doing their tasks, and advocating for them in situations where the interns are unable to adequately represent themselves. In instances where a disability or cultural difference best explains an inability to perform according to the employer's standards, the on-site instructor will need to be able to educate the employer. These types of mediations are discussed in more depth in chapter 4.

On-site instructors should make frequent calls to the significant others who came to the family meeting. A minimum of 70% of these calls should be to praise the interns for work well done, and for making progress toward vocational independence. When the positive aspects are emphasized, the family member can be an enthusiastic and cooperative key player in devising an intervention if a problem should arise. If there are no serious problems, a positive momentum toward postsecondary success can be built up through the ongoing communication with the home. On more than one occasion, a parent has responded to one of these calls with tears; in 12 years of public schooling, no one had ever called home to report on something their child had done right.

Data Collection and Intervention

Data collection serves a variety of functions: staff accountability, counseling, nonjudgmental feedback, intern involvement, fair grading procedures, appropriate input on Individualized Transition Plans, and documentation for future programming; it is a critical part of good instruction. This section will emphasize those aspects that directly affect the intern at the training site. In the beginning weeks of the semester, objectives are developed for all interns, usually two vocationally oriented objectives and one social objective. Data collection and interventions are the tools with which the on-site instructors enable the interns to meet these objectives.

Attendance and punctuality are the first and foremost areas where data collection serves an important function. If an intern is not meeting the standards set by the program and must be put on probation or terminated, accurate data are essential for making the case to the intern, teacher, and administrator who must handle the transition back to school. Charting attendance and punctuality in a jeopardized situation may help the intern rectify the problem. Most of the CLP job sites have time cards and time clocks, so these data are self-collected and are done so in a manner appropriate to the workplace.

Social skills comprise a domain of behaviors that is more subtle and sometimes difficult to describe. However, research and our experience have identified some social skills problems that typically occur. The CLP ''Quick'' On-the-Job Social Skills Assessment (see Appendix 2.11) is a tool the on-site instructor uses to report back to the manager, who can then develop and adapt the curriculum of the weekly workshop to the social skills needs of the interns. The assessment lists Conversing with Employees, Ordering Job Duties, Asking for Help or Instructions, Following Instructions, Giving Instructions, Accepting Positive Feedback, Accepting Negative Feedback, and Giving Negative Feedback. Certainly, some interns will have social skills needs beyond this short list.

The instructor may decide that each social skills objective includes behaviors that can be precisely defined, observed, and finally counted, by either the intern, a co-worker, or the instructor. These can then be recorded so that the effectiveness of any intervention is quickly noted or a lack of effectiveness eventually detected, in which case the intervention should be modified. For training to generalize social skills that have been taught and rehearsed in the Employment Skills Workshop, the same rating forms (see Appendix 2.12) can be used, and performance of each skill on the job is conveyed as a ''final exam.'' When co-workers, instructors, and interns all complete rating sheets on the same performance, interns and instructors can learn much by analyzing and comparing the three perspectives.

Like social skills, other job-keeping skills such as handling authority, being honest, leaving personal problems at home, and taking pride in your work can be the focus of objectives. If there are persistent problems, we strongly recommend that a key aspect (i.e., chronic negative complaining) be counted and charted in a nonjudgmental way so that the instructor can give feedback that will empower a youth to take responsibility for the problem and its solution.

The job tasks themselves, if they are routine, frequently require a combination of accuracy and speed. To help an intern meet the standards set for an entry-level employee, accuracy and speed can be charted and ultimately self-charted, with criteria goals set at the top of the chart. In the situation where an intern may not reach a criterion level of employability, these kinds of data are crucial to helping decide whether the intern should persist in the assigned task or move to another department. To leave interns in a position for a semester learning something they could never be hired to do is usually a waste of their time and a disservice to their vocational development.

In job situations where the assigned tasks vary from day to day, other approaches to data collection can train competency goals. If the intern has the objective of increasing general accuracy, the percentage of correct responses from a number of different tasks can be recorded on the same chart. If rate is an issue, the number of minutes beyond the expected time of completion can be recorded regardless of the task. If the intern's performance varies from task to task, supervisors can rate the quality of the work on checklists. This can help to identify areas in need of training, or data that can play a role in helping the intern to make career decisions. In one instance, an intern was able to stop his distracting behaviors and increase his rate on a clerical sorting task when he was given the opportunity to time himself and chart his performance. More complex jobs that demand problem solving and independent thinking can sometimes be quantified with decision trees, or addressed with correction and feedback strategies.

Evaluations of intern performance are conducted three times (every 6 weeks) during the semester, corresponding to the grading periods of the school. The form is individualized according to objectives (see Appendix 2.11, Intern Recording Sheet and Vocational Performance Record), but the merit review forms of the host company are also utilized. The first evaluation is usually conducted by the on-site instructor but is based largely on interviews with the sponsoring employer. The employer conducts the second evaluation, and the third is based on self-evaluation by the intern, using the same form. The concept guiding evaluations is to treat the intern just like any new employee at the company, and to request that employers maintain their usual standards. There is no point in saying that an intern is "doing well for a high school student" if that intern is about to become another young adult in the job marketplace, subject to the same standards and conditions as everyone else. Finally, the intern can learn the prevailing standards and apply them in the self-evaluation. This is probably the single most valuable counseling tool to see whether an intern is aware when he or she is not meeting employer expectations.

Data are pieces of information and can take many forms. A journal that is precise and avoids judgmental language can be as useful a source of data as charts and diagrams. The on-site instructor cannot balk at the task of configuring and counting behaviors and should be comfortable in the role of data taker. When designing interventions, the on-site instructor asks: Is the description precise, objective, and nonjudgmental? Is it in a form that is useful to the intern and to other instructors? Does it indicate strengths as well as areas in need of improvement? Are the data measuring behaviors that are relevant to the vocational independence of the intern?

Finally, data collection during the training period can teach an intern habits that will help when she or he embarks on a job search. Keeping track of the number of job leads, job interviews, and so forth can help maintain morale in this often frustrating process. If an intern knows ahead of time that it usually is necessary to follow up on fifteen job leads before a job is obtained, that intern will take pleasure in "beating the odds"; collecting data during the process will help keep the intern organized and build in satisfac-

tion. Many excellent resources on developing data-based applied behavioral interventions are available elsewhere and are not described here. However, Appendix 2.11 contains the data-collection tools developed for CLP on-site instructors.

Phases of the Training Semester

The semester is divided into three phases—the initial, middle, and ending weeks—and this section will help on-site instructors and managers to anticipate some of the moods and chronic events that typically accompany each phase. A timeline that the manager gives to the on-site instructors (see Appendix 2.13) serves as a summary of their duties and also corresponds to the chronology this section describes.

Initial Weeks

In the beginning of the semester, the on-site instructor is assiduously conducting evaluations of the interns' abilities and disabilities and shuffling placements. In some settings, most if not all interns are placed in one department for the first week or so and then assigned to the cosponsoring departments according to the assessment of their independence and ability to perform the tasks. Those in need of more supervision stay closer to the on-site instructor. Out of this assessment comes two work objectives and at least one social objective that address the job and social skills the interns will need to develop.

Attendance and punctuality are heavily emphasized, and the demand for high standards is made at this time. Sometimes interns will drop out or be terminated at this early stage if they cannot come to work consistently and on time. Good attendance and punctuality are most of what is required at this point in the semester, and failure to make the grade is not tolerated. Many interns will go through a "honeymoon" period, getting through the initial weeks but developing attendance problems during the middle weeks. Though an intern will not go on probation until he or she has had eight absences, a flag should go up after two or three absences in the very beginning weeks and the referring counselor and host teacher should be notified.

Within the first 2 weeks of the program, the family contact is called on the phone for the first progress report—almost always a positive one—and to establish what will be a cooperative, ongoing relationship. Good attendance should be praised and the priority of work reinforced.

In CLP, interns are paid a minimum wage through a statewide fund called Project WorkAbility. During the first 6 weeks, all interns are in an unpaid trial period.[1] This is why the objectives are so important. Graduation from the trial period into pay is based upon meeting objectives or making reasonable progress on them. This develops the concept of earning. Also, the unpaid trial period is a time to teach and learn about the rewarding aspects of work other than pay. We contend that anyone who works only for pay will not experience job or life satisfaction, and so, in these first weeks, we consider pay a distraction. Clearly, we do not condone exploitation through a manipulation of the volunteerist ethic. But we sincerely do believe that interns have much to gain from a period in which they cannot justify working simply as a way to get a paycheck. The trial period is a time for them to search, find, and express deeper and more satisfying reasons for wanting to participate in the work life of their community, such as pride, self-respect, participation, learning, community, friendships, contribution to society, and development of more lofty career goals.

Another aspect of CLP's particular pay program is the extensive amount of paperwork getting on the payroll entails. The skill of filling out forms is valuable, and understanding that paychecks cannot be generated without the proper paperwork is an important reality lesson. Interns need to already have social security cards and motor vehicle department identification, as the CLP staff is significantly affected by the organizational tasks of all the other paperwork demanded by the school district. Such preliminaries to working must be addressed in the earlier grades.

Finally, the end of this trial period signifies that the intern is actually making progress, is at least closer if not at the level of a typical entry-level employee with the sponsoring company, and has earned a paycheck.

Middle Weeks

The middle weeks make up the time period when the challenges of dealing with routine will be met by the interns. This is the time when stamina will be learned, when negative first impressions an intern may have made on the job can be reversed, and when the follow-through on positive first impressions can be reinforced. It is the time when a host employer may decide to hire an intern after graduation.

The first signs of tedium, which many experience at work, may emerge at this point. If the on-site instructor determines that the assigned job is nonetheless a good match, then an intervention to enable the intern to deal with these feelings and behaviors is called for. If attendance starts to slack off, breaks go on too long, or the intern starts showing up late for work, the on-site instructor should inform the CLP manager as soon as this appears to be a problem, and they may then consult to devise a strategy. Every individual is different, and there are many possible interventions, including calling the family and asking for their support; enlisting the employer as a confederate to articulate the demands of the workplace and set limits; counseling the intern and coming up with a contract, formal or informal; transferring the intern (though this is rarely recommended); putting the intern on probation; increasing or restructuring the work load; and analyzing with the intern the broader social arrangements that make it necessary for the intern to excel in this job.

We have heard interns tell us that their work is boring, that they are always given the dirty or most menial work, and that the work they are assigned is not essential to the business operation. Sometimes these complaints have merit. In a training program such as this, the staff are obliged to seek a challenging work opportunity that will advance the vocational potential of the interns, and the instructor needs to self-check on this principle. On the other hand, dealing with the tedium that many workers experience is one of the lessons offered, as is the fact that new and entry-level employees are often given the most menial tasks. Each situation is different, and the on-site instructor must perform a delicate balancing act. In addition, the instructor's job is to protect interns from exploitation, and while teaching job-keeping skills, the staff must also stay alert to exploitative situations.

During the middle weeks, job task rotation becomes a powerful instructional tool. In the instances where an intern is in a situation beyond her or his abilities, a social difficulty has not been resolved, or an intervention has not helped the intern to reach criterion, a transfer to another department may be appropriate. In the instances where an intern has excelled but the

---

[1]Unpaid work experience must be conducted in compliance with Department of Labor regulations (see chapter 6 for more discussion of this topic). In essence, this means that interns must not go into "production" to the point where the employer is obtaining free labor from the interns or other workers are being displaced from their jobs. Thus, the interns must be in either a learning or a training mode, in which they have not mastered the skill and the employer is expending resources to train them or work that they do must be "undone." We definitely support the ongoing learning of new skills throughout this 6-week probationary period. Once the intern is paid, by either the employer or a subsidy (like California's WorkAbility program), he or she may go into "production."

likelihood of a hire is low, or where the intern has mastered all the objectives, a transfer to another department can function like a promotion and can enrich the training experience. To maximize the likelihood of a hire after graduation, our very best interns are sometimes transferred to another company entirely—called a "satellite site"—with minimal supervision; even if the intern is not hired, maximal vocational independence will have been achieved.

Another educational aspect of transfer/promotion is that interns relearn how to enter a new situation. Many of them protest their transfers, but it is a lesson in an event that is likely to happen later in their career as well as practice for the inevitable transfer out of the community classroom and into the competitive work world.

Final Weeks

If the intern has not established a record of competence and dependability by the final weeks, it is usually too late to do so. Attendance and social problems may still occur, as the pressures that lead to them may have only been building, but not expressed, until now. In these cases, however, if a good track record has been established so far, the value of preserving it can be very convincing and can help the intern face situations with more maturity.

If there are interns who clearly are not likely candidates for hiring at the host company (regardless of whether or not there are openings), this is a last-chance but powerful opportunity to collect employer feedback and communicate to those interns the job-keeping skills they still need to develop. This is a difficult message to convey, but it is given at a time when an intern is open to hearing it and thus represents an educational opportunity that should not be missed.

School activities frequently punctuate the final weeks of the semester. On-site instructor supervision, in most cases, is nonetheless minimal, allowing the natural supervision of the workplace to take over. Some interns will, however, continue to need assistance and counseling. Because a top priority of the program is job placement, interns will be released from work to go to job interviews, conduct job searches, or meet with appropriate adult service agencies. In the fall semester, on-site instructors find out the high school completion status of each intern, to see which of them can take on a part-time job without jeopardizing their graduation.

When an intern is to be released for another job or a job search, employers should be given plenty of advance notice. An employer who complains about losing an intern should be encouraged to hire the youth. By this point in the semester, interns should have been trained in how to inquire about openings at the host site, or the on-site instructor should do this for those whose job search abilities are limited. Interviews should be arranged for top candidates. Those who are unlikely to be hired should be given the highest priority for developing a job search strategy.

CLP was originally structured to serve high school seniors, so the final weeks of the spring semester have always been difficult due to the celebratory activities that accompany graduation. One solution to these inherent problems is to serve seniors in the fall semester only, and juniors in the spring. This permits "senior-itis" to run its course and saves interns some of the conflicts that often arise between work and school activities at this time of year. To preserve the good work attendance records of our interns, the community classroom experience was shortened in the spring.

Another advantage of this configuration is that seniors can and should be ready to develop real jobs for themselves. They are offered a thrice-weekly job club, in which they share tales of job searches, network among themselves, share and develop job leads, prepare résumés and applications, rehearse interviews, and go out on supported job searches.

Supported job searches are for those youths who are capable of seeking out a job lead and passing a job interview, but who need some extra support to actually go out and do it. An on-site instructor will travel to a potential job and wait outside while the youth goes in to ask for an application or interview. The instructor also helps interns develop the leads and make cold calls. Youths who are known to be good workers but who may be handicapped by their inability to do a job search or handle an interview may actually have a job developed for them. A curriculum for a job search is described in chapter 3, and techniques of on-the-job support for those who obtain employment are discussed in chapter 4. It is expected that a few, and perhaps many, community classroom interns will seek and find jobs before the end of the training semester, graduating from the community classroom early, so these training and placement skills are definitely within the duties of the on-site instructor.

Postsecondary activities will be enabled and monitored by the transition specialist. Having visited the community classroom and the Employment Skills Workshop, the transition specialist has had a chance to start getting to know the interns. At this point, the on-site instructors brief the transition specialist, who can complete the case-opening procedures for the interns and begin working with those most in need. Thus the trauma and risk of the "pass-off" can be minimized. All efforts are made to make the process a friendly one and to allow the interns to see the on-site instructor, transition specialist, and manager as part of the same team. As graduates, the interns will continue to have access to that entire team. All staff have thus been identified as caring adults who are available to help the interns achieve career goals. The community classroom has introduced the interns to a real work experience and to valuable contacts in the work world. They understand the concept of work in an abstract way that has become part of themselves, in a concrete way through the work experience, and in an interpersonal way through the co-workers and professionals they have gotten to know during the training process.

Appendix 2.1
Community Classroom Flow Chart

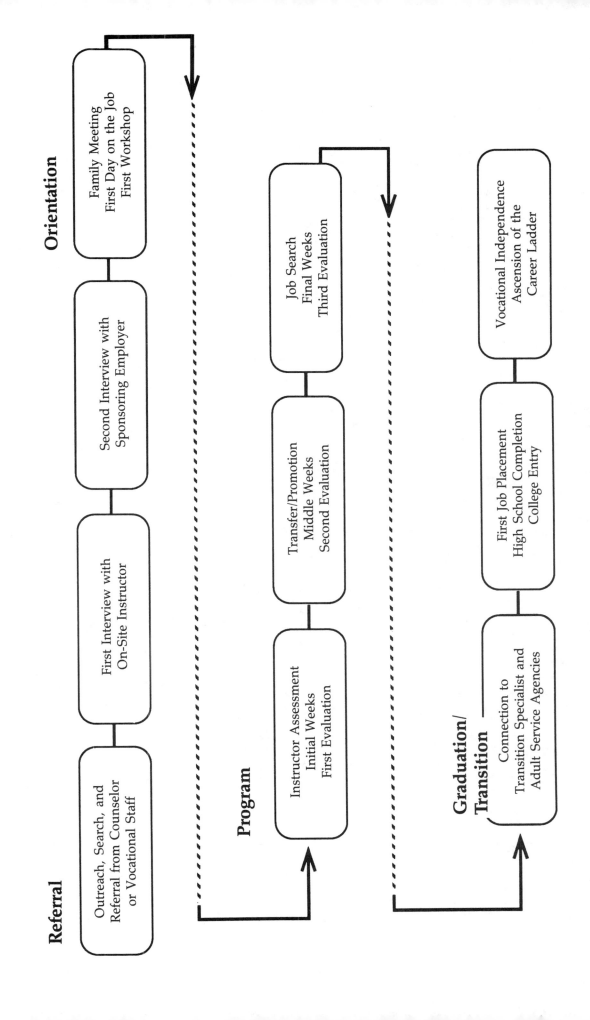

Referral

Outreach, Search, and Referral from Counselor or Vocational Staff

First Interview with On-Site Instructor

Second Interview with Sponsoring Employer

Orientation

Family Meeting
First Day on the Job
First Workshop

Program

Instructor Assessment
Initial Weeks
First Evaluation

Transfer/Promotion
Middle Weeks
Second Evaluation

Job Search
Final Weeks
Third Evaluation

Graduation/Transition

Connection to Transition Specialist and Adult Service Agencies

First Job Placement
High School Completion
College Entry

Vocational Independence
Ascension of the Career Ladder

Appendix 2.2
Initial Referral for Special Education Vocational Services

The following is an initial referral for special education vocational services. Our goal is to offer a vocational experience for students from any special education program within the district. The vocational staff will contact you for additional information to assist in student placement. Through this initial referral, students 16 years old or over could be accepted into the Career Ladder Program:

Student: _____ Birthdate: _____ Parent: _____

Home phone: _____ Counselor: _____ Phone/ext.: _____

Disability: _____ RSP SDC Expected grad. date: _____

Grade: _____ School: _____ Reading level: _____ Math level: _____

Previous job training/experience and goals: _____

_____

_____

Reason for referral/IEP or ITP goal: _____

_____

Will the student be able to work during the school day? _____

What are the best times for the vocational staff to contact you for additional information

about the referred student? _____

Please return this form by _____ to: The Transition Center
                                                 1441 10th Avenue
                                                 San Francisco, CA 94112

Additional comments: _____

_____

_____

Appendix 2.3
Referral Checklist

The referred student is particularly strong
or in need of assistance in the following areas:

Dealing with the public congenially				
Handling pressure				
Clear speech and language				
Eye contact				
Making friends				
Working with others				
Accepting criticism				
Resisting peer pressure				
Willingness to try new things				
Asking for help when needed				

Attendance				
Punctuality				
Awareness of safety				
Ability to make decisions				
Attention to task >5 minutes				
Attention to task >20 minutes				
Performing tasks at a consistent rate				
Attention to detail				
Working without supervision				
Performing repetitive or unpleasant tasks				

Memory of a motor task				
Memory of a rule (work or behavior)				
Ability to follow 1-step direction				
Ability to follow 2-step direction				
Ability to follow 3-step direction				
Ability to control hyperactivity				
Ability to screen out distractions				
Consistent behavior day-to-day				
Comprehension of spoken instructions				
Comprehension of written instructions				
Comprehension of modeled instructions				
Ability to alphabetize				
Ability to put in numerical order				
Ability to copy words and numbers accurately				
Ability to write a spoken message down accurately				
Ability to write legibly				
Coordination and dexterity				

Appendix 2.4
Referral: First Interview Notification

John Smith
Mary Jones
Career Ladder Program

November 2, 1992

Dear _____ :

Congratulations! You have been selected to interview for the Career Ladder Program. Please come to the Transition Center at 1441 10th Avenue, downstairs, at _____ on _____ . We recommend that you arrive five to ten minutes early. If you cannot make this time, call Mary Jones at 555-4979 immediately. See you there!

Sincerely,

John Smith   Mary Jones
CLP Coordinator   CLP Manager

Appendix 2.5
Second Interview Notification

John Smith
Mary Jones
Career Ladder Program

November 20, 1992

Dear _____ :

Congratulations! You have passed your first interview for the Career Ladder Program. The next step is your second interview with the corporate sponsor at the site you have selected. Your interview is with this company:

_____

at this address: _____

at this date and time: _____ .

Arrive five to ten minutes early, and ask for

_____ .

Bring your completed application with you. If you pass this interview, we will invite you to participate in the program and will ask to meet with you and one other person who is close to you. If there will be any problem making your interview, please call us immediately at 555-7851 between 8:30 A.M. and 3:30 P.M. If we are not there, please leave a message. Thank you and good luck!

Sincerely yours,

John Smith   Mary Jones
CLP Coordinator   CLP Manager

Career
Ladder
Program

Appendix 2.6
Final Acceptance and Notification of Family Meeting

John Smith
Mary Jones
Career Ladder Program

December 4, 1992

Dear _____ :

Congratulations! You have been selected as a candidate for the Career Ladder Program. If you are successful, you will have the chance to get job training for school credit. Even more important, the Program will do everything it can to help you develop your career after you graduate.

If you want to remain eligible, you must attend a meeting where you will receive an introduction to the Program. Please bring with you the person who cares most about your success after high school. We would be happy to meet with a parent, brother or sister, aunt or uncle, or anyone over 18 who is close to you and will continue to be in your life after high school.

The meeting will take place on Wednesday, December 16, at 7:30 P.M., in Room 107 at Abraham Lincoln High School, 2122 25th Avenue. If you cannot make it, please leave a message for Ms. Jones at 555-2190 or Mr. Smith at 555-1161, during business hours. If you do not come to the meeting, or you do not call, we will have to disqualify you from the Program, so please come to find out more. We are eager to meet you and your family, and we wish you the greatest success and fortune.

Sincerely yours,

John Smith   Mary Jones
CLP Coordinator   CLP Manager

Appendix 2.7
Job Duties of CLP Staff Members

CLP On-Site Instructor

I. On-the-job training
- A. Prepare work site
  1. Supervision
  2. Tasks
  3. Fading plan
- B. Instruct and fade
- C. Make written evaluations—objective and behaviorally stated
  1. Goals
  2. Social skills
  3. All other relevant factors

II. Work with entire ecosystem
- A. Student
- B. Family
- C. Employer
- D. Peers
- E. Relevant agencies

III. Maintain positive images
- A. Self
- B. Student
- C. Program

IV. Facilitate job searches

V. Join the team
- A. Report to manager
- B. Work with transition specialist
- C. Work with coordinator
- D. Attend and participate in staff meetings

VI. Help in Employment Skills Workshop (seminar)

VII. Process paperwork

Career
Ladder
Program

CLP Head Teacher/Program Manager

I. Supervise on-site instructors
   A. Provide timeline; monitor
   B. Facilitate/consult on behavioral, vocational, and social intern objectives
   C. Consult on employee relationships
   D. Train in supported job search techniques
   E. Communicate information on meetings and other activities
   F. Orient new staff

II. Teach Employment Skills Workshop
   A. Prepare and develop curriculum; preview with project coordinator
   B. Outline workshop duties for on-site instructors
   C. Coordinate job searches

III. Supervise transitions
   A. Brief transition specialist
   B. Identify interns in need of more intensive support
   C. Coordinate postsecondary services: city college, Department of Vocational Rehabilitation, temporary employment, and so on
   D. Process WorkAbility paperwork

IV. Recruit new interns
   A. Solicit referrals from all high schools
   B. Conduct initial interviews; screen
   C. Set up employer interviews; consult and screen with employers
   D. Set up parent meeting, orientation

V. Develop program
   A. Collaborate with project coordinator on presenior trainings
   B. Develop new sites
   C. Construct plans to increase success rate and number of students served

CLP Transition Specialist

The transition specialist assumes responsibility for the career development of youths who are exiting school and have succeeded in the Career Ladder Program community classroom as high school seniors. These duties are explained in detail in chapter 4.

I. Visit sites

II. Visit Employment Skills Workshop

III. Develop curriculum, provide Department of Vocational Rehabilitation curriculum for 10-key, job search, and so on

IV. Follow up on former interns
   A. Consult with current employers
   B. Facilitate job search or postsecondary school
   C. Train, retrain, and mediate on-the-job problems
   D. Maintain follow-up statistics

V. Expand and coordinate job club with program manager/head teacher

VI. Initiate contact with previous fall interns in late spring

VII. Coordinate rehabilitation case openings and closures

VIII. Conduct job search with current interns

IX. Write monthly reports

X. Attend staff meetings

XI. Collect assessment data

XII. Deliver transition services (see chapter 4)

XIII. Perform other duties as assigned by case worker and project coordinator

CLP Project Coordinator

When the Career Ladder Program is replicated by a school district or similar organization, the project coordinator's duties should be assumed by an administrator and adapted to that change as needed. This job description was written to fit the situation of a model demonstration project and a university/school district collaboration.

I. Maintain liaisons between university, Department of Rehabilitation, unified school district (USD), and host employers
   A. Contact USD administrators regularly; consult before changing policies and plan future of program collaboratively
   B. Conduct site visits with employers and host employees; get informal feedback on acceptance of program and attitudes toward it; consult before changing policies that will affect the site; advocate for students and processes of formalizing student placement in permanent jobs; aid program manager in development of new sites and negotiations in current sites when necessary
   C. Provide ongoing services and appropriate research findings to staff, district, and employers; facilitate appropriate applied research efforts at CLP sites; provide internships for special education university students

II. Provide leadership for CLP staff
   A. Review program manager's performance and delegate responsibilities
   B. Select new staff in collaboration with district; facilitate orientation of new staff; maintain regular contact with staff, primarily through staff meetings; maintain close advisory relationship with program manager; review and evaluate staff performance; terminate staff in collaboration with district when necessary
   C. Advise staff on instructional methods, on-site problems, site development, job placement strategies, and intern assessment

III. Develop and manage program policy
   A. Communicate with interns and develop role model of work instructor; maintain worklike environment of program
   B. Develop philosophy and set CLP policy: targeted populations, pay issues, school credit, liaison with other programs, parent and community policy, and so on
   C. Set guidelines for intern selection collaboratively with district and program manager; advise on site placement, movement, and termination of interns when necessary; review social and vocational objectives of interns, revise when necessary; provide guidance and instructional technology for training and attaining intern objectives; set objectives for Employment Skills Workshop; advocate and direct strategies for job placement

Appendix 2.8
Career Ladder Program Rules

Interns who are going to be absent must call in to the work site ahead of time.

Interns must follow the dress code at work. Interns are requested to remove heavy coats and hats.

Interns cannot borrow money either from other employees or the on-site instructor.

Interns are allowed a 15-minute break.

No portable radios or tape players are allowed during the Employment Skills Workshop. Their use is determined by supervisor discretion on the job site.

Interns are advised not to bring valuables to work.

No eating in the workshop or at work unless on break.

Interns do not lose pay for visits related to the Department of Rehabilitation that are during work hours.

Attendance Policy

Five excused days absent in one semester allowable (interns must call in).

Every 2 days over 5 days absent: one-half grade lowered.

Eight days missed: intern is on probation.

Ten days missed: intern is terminated.

Parents and teachers must be contacted if intern has missed over 3 days in less than 2 months.

One unexcused absence: one grade lowered.

Two unexcused absences: pay is docked.

Three unexcused absences: probation.

Four unexcused absences: intern is terminated.

© 1993 by PRO-ED, Inc.

Appendix 2.9
Counseling Checklist

Intern: _____

On-site instructor: _____

Date: _____ Site: _____

1. Did the intern apply suggestions from the last session?

2. Did the intern receive and understand the current feedback as well (how did the intern express this)?

3. Did the intern review self-monitoring? objectives? recording sheets? graphs?

4. Did the on-site instructor discuss strengths (reinforce)?

5. Did the on-site instructor address weaknesses or areas in need of improvement?

6. What specific advice did the on-site instructor provide?

7. How does the on-site instructor feel about the intern's overall job performance?

8. How does the intern perform relative to the regular employees?

9. Was a problem-solving approach used in the counseling session?

10. Was role playing used successfully in terms of behaviors performed and understanding?

11. What ecological interventions are being used in concert with the intern?

12. Have all the data been updated in the on-site instructor's notebook?

Appendix 2.10
Orientation to Lights and Action

by Eric Gidal

In determining one's role as an on-site instructor at any of the sites, it is important not only to understand the basic job description but to gain knowledge about the work site itself. The following is written to assist a new instructor at Lights and Action in getting to know the work site and the various dynamics therein. As a new instructor myself this year, such a guide would have been extremely helpful and I hope any new instructor will take time to read this orientation document.

I would also recommend that the instructor take about 2 weeks before the start of the school year to become familiar with the company and the people who work there, to get a feeling for the jobs required of the interns, and to plan with the supervisors possible long-term projects for the interns. The school district will allot the 2 weeks' pay to enable the instructor to do this.

This year [1988–1989], we had interns in three departments: Rental and Convention Services, Service, and Parts and Supplies. Each department works differently and the interns' duties and responsibilities vary as well. Accordingly, the instructor's role in each of the departments will differ in several respects.

The rental and convention services department has three internships and the interns are given a wide variety of tasks. These include checking and cleaning equipment, organizing equipment on the shelves, some inventory of parts and equipment, occasional paperwork, helping to load and unload equipment onto and from vans, assisting in deliveries of equipment, and general cleanup work. There is no daily routine. Things are done when they need to be done, and some days are very busy while others are painfully slow. The atmosphere in the department in terms of job task assignments is loosely organized and the interns therefore need to be able to put out a good amount of initiative in order to stay busy and get assigned to the more interesting job tasks.

This atmosphere requires the instructor to help supervisors develop job tasks for the interns and to keep on top of what needs to be done so that he or she can have work for the interns on occasions when there is no supervisor present. It also requires the instructor to act as a backup supervisor, particularly at the beginning of the semester, in order to provide the necessary amount of structure to enable the interns to succeed. Once the interns have acquired the concepts of initiative and keeping busy, this role can be faded out.

There were two internship positions in the service department this year, a clerical assistant and a technical assistant. The clerical assistant is responsible for filling service reports, calling clients when services have been completed, answering the phone, directing calls, and entering data in the computer. Occasionally, other tasks may be assigned but the duties remain relatively constant. This intern is given a good amount of one-on-one supervision from Marcia Palermo and therefore the instructor does not need to take a very strong supervisory role. Where the on-site instructor is needed, however, is in reinforcing instructions; Marcia is very busy and does not have the time to go over instructions repeatedly or give extra training in the above-mentioned tasks. What worked well this year was keeping in contact with Marcia and, when the intern was having difficulty in a certain area, working out a time we could spend together in the front office space or providing some backup training (i.e., in answering phones and taking messages) during the Employment Skills Workshop.

The second internship in the service department is a real jack-of-all-trades position. The duties range from organizing parts and labeling catalogs to helping disassemble computers and video equipment. The intern this year has also had opportunities to help set up computer hardware and software and salvage transistors from broken equipment. The job tasks range from the very menial to a high level of technical performance. Ron Albright, the supervisor of the service department, is also very busy but is willing to spend time with the intern when he can. When he can't, this role is delegated to various technicians who differ in the kinds of tasks they assign the intern (some are more inclined than others to give interns challenging and interesting tasks). Like the rental and convention services department, the service department has its very slow days as well as very busy ones, and the interns occasionally have very little to do. In these positions, it is more difficult for them to find work for themselves than it is for the interns in Rental and Convention Services. It is therefore necessary to occasionally brainstorm ideas with the supervisors (Ron and Marcia) concerning new types of projects for the interns. The interns' lack of technical training places certain limitations on the range of possible duties, but this year we have been able to think up quite a variety of semitechnical tasks for the interns to work on.

The last department we have placed interns in this year is the parts and supplies department. Although there were two available positions, we only had one intern placed there each semester. The role of the intern changed in the spring from a loosely defined one to a more clearly defined one in terms of duties and responsibilities. This was due to policy changes in the department and has had its advantages as well as its drawbacks. As it stands at the end of this year, the interns in the parts and supplies department are responsible for shipping out equipment and parts to various clients and other Lights and Action sites. This involves filling out shipping orders, looking up prices on the computers, and actually packaging the equipment to be sent out. It is a good position that helps develop such skills as paying attention to detail and accuracy, maintaining a high production rate, and taking personal responsibility; it also exposes the interns to basic data entry and retrieval on the computer. However, the work is very repetitive from day to day and does not provide the variety of job duties found in some of the other positions.

The supervisors and regular workers in the parts and supplies department are very cooperative about the program and try to do as much as they can to make the interns' semester a good one. But they are less willing to take chances with the interns and to make exceptions or accommodations to fit the interns' specific needs. It is recommended, therefore, that the interns placed in Parts and Supplies should be those who show higher degrees of responsibility and commitment and whose special needs do not require as much attention. It is often difficult for the instructor to spend time with the interns in this department as the work space is quite confined and busy. The parts and supplies department seems to have very few slow days, although certain times during the day are less busy than others.

One of the major difficulties of working as an instructor in a work setting is the different perspectives of the supervisors and the instructor. As an instructor, the primary goal is to teach the interns as much as possible while making the internship challenging and exciting for them. The supervisor's primary goal is to keep the department running smoothly and efficiently. These two goals do not always complement each other. As an outsider to the company, your only control over the job site is your ability to suggest and to persuade the supervisors to go along with your ideas. This is not always possible. Often, the interns are given very menial duties or left with nothing to do, and much of the time there is very little the instructor can do about this. However, such experiences can be viewed as educational to the interns, as almost any job has aspects that are either uninteresting or unpleasant; learning to accept this and understand the necessity of even the most routine job tasks is an important lesson.

I do not mean to present a scenario of confrontation or conflict between the supervisors and the instructor. This is not the case. The supervisors are all very willing to help out with the program and derive a good deal of satisfaction from seeing our interns succeed. Lights and Action has volunteered to participate in this program; it is not being forced upon them. While I have actively met with supervisors and put forth many suggestions this year, I have also recognized and respected their needs and goals and have been willing to compromise in certain areas for the overall success of the program.

Certain supervisors and employees should be named who are particularly helpful to talk with and get suggestions from and who will put out that extra effort for the interns. In Rental and Convention Services, A. J. Worthy has played a very active role with the interns this year and is fully committed to helping them. Many of the technicians relate very well to the interns and often play the role of counselor as well as instructor for the interns. In the service department, both Ron and Marcia are very committed to helping the interns but are very busy and cannot always give the interns as much time as is needed. The parts and supplies department is in a state of flux right now as John Cone, the old supervisor, left unexpectedly and no replacement has yet been found. Herbert Flanders, the second-in-command supervisor, has been helpful but, as previously stated, hasn't been willing to take as many chances with the interns.

Several times this year, I was told one thing by a supervisor and later discovered or realized that I was not being told the whole truth. I present these examples not to foster mistrust, but to make the point that, in the end, it is the instructor who is most concerned with the interns' welfare and that therefore the ultimate responsibility for their success lies with the instructor and themselves.

During the first semester of this year, I was advocating with Geoff Dunn to have the interns in Rental and Convention Services be given more responsibility and initiative. He agreed with me and said that he would speak with the various technicians about this. I also spoke with the technicians, who agreed but said that they needed to be given the time to spend with the interns from Geoff and the other people in management. After a few weeks there was no noticeable change in the interns' job assignments and I spoke with two of the technicians about this. They said, truthfully I believe, that Geoff had told them not to give the interns any real responsibility and to simply "babysit" them. There was obviously no real commitment to giving the interns a meaningful semester's experience and the results of this attitude were obvious by the end of the semester when the interns in this department all but stopped attending, feeling unneeded and unchallenged.

This episode needs qualification, however. The interns in the rental and convention services department that semester showed very little initiative or responsibility almost from the start and this created a vicious cycle in which expectations were lowered by both the interns and the technicians. Also, before the beginning of the spring semester, A. J. Worthy was hired by Geoff Dunn as a quality control specialist and was given, as one of his stated duties, responsibility for making the intern program a success. A. J. has put out a great effort to get the interns more involved in the department and the results have been fantastic—a complete turnaround from the previous semester.

A second episode worth mentioning also occurred during the fall semester in the parts and supplies department. We had brought a new intern in after the first grading period who was very articulate and showed a good degree of initiative. After his first week in Parts and Supplies, I met with John Cone, who said he was very happy with this intern's performance; I had much the same impression. A week later, totally out of the blue, John announced that the intern had to leave as he was "belligerent and sloppy in his work." John was completely unwilling to let me work with the intern and, in order to keep the intern in the program, I was forced to move him over to Rental and Convention Services. The intern did not want to work there and the move created a negative attitude that lasted throughout the semester. In fact, as I came to observe the intern more carefully, I, too, found him to be belligerent and sloppy at times. Yet these were problems that were to some degree being addressed and that I believe could have been worked out even better if the intern had been allowed to remain in the parts and supplies department.

Both of these episodes left a sour taste in my mouth as far as establishing a trusting working relationship with these two supervisors. John Cone is no longer with the company and Geoff has given this semester's interns more guidance, mostly indirectly through A. J. However, these incidents point to the fact that in many ways, the on-site instructor is an outsider to the company and when push comes to shove, the company's interests come first.

Finally, I need to emphasize the most important rule for helping the interns to succeed: Challenge them as much as possible. The more responsibility they are given and the more they are given tasks that require a real effort on their part, the more they will rise to the occasion. This seems like obvious advice, but it is very important for the interns' success. They do have limitations and disabilities that make it harder for them to excel, but they all have the ability to succeed and to raise themselves up to the level of the other employees at Lights and Action. They only fail when they are put in situations where they are expected to fail. Given the proper supervision and understanding they can, in time, succeed.

Appendix 2.11
CLP Data Collection Handbook

CLP "Quick" On-the-Job Social Skills Assessment

INTERNS	Conversing wth Employees	Ordering Job Duties	Asking for Help or Instructions	Following Instructions	Giving Instructions	Accepting Positive Feedback	Accepting Negative Feedback	Giving Negative Feedback	Others

Key

* Is excellent in this skill; needs no instruction.

\+ Is adequate in this skill; some feedback and training may help.

O Is apparently adequate.

? I don't know.

\- Has had some problems in this area that I have noticed.

! Has serious problems in this area.

∞ I need to explain what the student's difficulty is in this area.

P I have received peer (employee) feedback that confirms my rating.

Career **L**adder **P**rogram

Intern Recording Sheet

Intern: _____ Recorder: _____

Circle one: teacher   intern   co-worker/employer

Job Tasks	Superior 4	Good 3	Improving 2	Poor 1	
1. _____	____	____	____	____	quality
average _____	____	____	____	____	quantity
2. _____	____	____	____	____	quality
average _____	____	____	____	____	quantity
3. _____	____	____	____	____	quality
average _____	____	____	____	____	quantity
4. _____	____	____	____	____	quality
average _____	____	____	____	____	quantity

Total ____

General Work Behaviors

5. Grooming	____	____	____	____
6. Punctuality/attendance	____	____	____	____
7. Follows directions	____	____	____	____
8. Seeks assistance	____	____	____	____
9. Production rate	____	____	____	____
10. Cooperative, team player	____	____	____	____

Total ____

Social Behaviors

11. Initiates interactions	____	____	____	____
12. Converses, responds, and takes turns in conversations	____	____	____	____
13. Terminates interactions	____	____	____	____
14. Eye contact and body posture	____	____	____	____
15. Speaks clearly and loudly	____	____	____	____
16. Has pleasant demeanor and gives respect	____	____	____	____
17. Negotiates well and resists peer pressure	____	____	____	____

Total ____

Career
  Ladder
    Program

Problem Behaviors	Never 4	Rarely 3	Sometimes 2	Often 1
18. Shows verbal or physical aggression	____	____	____	____
19. Temperament is moody or insulting	____	____	____	____
20. Manipulates and takes advantage of others	____	____	____	____
21. Breaks social rules (e.g., interrupts)	____	____	____	____

Total ____

Grand Total _____

Comments: _____

_____

_____

_____

_____

_____

CLP Comments: _____

_____

_____

_____

Employment Skills Workshop: _____

_____

_____

_____

CLP On-the-Job Performance
SUMMARY GRAPH

NAME _____ PROFESSIONAL _____ DATE _____

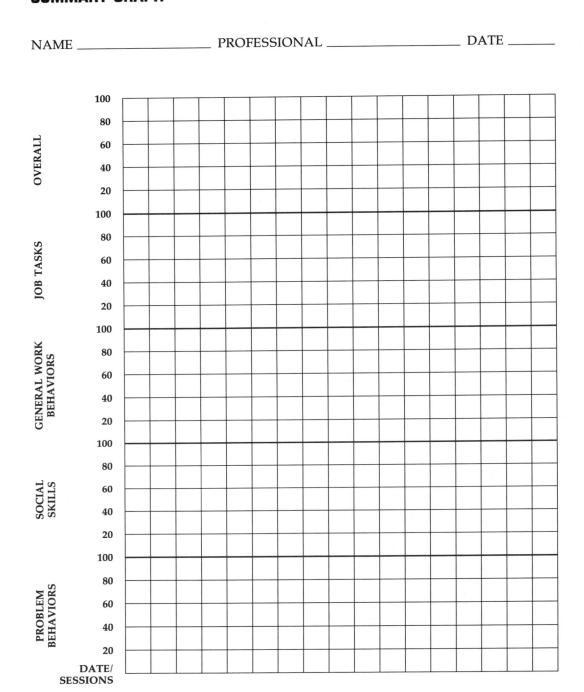

Vocational Performance Record

Intern: _____ Training Site: _____

School: _____ Counselor: _____ Phone: _____

Family Contact: _____ Phone: _____

Intern meetings to present and review objectives:

___/___ ___/___ ___/___ ___/___ ___/___ ___/___

___/___ ___/___ ___/___ ___/___ ___/___ ___/___

Phone calls home to report on intern progress and coordinate support:

___/___ ___/___ ___/___ ___/___ ___/___ ___/___

___/___ ___/___ ___/___ ___/___ ___/___ ___/___

Phone calls to school to report on intern progress and intern support:

___/___ ___/___ ___/___ ___/___ ___/___ ___/___

___/___ ___/___ ___/___ ___/___ ___/___ ___/___

Objectives (always include conditions, behavior, and criterion):

```
┌─────────────────────────────────────────────────────────────┐
│  Weeks 1–6                                                   │
│  1. _____ │
│     _____ │
│  2. _____ │
│     _____ │
└─────────────────────────────────────────────────────────────┘
```

```
┌─────────────────────────────────────────────────────────────┐
│  Weeks 7–12                                                  │
│  3. _____ │
│     _____ │
│  4. _____ │
│     _____ │
└─────────────────────────────────────────────────────────────┘
```

```
┌─────────────────────────────────────────────────────────────┐
│  Weeks 13–18                                                 │
│  5. _____ │
│     _____ │
│  6. _____ │
│     _____ │
└─────────────────────────────────────────────────────────────┘
```

Program

Describe in a few sentences what program (including nonintervention, counseling, or transfer to co-worker) you have designed for each intern objective.

Objective Number _____   Date: ____/____

Program:

_____

_____

Objective Number _____   Date: ____/____

Program:

_____

_____

Objective Number _____   Date: ____/____

Program:

_____

_____

Objective Number _____   Date: ____/____

Program:

_____

_____

Objective Number _____   Date: ____/____

Program:

_____

_____

Objective Number _____ Date: ____/____

Program:

_____

_____

Objective Number _____ Date: ____/____

Program:

_____

_____

Objective Number _____ Date: ____/____

Program:

_____

_____

Objective Number _____ Date: ____/____

Program:

_____

_____

Objective Number _____ Date: ____/____

Program:

_____

_____

Objective Number _____ Date: ____/____

Program:

_____

_____

Recording the Data

If the intern will meet the objective by increasing
Rate .... use Chart 1
Accuracy .... use Chart 2
Quantity (frequency, duration, or amount) .... use Chart 3
None of the above .... continue to next section

Social Skills

Use the "Quick" On-the-Job Social Skills Assessment to discover any need for social skills objectives.

Discuss the results with the supervising teacher. Write an objective, measurable, and non-judgmental objective.

For many social skills objectives, a recording sheet from the Employment Skills Workshop (ESW) can be used.

If the objective is not covered by one of the ESW recording sheets and cannot be easily charted by one of the charts, go to Journal Entry.

Journal Entry

Keep dated notes on intern behavior. Always keep comments focused on the behavior(s) addressed in the objective. If observations reveal new issues, write new objectives. Avoid subjective or judgmental language. Report facts. If, for example, an intern behavior is provoking a negative response from the employer, describe the employer behavior. "John's supervisor was clearly distressed when John was 15 minutes late for the third time this week, but the supervisor did not say anything to John. I gave the information to John when he did arrive . . ." instead of "John screwed up again today. I told him to shape up when he finally got here . . ."

Reporting the Data

After each six-week period, complete a Client Recording Sheet. It is recommended that the on-site instructor complete the first sheet, a co-worker the second, and that the intern self-evaluate for the third. More frequent data may be recorded on these sheets and charted on the Summary Graph. Copies of the trimester interval sheets go to the supervising teacher, or directly to the school counselor and home. Arrange the reports with the supervising teacher, and make sure that the personal calls home to the family are consistent with what the data show. At the end of the semester, complete an End-of-Year Transition Referral and Report.

Journal Entry

Intern: _____ Date: _____ Objective Number _____

_____

_____

_____

_____

_____

_____

_____

_____

Intern: _____ Date: _____ Objective Number _____

_____

_____

_____

_____

_____

_____

_____

_____

Intern: _____ Date: _____ Objective Number _____

_____

_____

_____

_____

_____

_____

_____

_____

End-of-Year Transition Referral and Report

Intern: _____ Evaluator: _____ Date: _____

Attach additional sheets if necessary.

Work History: _____

_____

_____

_____

_____

Appearance/grooming: _____

_____

_____

_____

_____

Interpersonal skills: _____

_____

_____

_____

_____

Vocational strengths: _____

_____

_____

_____

_____

Punctuality/attendance: _____

_____

_____

_____

_____

Communication skills: _____

_____

_____

_____

_____

Learning strengths/ability to generalize and follow directions: _____

_____

_____

_____

_____

Interests: _____

_____

_____

_____

_____

Family: _____

_____

_____

_____

_____

Personal needs: _____

_____

_____

_____

_____

Other: _____

_____

_____

_____

_____

Intern's goals: _____

_____

_____

_____

_____

Evaluator's recommendations:: _____

_____

_____

_____

_____

Career
Ladder
Program

Chart 1. Rate

Intern _____

Objective Number _____ Task _____

Units of measurement: Time increment _____ or Quantity _____

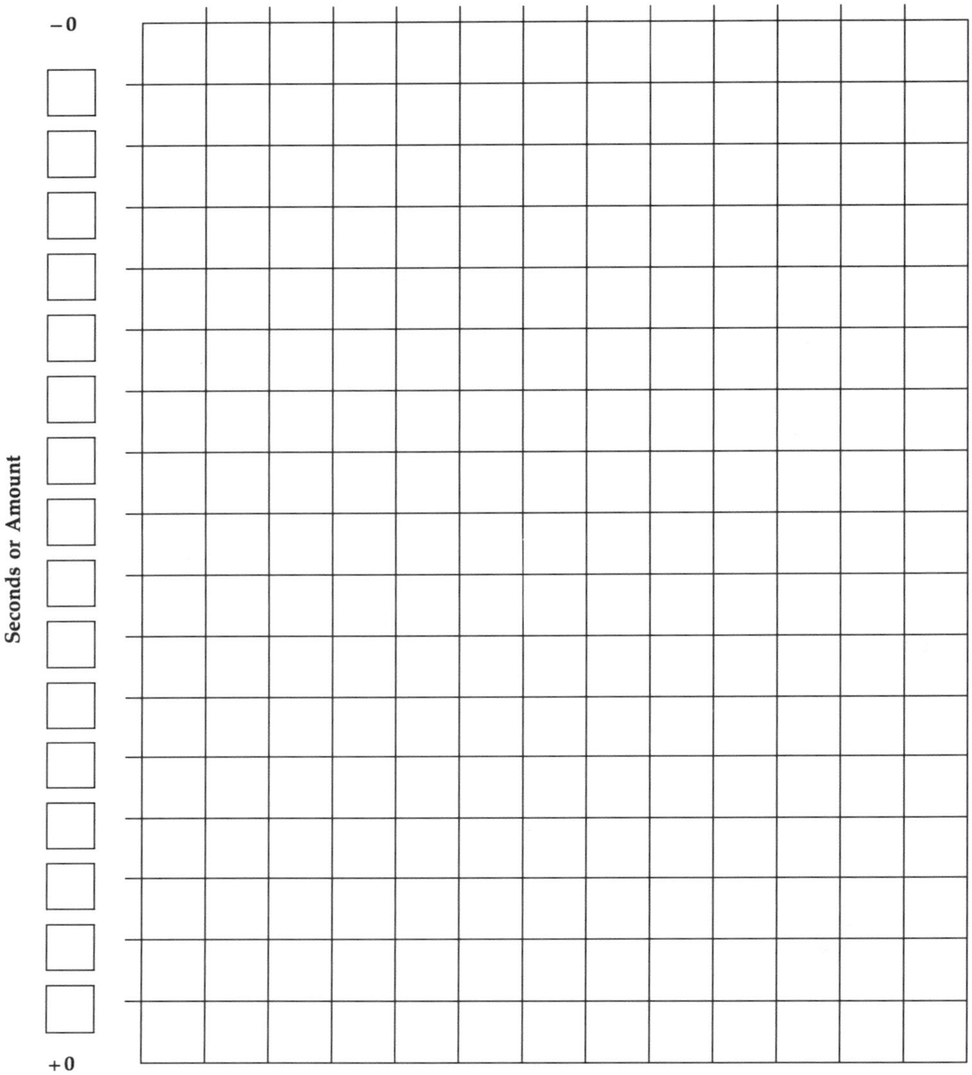

-0

Seconds or Amount

+0

© 1993 by PRO-ED, Inc.

Chart 2. Accuracy

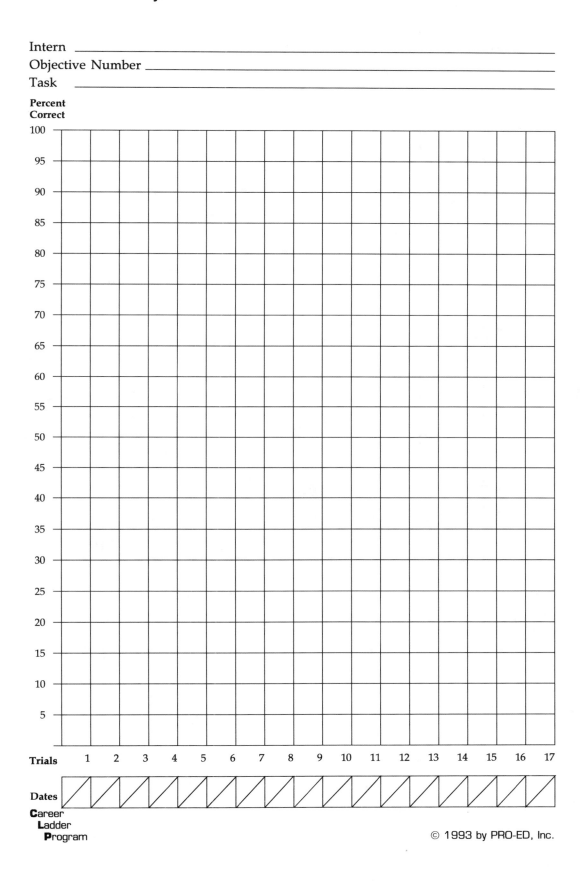

Intern _____

Objective Number _____

Task _____

Chart 3. Quantity

Circle one:

Amount
Duration
Frequency

Intern _____

Objective Number _____

Task _____

Trials   1   2   3   4   5   6   7   8   9   10   11   12   13

Dates

Career
Ladder
Program

Appendix 2.12
Social Skills Training (SST) Rating Forms

SST Rating Form
Ordering Job Duties

	yes	no	yes	no	yes	no	yes	no
FACE the person								
WAIT for the question								
BEGIN job duties with the word "I"								
TELL them your job title								
LIST a few of the things you do								
ASK if your answer is complete								

Use professional job terminology

1 – – – 2 – – – 3 – – – 4
poor   good

Eye contact

1 – – – 2 – – – 3 – – – 4
poor   good

Speech loudness

1 – – – 2 – – – 3 – – – 4
poor   good

Hands away from face

1 – – – 2 – – – 3 – – – 4
poor   good

Confident voice tone

1 – – – 2 – – – 3 – – – 4
poor   good

Straight body posture

1 – – – 2 – – – 3 – – – 4
poor   good

Full sentences

1 – – – 2 – – – 3 – – – 4
poor   good

SST Rating Form
Starting a Conversation, Giving Positive Feedback

	yes	no	yes	no	yes	no	yes	no
FACE the person								
INITIATE the conversation								
RETURN the greeting								
GIVE the feedback								
WAIT for the person to respond								
Make SMALL TALK								
DECIDE if the other person is listening								
Bring up the MAIN TOPIC								

Number of conversational questions   1 – – – 2 – – – 3 – – – 4
    poor   good

Number of complimentary comments   1 – – – 2 – – – 3 – – – 4
    poor   good

Eye contact   1 – – – 2 – – – 3 – – – 4
    poor   good

Personal presence (smiling, enthusiastic, sincere)   1 – – – 2 – – – 3 – – – 4
    poor   good

Speech loudness   1 – – – 2 – – – 3 – – – 4
    poor   good

Relaxed posture and hands away from face   1 – – – 2 – – – 3 – – – 4
    poor   good

SST Rating Form
Giving Negative Feedback

	yes	no	yes	no	yes	no	yes	no
ASK if you can talk for a minute								
First SAY SOMETHING POSITIVE								
TELL how you feel or what was done wrong								
GIVE the person A REASON for changing								
ASK if the person UNDERSTOOD								
(If not, EXPLAIN AGAIN)								
ASK how the person FEELS								
GIVE the person SUGGESTIONS for changing								
THANK the person for listening								
CHANGE the topic								
TELL the person you are concerned								

Don't put down the other person

1 – – – 2 – – – 3 – – – 4
poor   good

Face the person

1 – – – 2 – – – 3 – – – 4
poor   good

Keep a serious facial expression

1 – – – 2 – – – 3 – – – 4
poor   good

Use a serious voice tone

1 – – – 2 – – – 3 – – – 4
poor   good

Straight posture and hands away from face

1 – – – 2 – – – 3 – – – 4
poor   good

Career
Ladder
Program

SST Rating Form
Accepting Negative Feedback

	yes	no	yes	no	yes	no	yes	no
STAY NEAR the person								
LISTEN to the person								
(ASK for clarification)								
If you agree, APOLOGIZE								
SAY you understand								
ASK for suggestions								
If you don't agree, SAY you understand								
ASK permission to tell your side								
TELL your side with facts								
If it is an authority figure, ACCEPT THE FEEDBACK								

Face the person

1 – – – 2 – – – 3 – – – 4
poor   good

Eye contact

1 – – – 2 – – – 3 – – – 4
poor   good

Neutral expression

1 – – – 2 – – – 3 – – – 4
poor   good

Normal voice tone

1 – – – 2 – – – 3 – – – 4
poor   good

Straight posture and hands away
from face

1 – – – 2 – – – 3 – – – 4
poor   good

Don't interrupt

1 – – – 2 – – – 3 – – – 4
poor   good

Career
  Ladder
    Program

SST Rating Form
Asking for Help or Instructions

	yes	no	yes	no	yes	no	yes	no
DECIDE what the problem is								
DECIDE if you want help								
THINK about who to ask								
TELL the person about the problem								
ASK the person to help you								

Eye contact

1 – – – 2 – – – 3 – – – 4
poor   good

Hands away from face

1 – – – 2 – – – 3 – – – 4
poor   good

Enthusiastic voice tone

1 – – – 2 – – – 3 – – – 4
poor   good

Don't sound frustrated

1 – – – 2 – – – 3 – – – 4
poor   good

Neutral expression

1 – – – 2 – – – 3 – – – 4
poor   good

Career
Ladder
Program

SST Rating Form
Following Instructions

	yes	no	yes	no	yes	no	yes	no
LISTEN carefully								
ASK questions if you don't understand								
DECIDE if you want to follow the instructions								
REPEAT the instructions to yourself								
DO what you have been asked to do								

Neutral expression   1 - - - 2 - - - 3 - - - 4
                            poor   good

Eyes on person or work   1 - - - 2 - - - 3 - - - 4
                            poor   good

Nod your head when listening 1 - - - 2 - - - 3 - - - 4
                            poor   good

Say "mm-hmm"   1 - - - 2 - - - 3 - - - 4
                            poor   good

Hands away from face   1 - - - 2 - - - 3 - - - 4
                            poor   good

Straight body posture   1 - - - 2 - - - 3 - - - 4
                            poor   good

SST Rating Form
Giving Instructions

	yes	no	yes	no	yes	no	yes	no
DECIDE what needs to be done								
LABEL the job or task								
THINK about who could do it								
CHOOSE a person								
ASK what you want done								
EXPLAIN the purpose of the job								
SHOW all the materials								
GIVE INSTRUCTIONS step by step (CHANGE or REPEAT instructions if you need to)								
ASK if there are any questions								

Eye contact

1 – – – 2 – – – 3 – – – 4
poor   good

Hands away from face

1 – – – 2 – – – 3 – – – 4
poor   good

Patient voice tone

1 – – – 2 – – – 3 – – – 4
poor   good

Be willing to repeat

1 – – – 2 – – – 3 – – – 4
poor   good

Speak slowly enough

1 – – – 2 – – – 3 – – – 4
poor   good

Career
Ladder
Program

Appendix 2.13
Timeline for CLP On-Site Instructors
(Spring Semester)

1–2 weeks prior to
interns starting:

- Visit job site, learn interns' job duties, and meet co-workers.

1 week prior to
interns starting:

- Attend the scheduled family meeting.

1st instructional
day of semester:

- First day on job.
- Student orientation.
- Teacher/supervisor evaluation of students' abilities.

Weeks 1–2:

- A minimum of two work and one social objectives for each student (due Feb. 17). Discuss objectives with each student; remind them that objectives must be met before pay starts.
- Phone parents to report on students' progress (positive call).

Weeks 2–3:

- Fade supervision.
- Develop alternative work sites for students within the company (promotion for qualified students).
- Feb. 17: List of job duties for each student.

Week 4:

- Phone family to report on progress. Request that they help intern memorize his or her job duties.
- Week of Feb. 24: Conference with students; have objectives been met?

Week 5:

- Wednesday, March 3: Pay begins (tentative).
- Complete evaluations on the students' job performance; discuss evaluations with each student. Make three copies: original to CLP files, one copy to the student's special education teacher, one copy to parents.
- Phone parents to discuss evaluation.

Week 6:

- Monday, March 10: Grades due, turn in to CLP manager.
- Phone parents; report on progress.

Weeks 7–16:

- Take a few students out on job search, each day, as time permits.
- Continue to call family every 2 weeks.

Week 10:

- Ask supervisors to complete intern evaluations (due Friday).

Week 11:

- Monday, April 14: Complete CLP evaluations on each student.

Week 12:

- Monday, April 21: Grades due to CLP manager.

Weeks 13–14:

- Keep up the good work!

Week 15:

- Ask supervisors to do evaluations on each student.

Week 16:

- Complete CLP evaluations on each student.
- Tuesday, May 20: Grades due.

Weeks 17–18:

- Interns dismissed for graduation! Friday, May 31: Last day.

3

CHAPTER

The Employment Skills Workshop

Shepherd Siegel and Karen Greener ■

In chapter 2, the core experience of CLP, the community classroom, was explained and described. In fact, there are hundreds of similar work experience programs throughout the nation. The purpose of the previous chapter was to offer some tools that will enable teachers and supervisors of such programs to manage them efficiently, so that interns will derive the maximum benefit from the experience. That is, they will have an experience that is "worklike," where they respond to adult demands in an integrated adult environment; they learn real job skills; they learn to function well in an adult, work environment; they focus on what their real career interests are; they develop a work ethic; and they are exposed to and make friends with legitimate and heroic role models. But the community classroom experience alone is no guarantee that interns will fully connect their own lives with the idea of a work life.

Going to work can be a shocking experience, and one that needs to be processed, reconciled, justified, and shared. The effectiveness of a community classroom training can be greatly multiplied—more interns will get more out of it—if interns are periodically able to meet in a safe environment with peers who are in the same program. In CLP, interns met weekly in a school classroom and were taught a curriculum, called the Employment Skills Workshop, which is the subject of this chapter. Above and beyond, and underlying, the curriculum itself, the weekly meeting is an opportunity for the interns to solidify their

career wills in a group of peers. They learn to give each other support, and they make their decisions to have a legitimate career in an atmosphere of shared reactions to the tumult of leaving public school and entering the adult world of work. This chapter presents a curriculum intended to help the intern to make the most of this experience and to make sense of it.

The Curriculum

Information for the Teacher

The purpose of the curriculum for this course is a simple one. Whatever will enable an exiting student to better make the transition from school to work and adult life is appropriate for the course. In many cases, this translates into asking whether the behaviors demanded of an intern by the course will help that person to get and keep a job that is satisfactory to all concerned parties. This is the priority of the program. On the level of curriculum, any activities that do not serve this purpose should be discarded or given a low priority.

For example, reading, writing, and math skills are critical, but during the last semester of secondary school, it is difficult to effectively address them. CLP is structured to work with whatever 12 years of public instruction have taught so far. Referral to a postsecondary institution that addresses these skills is usually more appropriate. When academic learning is a concern of the soon-to-be-adult graduate, referral to the community college system and procedures for enrollment are more appropriate than actual instruction. The intern must be prepared to meet the demands of the adult world and to utilize community resources. The Career Ladder Program Pyramid (Figure 2.1), building from the bottom up, identifies the curricular components that are most critical at this point in the interns' lives.

All interns should have social security cards. Most should have driver's licenses. Clearly, this is one task that the family and school can complete before the interns' senior year. In the event that an intern does not have this documentation, a large part of his or her curriculum is probably going to consist of learning these skills. We live in a highly complex society, and the larger the gap between the skills a youth presents and the legal requirements for activating services, the more serious the struggle to survive will be. In one semester, a single intern may have to obtain the following documentation: birth certificate, social security card, driver's license, I-9 form (proof of citizenship), psychological evaluation, medical examination, all other documentation to get on the school payroll (in a stipended program), all other documentation to have a case opened at the Department of Rehabilitation, all documentation to enroll in a community college, two to four signed parental consent forms, and so forth. This ''documenting'' is a curriculum in and of itself. To the extent that these skills have not already been taught, CLP staff work is necessarily reduced to the critical and regrettably clerical function of just getting onto the career ladder. When these skills in conducting the paper chase are addressed in the earlier grades, CLP staff can put more effort into enabling interns to climb the career ladder.

On the emotional level, CLP interns are going through a transition as well. The exhilaration of independence and the burden of self-support can create a pressured situation. Interns react in a variety of ways: enthusiasm, withdrawal, aggression, immaturity, self-destruction, ambition, crime, boredom, truancy, and fantasy. All are growth responses, and all indicate some awareness of the magnitude of the imminent change in their lives. Thus the other critical task facing the CLP staff is to make a personal bond with the interns that reassures them that they are not alone during this time, and that the CLP will reward their efforts with an ongoing commitment. People are not used to having the assistance CLP provides, and it takes consistent effort to connect with the intern, the

intern's family, and the intern's employer and gain the trust that will encourage their best effort. Thus, affective or personal growth curricula such as peer counseling, counseling, parent or family contact, and mediation will bring the intern emotionally into the transition process, while the functional curriculum makes the intern a legitimate player in the work world. Both of these domains must be addressed if the CLP is to enable success and empowerment.

All of the curriculum strands of the Employment Skills Workshop (ESW) follow a sequence of three stages. First, lessons are keyed to heighten and develop an intern's sense of self. Next, sensitivity to others is emphasized. Finally, interns are given opportunities to develop and express values. Many of the peer counseling activities take the intern out of the vocational context temporarily, to ease the strain of transition and to build trust and bonding in the group. However, the purpose of the curriculum is to enable the interns to redefine themselves, improve and refine their sensitivity to others, and develop values that include vocational development and make it a priority. Regardless of the high success rate the CLP has demonstrated so far, the real success occurs when every intern has taken the notion of career and of being respected to heart as a result of the experiences CLP offers.

This curriculum does *not* stand alone. It reinforces and enables interns to maximize the core vocational training, the community classroom, described in the previous chapter. Failing to integrate this curriculum with a community-based work experience and job search negates its purpose.

Finally, the writers of this book realize that by themselves, social skills training, peer counseling, interview skills, and so forth are not new concepts; therefore, the curriculum borrows heavily from all of the writers' best influences. The innovative and critical quality of the CLP curriculum is its holistic organization of these components in a way that integrates them with other services and with the transition phase of life for adolescents exiting secondary school. When it is well executed, the curriculum should ease and empower interns in that process and enable them to best utilize available social services.

Information for the Intern

This course will provide you with the latest information and training on how to:

- Identify and express your feelings about leaving high school
- Know the importance of having a good attendance record

- Make friends on the job
- Be the type of worker an employer wants to hire
- Find a job opening
- Apply for a job
- Interview for a job
- Keep a job
- Make a career plan
- Get promoted and advanced in your job
- Get the best education for your career
- Make friends with other interns facing the same challenges as you

You will learn the most common reasons people are fired and how to avoid that situation. You will learn how to operate office equipment such as calculators, telephones, cash registers, and typewriters. You will be introduced to the computer. You will learn how to be honest about your feelings and how to use this skill to your best advantage on the job. You will learn how to get along with co-workers, supervisors, customers, and people who work for you. During the second half of the semester, after you show that you understand what is expected from you on the job and that you have the skills to look for one, you will be given a chance to conduct a job search. If you get a job before the semester ends and have met all of your objectives, you will be released from the program so that you can go to work. You will still get credit for the course.

Course Objectives

By the end of the semester, all students with 95% attendance will be able to perform 90% of the objectives listed below:

- Operate a cash register
- Take a telephone message
- Use a 10-key calculator "by sight"
- Recite their job title and job duties using correct job terminology
- Have a conversation with a co-worker
- Formulate a job search strategy and begin to conduct a job search
- State the purpose of a personal data sheet and be able to use it in the application process

- Complete a résumé
- Analyze the three most common reasons people get fired and identify how to avoid being fired
- Know how to contact appropriate adult service agencies (Department of Rehabilitation, community college, temporary employment agencies, Planned Parenthood, Department of Social Services, social security office, hospital, counseling services, etc.)

Methods, Strategies, Procedures, and Techniques

The course uses the following methods:

Role playing	Guest speakers
Lectures	Problem solving
Videotaping	Group process
Supported job search	Films
Drill and practice	Group discussion
Self-evaluation	Self-monitoring

Instructional Materials

The course utilizes the following instructional materials:

Overhead projector	Videotaping equipment
Films	Job announcements
Computers	Filmstrips
Calculators	Job applications
Agency brochures	Cash registers
Handouts	Career workbooks
Newspapers	Employer's materials
Typewriters	

Curriculum Note

Clerical tasks receive special emphasis because so many jobs require some clerical ability, and because such tasks are easily transferred to a classroom setting. Some schools may have access to other job-training activities, and as long as they are relevant to the current regional job market, their use is encouraged.

Many curricular materials exist that are not directly recommended or included in the reference section of this book. This book utilizes those materials that have suited the teaching styles of CLP staff over the past several years, but instructors are encouraged to add other materials that will serve the same purpose. The appendixes to this chapter include sample materials (i.e., intern questions, intern rating sheet) that can be generated (and owned) by the interns' group process. In these cases, the appendix materials are guidelines, and their use is more optional. If the book has at least communicated what it means to make real vocational development a priority in programming and instruction, then the use and adaptation of materials to that priority is encouraged and applauded. Some objectives, such as social skills, peer counseling, the use of a cash register, or receptionist skills may require more depth and detail than is provided here, and instructors are encouraged to locate and use other materials, as long as the overriding goal of vocational adjustment is not compromised.

Week 7 is a critical week for sustaining interest in the workshop for the second two-thirds of the semester. It is packed with activities that will set a more serious and hardworking tone, and it presents procedures that will be used for the rest of the semester. Thorough preparation for Week 7's presentation is strongly recommended.

To implement this curriculum with greater rigor and ease, familiarity with the following materials is recommended. These books, or books covering the same curriculum areas (job-keeping skills, social skills training, and peer counseling/cooperative learning), are especially critical to full implementation of the workshop.

- *Don't Get Fired! How to Keep a Job,* by Durlynn Anema and William Lefkowitz (1990) (DGF)

- *Performance Based Placement Manual: Job Development Techniques That Work!* by Denise Bissonnette and Rich Pimentel (1984)

- *Tribes: A Process for Social Development and Cooperative Learning,* by Jeanne Gibbs (1987)

- *Skillstreaming the Adolescent,* by A. P. Goldstein, R. P. Sprafkin, N. J. Gershaw, and P. Klein (1980)

- *Curriculum Guide for Student Peer Counseling Training,* by Barbara B. Varenhorst (1980) (PCT)

The Instructor's Stance

The relationship formed between the staff and the interns is critical to enablement of the interns. Staff members who are looking for a job that takes less than a serious, heartfelt commitment to the impor-

tance of the work will not be effective. Likewise, staff members who are looking for opportunities to make youths dependent upon them or who want to take care of helpless people will not be effective. The same delicate point of balance is sought for each intern, but for each intern the balance will be found in a different place.

That balance is the point where a youth is enabled; in other words, when an intern presents an authentic inability to perform what is normally expected from the workplace or other adult organization, the staff person is able to creatively invent an accommodation that is placed as much as possible within the control of the intern. When an intern presents an authentic ability to perform, the staff person is able to praise, and then leave the intern to function independently.

The staff must be constantly alert to when they are crossing into a region of making an intern dependent—caring too much—or into a region of not being there to accommodate when assistance is in fact called for. With each intern, the point of balance will be unique; when it is known and decisions are made based on that knowledge, interns will grow into independence and self-sufficiency.

The relationship that critically involves the staff person, and then allows that person to fade out, moves in a progression from *telling* to *joining*. This progression takes place in a microcosmic form over every daily period of instruction, and in a larger arc extending over the course of the entire semester. It can be roughly described as follows.

Weeks 1–4: Telling

You are now an intern in the Career Ladder Program. This is part of your school course, and it is the beginning of your adult life independent of school. We will be making some demands of you, and if you want to remain in the program and succeed in it, you will meet those demands. They are not negotiable.

Weeks 5–7: Selling

We believe that the skills we are teaching and the opportunities we are providing are essential to your success as a work- or college-bound individual, and that they will make you powerful, responsible, and successful. The Career Ladder Program is a particularly good deal for you.

Weeks 8–11: Testing

By now we expect that you have some idea of what this program is about: responsible and productive adult behavior in the work world. We are giving you some opportunities to show us that you have that understanding. We reserve the right to observe you, and to provide you with feedback and direction.

Weeks 12–15: Consulting

You have proved that you understand what we and the work world expect of you, and you are pretty much on your own. We know that you will respect our opinions and advice. We appreciate being consulted when you are faced with a tough decision, or even when you need some help getting your career plan going.

Weeks 16–18: Joining

You've really shown growth and you have learned what you need to do to succeed. You are in charge of your destiny, and we hope that you will use your power wisely and effectively. We are still here with you, but more as partners than as teachers or supervisors. We are always available if you need us, but we have so much faith in your abilities that this should hardly be necessary.

The Curriculum

The curricular content is divided into six strands: Job-Keeping, Job, and Job Search Skills; Personal and Interpersonal Growth; and Timely Topics. They can each be briefly described:

Job Skills

Job Skills are any that could be found on a job description. These are skills that are directly related to the performance of job tasks, such as typing, filing, sorting, labeling, cooking, taking inventory, answering telephones, knowing a lexicon, and processing an order.

Job-Keeping Skills (or Employer-Pleasing Behaviors)

Job-Keeping Skills are those behaviors that are pleasing to employers and that have been found by experience, employers, and educators to correlate highly with job retention, including handling authority, being on time, being responsible, keeping yourself busy, being honest, staying on the job, and asking for work when an assigned task is done.

Job Search Skills

Job Search Skills are those behaviors and strategies that can increase the likelihood that an intern will be hired by an employer. These skills include using the self-family-friend network, filling out applications, preparing a résumé, performing in a job interview, and using employment agencies.

Personal Growth

Personal Growth refers to those activities that enable interns to identify and express their feelings in an honest and responsible fashion, create personal bonds and nonjudgmental postures, take control of their own group process, make wise decisions, own their problems, gain perspective on their own life continuum, and so on. Personal Growth exercises demonstrate a recognition that feelings are deeply interior, yet do not exist without the interaction of others. This curriculum includes tasks or activities that use role play, simulation games, and modeling to generate a flow of primary (feelings, emotions, fantasies, dreams, imagination) and secondary (reason, logic, intellect, and thought) process data from the group, the results of which are totally within interns' control. This, combined with the Interpersonal Growth curriculum described below, comprises a movement from self-awareness to sensitivity to others to affirmation of values.

Interpersonal Growth

Often referred to as social skills training, Interpersonal Growth activities are a rehearsal of those behaviors that have been found by experience, employers, and educators to correlate highly with social acceptance on the job. These include having a conversation, giving and accepting negative feedback, giving and accepting positive feedback, following instructions, and giving instructions. Skill sheets for teaching social skills are found in Appendix 2.12.

Timely Topics

Timely Topics refer to special lessons, usually group discussions or lectures, that are best delivered at specific points during the semester. They are designed to reinforce other lessons and to anticipate and avert problems that we have found to frequently occur during the semester-long course. Topics include: Why work without pay? Why practice social skills? The CLP Pyramid, How does capitalism work? Job search strategies, and Realities of the work world.

Curriculum Matrix

Table 3.1 gives a week-by-week breakdown of the lesson plans. A matrix that summarizes the emphasis on attendance and five of the six curriculum strands is depicted by Table 3.2. Highest emphasis

TABLE 3.1

Lesson Plans for Employment Skills Workshop

Week	Job Skills	Job-Keeping Skills	Job Search Skills	Personal Growth	Interpersonal Growth	Timely Topics
1	Basic Clerical	First Day on the Job, Part 1		Confidentiality		Warmup and First Impressions
2	Basic Clerical	First Day on the Job, Part 2		Introductions		CLP Pyramid, Rules, and Agreements
3	Basic Clerical	Be Aware of Time		Animal, Color, Water, White Room	Learning Your Job Duties	Pioneer, Warrior, Hero
4	Basic Clerical	Be Responsible		Problem Solving; Having a Conversation	Ordering Job Duties	Why Work Without Pay? Why Be Supervised?
5	Basic Clerical	Follow the Schedule		Making "I" Statements	Ordering Job Duties	Stamina and Determination
6	Basic Clerical	Follow Directions	Job Interview Questions: Brainstorming for a Résumé	Exchanging Positives; Having a Conversation	Ordering Job Duties	Tolerance and Terminations
7	Intermediate Clerical	Be Helpful and Friendly to Everyone at Work	Learning How to Do a Job Interview	Asking Open and Feeling Questions	First Session and Overall Session Format	Social Skills—Why Have a Workshop on Them?
8	Intermediate Clerical	Don't Talk to Friends While Working	The Personal Data Sheet	Making Nonjudgmental Observations	Ordering Job Duties	Working with Vocational Rehabilitation
9	Intermediate Clerical	Keep Yourself Busy	Complete a Personal Résumé	Crocodile Creek	Asking for Help or Instructions	Beginning the Job Search
10	Intermediate Clerical	Following Directions and Making an Extra Effort	Baseline Job Interviews	Decision Agent	Asking for Help or Instructions	Reevaluating Career Objectives
11	Intermediate Clerical	Give Good Service	Mock Interviews	Values Ranking	Having a Conversation	Past Interns' Anecdotes
12	Intermediate Clerical	Leave Your Personal Problems at Home	Mock Interviews		Giving Negative Feedback	Capitalism 101
13	Site-Related Tasks	Get Along with Others	Mock Interviews		Giving Negative Feedback	Job Search Strategies
14	Site-Related Tasks	Take Pride in Your Work	Mock Interviews		Giving Negative Feedback	Waiting for the Job You Want
15	Site-Related Tasks	Don't Talk Back to Your Boss	Mock Interviews		Accepting Negative Feedback	Realities of the Work World
16	Site-Related Tasks		Mock Interviews		Accepting Negative Feedback	What is Postsecondary Life Like?
17	Continuing Development		"Real" Mock Interviews		Accepting Negative Feedback	Open Forum
18		Using an Appointment Calendar				Making Choices

TABLE 3.2
Matrix Defining Emphasis on Attendance and Curriculum Strands

Weeks Emphasis	1–4 Telling	5–7 Selling	8–11 Testing	12–15 Consulting	16–18 Joining
Attendance	••••	••	•		
Personal	•••	••••	••••	••	•
Interpersonal	•	••	•••	•••	••••
Job Keeping	••	•••	••••	•••	••
Job	•	••	••••	••••	••
Job Search			•	••	••••

is represented by four dots and little-to-no emphasis by none. The chart divides the 18-week semester into five segments that roughly correlate with the progression of the instructor's stance from telling to joining. Actual lesson plans follow.

Week 1

```
              LESSONS IN
|X| Job Keeping   |X| Personal Growth
|X| Job           | | Interpersonal Growth
| | Job Search    |X| Timely Topics
```

Job: Basic Clerical

On-site instructors should be ready to teach individually on cash registers, calculators, and typewriters 10 minutes before class is scheduled to begin. Interns want to learn. They want to work. Those interns with attendance and punctuality problems will not devalue the experience of those with good attendance habits if individualized tasks are available 10 minutes before class. For cash registers, have mock food products priced and available for checkout. The first few weeks, have interns work on accuracy of checkout, then accuracy of checkout and making change; next, setup of timings with rate charts (see Appendix 2.11) and work on speed. When using self-charting and data sheets, encourage interns to compete with their own "personal best" time. For calculators, use worksheets with long lists of numbers to add (this improves data entry skills) and lessons related to budget keeping. Emphasis on methodical sequences will make these activities more transferable to data entry and computer-related skills. For typewriters, use standard typing manuals or typing tutorial software, emphasiz-

ing accuracy first and speed later. Interns with typing potential (able to exceed 30 words per minute with a little practice) should be identified and allowed to practice typing during this period for the entire semester. After all interns have arrived, implement the following lesson.

Rationale/Warmup/Review

The basic skill objectives are to count by 25s, 10s, 5s, and 1s. Ask interns to brainstorm jobs that might require an employee to operate a cash register or handle money. Ask how many interns have had experience handling money. How did they learn? Did they get better with practice?

Presentation

Write on the board the steps to becoming a good cashier: courtesy, speed, security, and accuracy. Define the terms.

Guided Practice

Have interns pair off and practice cashiering. Pair experienced and inexperienced interns for peer tutoring. Purchase products from a cabinet that has priced food containers.

Life-Skill Competency Application

Have interns work as cashiers, with the teacher being the customer. Rate their accuracy, courtesy, speed, and understanding of security.

Timely Topic: Warmup and First Impressions

Expect that special circumstances will reduce the likelihood of a complete group on the first day. Perhaps the recruitment process from the previous semester was not complete, or some interns have not yet made it to the job site, or staff may be deliberately staggering the first day of work to manage the flow of new people onto the work site. Therefore, a full orientation to program policies and expectations can and should be delayed until the second week to avoid incomplete communication. However, praise for making good first impressions, basic concepts, and expectations of attendance can and should be addressed. The contract nature of the commitment and services interns receive in exchange for satisfactory performance can be introduced and developed in detail in Week 2. Complete the paperwork process that was begun at the family meeting (see chapter 2) and continue the same process used for opening Vocational Rehabilitation cases.

Job Keeping: First Day on the Job, Part 1

This lesson can be enriched by having the interns observe and analyze the similarities between their first day on the job and behaviors that welcome a stranger.

Rationale/Warmup/Review

Ask how many interns remember their first job. Ask them to remember back farther to the first day on the job. Discuss what it felt like, what they had to know, how they found out what they needed to know. Discuss good and bad experiences. Have the interns discuss the importance of first impressions, perhaps sharing stories from an important first impression they may have made or failed to make. Ask about the impressions they may have made so far on the job or with their co-interns.

Presentation

Watch the filmstrip ''Your First Days on the Job'' (*Entering the World of Work*, 1979).

Guided Practice

Discuss different situations in which interns might find themselves where they would be concerned with making a good first impression and where another intern might be helping them get acquainted. Responses might include first dates or blind dates, a new school, a new neighborhood, or being a new club member. What do they need to do to welcome the new person? Responses might include introducing themself and others, showing the person around, or showing the person how to do something. Pair or group interns to select and practice the task. Discuss the outcome with the class.

Life-Skill Competency Application

Have interns practice what they have learned with a co-worker (not another intern) and give feedback to the on-site instructor or volunteer feedback to the group at the next workshop. During the coming week, have on-site instructors give nonjudgmental feedback to interns regarding the impressions they are making on the job.

Personal Growth: Confidentiality

The purpose of doing activities with feelings and group process can also be introduced, but briefly. Although a fuller introduction is delayed until Week 2, the process can begin now. First, establish confidentiality and explain the trust that can grow from it. Varenhorst's (1980) *Curriculum Guide for Student Peer Counseling Training* (PCT) addresses this (p. 78) as does the *Tribes* curriculum (Gibbs, 1987). Interns are experiencing the feeling of being a stranger, to each other and on the job. This is an excellent opportunity to demonstrate the usefulness of the deliberate self-consciousness, self-monitoring, and self-evaluation that makes the workshop powerful. The Personal Growth exercise, ''Welcoming a Stranger,'' is integrated with the Job-Keeping lesson for the next week. The exercise can be prepared for this week by (a) doing the ''Introduction to Session Topic'' (PCT, p. 23); (b) evaluating what co-workers did to make the interns feel welcome during their first days on the job; and (c) assigning the interns the task of making new interns who will be on the job and at the workshop in Week 2 feel welcome by using the methods discussed and learned in the lesson. On-site instructors have the responsibility of prompting responses from interns during the coming week on the job, and during Week 2's seminar.

Week 2

LESSONS IN		
[X] Job Keeping	[X] Personal Growth	
[X] Job	[ ] Interpersonal Growth	
[ ] Job Search	[X] Timely Topics	

Job: Basic Clerical

See Week 1. Emphasize the act of referring back to performance from the previous week, so that interns can see their progress and practice memory tasks that they will need to be successful in the job.

Personal Growth: Introductions

Review concepts of confidentiality and trust. Review the "Welcoming a Stranger" concepts and have interns share observations and reports of welcoming behaviors on the job and at the seminar. Discuss how interns who attended the previous week's seminar welcomed the newcomers. Praise follow-through heavily. With what is now the complete group for the seminar, repeat the purpose of the peer counseling activities: to learn how to better share feelings, to learn how to support each other, and to get through the transition from school more successfully. The overall context is the transition from school to adult life. The power that comes from the communication skills learned in the peer counseling activities will certainly increase success on the job, but the group will be more effectively built if peer counseling is introduced as a set of activities that have their own merit and are *not* directly related to work and vocation. Knowing that there is a safe place for feelings and for building relationships will multiply the overall power of the vocational curriculum. For today, students can introduce themselves to each other by talking about their names, where they came from, and other autobiographical information that is safe to share and that will make them more memorable to other members of the group. Gibbs (1987) and Varenhorst (1980) both offer exercises that structure and facilitate the process of getting acquainted with other people.

Timely Topic: CLP Pyramid, Rules, and Agreements

Explain the CLP Pyramid of skills (see Figure 2.1). This illustrates what the curriculum is about and shows how it must be built from the ground up. The intent is not to make interns pass a class or get a grade. Rather, the purpose is for them to find a job or get into college or both by the time they leave the program. We are providing what they have told us they want. Explain the ongoing commitment, mention that they will be meeting their transition

specialist the following week, and say that this is how we live up to that commitment. Explain their right to challenge the curriculum and our right to justify it. At this point, we are not "selling," we are telling them what must be done.

Pass out and discuss the CLP Rules (see Appendix 2.8). Make the presentation concise, clear, and direct.

Job Keeping: First Day on the Job, Part 2

This lesson is an excellent opportunity for those who attended last week to be competent and confident, and for the newcomers not to feel that they are being left out or are lagging behind.

Rationale/Warmup/Review

Ask who in the class knows everyone there (no one will know everyone). Explain that the group is going to do an exercise called "Welcoming a Stranger." Ask interns to guess what the exercise is about and what we might do in the exercise. Review last week's relevant points.

Presentation and Guided Practice

Do the PCT lesson "Welcoming a Stranger" (PCT, pp. 22–26). This is an exercise that simulates the feelings of being an unoriented newcomer in a group. Interns are broken down into small groups of six or less. A single intern is asked to leave the room and return. The group role-plays the CLP community classroom, and the members are left to their own devices, after being asked to do only what they would in order to welcome a newcomer. The participants are finally debriefed with questions that address how it felt to be treated as a stranger, and what techniques were effective in making a person feel comfortable.

Life-Skill Competency Application

Ask the interns to decide where and how they will adapt and use what they've learned, preferably at the work site. Have them negotiate with their on-site instructors how they will report the results of their efforts.

Week 3

LESSONS IN	
|X| Job Keeping	|X| Personal Growth
|X| Job	|X| Interpersonal Growth
| | Job Search	|X| Timely Topics

Job: Basic Clerical

Remember to have materials and instructors ready for the interns 10 minutes before class is scheduled to begin.

See Week 1. Those who have gained some speed and accuracy in checking food items should move into making change. Carefully monitor calculator and typing interns to make sure that they are challenged and making progress. Interns with typing potential—they should be able to exceed 30 words per minute with a little practice—should be identified and allowed to practice typing during this period for the entire semester. Assign a small group of interns to the following lesson in taking phone messages.

Taking Phone Messages

The goal is to teach interns how to identify an occupied line, an incoming call, and a call on hold by the rate of flashes; to learn how to use the intercom; and to learn the parts of a message notepad.

Rationale/Warmup/Review

The interns generate a list of job skills that are helpful to learn. The teacher writes their answers on the board. Possible responses are answering phones, typing, operation of a cash register, and operation of a calculator.

Presentation

Demonstrate message taking to the interns. Using a transparency of a message pad, teach these steps: Identify information that must be taken right away (the name of the person calling, the person the message is for, the phone number, and a short message); repeat back the information recorded on the message pad; hang up and finish completing the message, with the date and time of the call and the message taker's signature.

Teach interns tips to slow down a fast caller and how to take the message as quickly as possible. Demonstrate shortcuts.

Guided Practice

Have interns form a triad. Using a telephone trainer, have one intern take a message, one intern call, and one intern operate the telephone trainer. Have the interns rotate in the roles.

Life-Skill Competency Application

Have the interns answer the phone in the school office, with supervision as necessary. Request that supervisors at the work site allow the interns to answer phones.

Job Keeping: Be Aware of Time

Review the first step on the Pyramid. Use the *Don't Get Fired!* (DGF) lesson (Anema & Lefkowitz, 1990) and have a serious discussion of the importance of good attendance habits. Review the CLP policy on attendance—rewards for good attendance; warnings, probation, and termination for unexcused absences—and explain that CLP is more tolerant than most employers, but different in quality from schools, and stricter. Make sure the interns have the correct phone numbers and contact people for calling in when they cannot get to work, and remind them that there is no excuse not to call. Drill responses to hypothetical situations. Ask the interns what they would do if they were an employer with an employee who was late or absent frequently.

Personal Growth: Animal, Color, Water, White Room

Begin to develop a sense of self among the interns. Do the following exercise, in which interns write adjectives describing their favorite animal, color, body of water, and reactions to being in a white, enclosed room. Have every intern seated with a pencil and piece of paper. Explain to the interns that this is an exploration apart from their vocational training. Review what an adjective is and give several examples. Ask the interns to write down their favorite animal and three to five adjectives that describe it, and to explain why they like it. Keep the room quiet, and help the interns search for the best words without disturbing the peaceful ambience. Then have them write their favorite color and list adjectives that disclose why they like it. Do the same for the interns' favorite form of water (e.g., lake, steam, ice, rain) and have them list adjectives that describe why they like it. Finally, ask the interns to imagine themselves in a white, enclosed room with no windows or doors. Let them write adjectives that describe how that feels. Give the interns adequate time to respond.

Now find a volunteer to share her or his favorite animals and the accompanying adjectives. Ask for a few more. Share the idea that these answers are thought by some to reveal what people think of themselves. Keeping this in mind, the last volunteer to speak should be one who has communicated high self-esteem. Ask for more volunteers. Draw in the ones who don't want to share. Ask for volunteers to share their favorite color and accompanying adjectives. After a few have volunteered, perhaps all, tell the group that these answers are believed by some to tell how others would like to be perceived, or how they believe they are perceived. Repeat this process again for water. This one reveals sexual self-image, or intimate relationships. Finally, the white room tells how we feel about death, transformation, or drastic change.

Let the information be shared, the feelings felt. No coercion. No lecturing. No judging. No explaining.

Interpersonal Growth: Learning Your Job Duties

Have the interns write out their job title and job duties. This will later be taught as a job search skill as well. Before dismissing the interns, have them recite their name, job title, and at least three job duties. On-site instructors should prompt them in the coming week at the community classroom sites. Give each intern a copy of his or her "job description." Always deliver praise to each intern for good voice, pleasant presence, precise reciting, sincere tone, or any combination of these qualities. Give some general feedback and modeling on how you would like to see this performed, but remarks to individuals should only praise. Just make sure the interns all recite their job duties at least once before being dismissed.

Timely Topic: Pioneer, Warrior, Hero

Have the interns define what a Pioneer is, what a Warrior is, and what a Hero is, and put their ideas on the board. Whatever they say is essentially correct. After each term is defined, offer your own definition, and explain that you are looking for those qualities in a work personality. Pioneers venture into unexplored territories (like work). Warriors are prepared to fight and struggle, but are wise in picking their battles and only fight when they absolutely have to. Heroes rescue others in need of help and are able to rise to a challenge and overcome odds. Clearly, interns with serious learning, behavior, family, or neighborhood problems must develop these qualities if they are to succeed. This is an opportunity to praise them heavily for trying.

Ask for feedback on the curriculum so far, and write down what the interns say. Do not respond to the comments, defend, or "sell" the program. Just take in the feedback and let the interns see that their comments are being recorded. Let them know that they are free to say whatever they want.

Introduce the transition specialist, who visits today. The transition specialist's presentation should explain:

- How he or she keeps the CLP promise of an ongoing commitment

- The benign nature of opening a case with the Department of Rehabilitation
- The advantages of rehabilitation services
- Several "success story" anecdotes
- Ways in which the transition specialist can be contacted, and ways in which a relationship can develop

Week 4

LESSONS IN	
|X| Job Keeping	|X| Personal Growth
|X| Job	|X| Interpersonal Growth
		Job Search	|X| Timely Topics

Job: Basic Clerical

See Week 3.

Job Keeping: Be Responsible

Rationale/Warmup/Review

Use the DGF lesson. Have the class brainstorm what being responsible means, and then test and organize the concept.

Presentation

Do the DGF lesson, assigning interns to parts.

Guided Practice

Lead a discussion based on the DGF questions (Decision Time and Discussion Questions) at the end of the lesson.

Life-Skill Competency Application

During the coming week, have the on-site instructors give nonjudgmental feedback to the interns based on the points of this lesson.

Personal Growth: Problem Solving

Introduce problem-solving skills. Begin with a discussion of how the interns are feeling about their jobs. If any interns have had problems they want to share, make note of them and return to these interns later to demonstrate the skill. Remember that this is not the place to lecture or to tell interns the solutions to on-the-job or other communication problems. It is the place to show them how they can generate strategies and experience satisfaction and competence. Teach and show the process in the following way:

1. *Identify the feelings* that a person is having (introduce the List of Feelings in Appendix 3.1) by modeling ''I'' statements—these are taught in Week 5, but should be modeled and introduced in this lesson. Interns can become desensitized to the idea of ''I'' statements and can also grasp the first step in making an ''I'' statement, identifying and speaking the feeling. (Later, when ''I'' statements are taught directly, problem-solving sessions will delve into them more deeply.)

2. *Identify the issues* around the problem, learning how to make an abstraction, form a concept, and get some distance from the problem, taking control of it.

3. *Generate alternatives* in a free-for-all brainstorm where all suggestions are acceptable, and put all of them on the board, making sure that extreme solutions are included. Do not lecture or restrict the options.

4. *Test alternatives*, letting the interns set the standards of what are and are not reasonable courses of action.

5. *Make a strategic plan* to act on some of the better alternatives.

When the group understands these steps, return to the problems that have been shared, or ask again for other problems, and facilitate the group going through this process at least two more times, using real on-the-job problems.

Do the ''Having a Conversation'' exercise (PCT, pp. 1–6) or *Tribes* (Gibbs, 1987). This is an opportunity for the interns to simply spend unstructured time in pairs and have conversations. Encourage them to select people they do not know. As with all Personal Growth exercises, this is an opportunity for the on-site instructors to let go of their authoritarian role and let the ESW teacher lead the group. This is an important opportunity for the community classroom teachers to join the group and relate to the interns as a peer.

Interpersonal Growth: Ordering Job Duties

Have interns practice ''Ordering Job Duties'' (see Week 3).

Timely Topics: Why Work Without Pay?

Begin to move from a ''telling'' to a ''selling'' stance with the group by asking them to brainstorm reasons

they might ever be willing to work without pay. The idea is to tease out some of the other reasons we all have for working, and to help the interns get in touch with some of the satisfactions of work that go beyond pay. The program fails when an intern views it as merely a way to make some extra money. CLP pays too little, and interns must understand that the real value of CLP is that it will enable them to get and keep a better-paying and more satisfying job.

One of the things CLP does offer is on-the-job supervision, and ''selling'' this to interns is one of the very tricky tasks the staff must face. There must be open channels that allow the staff to give interns specific feedback, enabling them to improve their performance. It is important to avoid the humiliation of criticizing interns on their lack of employability. At the same time, we cannot let them believe that they are more competent and job-ready than they really are. Developing good on-the-job supervisory skills is one way the staff can achieve this delicate balance. Here the ESW teacher can ''sell'' the idea of supervision. It is up to the on-site instructors to make good on the benevolence and educational merit of their presence on the job.

Reward and praise heavily interns who have completed and processed their paperwork. Use a posted chart to record their progress (see Appendix 3.2). Keep interns who have not kept pace with their paperwork after the workshop, and make a contract with them, explaining the consequences clearly—by the time the work experience becomes paid employment, interns without completed paperwork will return to their schools until it is done. This is probably occurring this week. Legally, interns cannot continue to work when other interns at the same site are being paid. Ethically, they have earned the right to receive pay if they have been making progress. Educationally, they must experience real consequences for not processing paperwork in a timely fashion. Give a 3- to 5-day deadline, and return to school any interns who have not completed their paperwork at that time, with no exceptions.

Before dismissing the interns, have them recite their name, job title, and at least three job duties. On-site instructors can prompt them to recite duties on the job during the coming week.

Week 5

LESSONS IN	
|X| Job Keeping	|X| Personal Growth
|X| Job	|X| Interpersonal Growth
| | Job Search	|X| Timely Topics

Job: Basic Clerical

See Week 3. Remind the interns that they will be rotating to new job skill activities in two weeks (beginning Week 7), and that this is an opportunity to really master the skills they are working on. If any interns have achieved mastery, either move them to more advanced activities or rotate them early.

Job Keeping: Follow the Schedule

Rationale/Warmup/Review

Use the DGF lesson. Use actual events that have happened during the semester, letting the group define and explain the concept and consequences of sticking to the schedule.

Presentation

Do the DGF lesson.

Guided Practice

Have a discussion based on the questions at the end of the lesson.

Life-Skill Competency Application

Have on-site instructors give nonjudgmental feedback during the week based on the points of this lesson.

Timely Topics: Stamina and Determination

The novelty of going to work is wearing off for some of the interns at this point, and the first cases of boredom are probably emerging. The concepts of stamina and determination need to be developed. In this particular instance, examples of athletes and popular celebrities are effective as reinforcers and as easily understood examples. The continuum from the CLP internship to vocational success (internship to entry-level job to postsecondary training to promotion to career change, etc.), *not* to celebrity status (which should not be excluded, but certainly not emphasized), should be simply and clearly laid out. Then return to the issue of the day, which is developing the skill of getting through the work week at a job that is good but less than ultimate in satisfaction.

If this lecture/discussion is going well, it can be extended to discuss the line between tolerance and stamina on the job and more serious job dissatisfaction, which may lead to job change. Give examples. However, in 99% of the cases, the CLP internship should be an experience and lesson in following through, and only the very most extreme cases of dis-

satisfaction or potential failures should result in an intern transferring, quitting, or being terminated. For those who are less than satisfied with their CLP placement, this is an important lesson in sticking it out for a semester and building a résumé and a good reference that will get them to the job they want. It is crucial not to back down on this point. The fundamentals of stamina, determination, and delayed gratification, as illustrated by example, are the key lessons here.

Before dismissing the interns, have them recite their name, job title, and at least three job duties. On-site instructors should prompt them to recite duties on the job during the coming week.

Personal Growth: Making "I" Statements

"I" statements are a key tool to assertive social skills, problem-solving skills, self-awareness, and overall clear communication. This day, they should be presented outside of a vocational context. They should be modeled, with several examples, using the List of Feelings (Appendix 3.1).

An "I" statement has three parts: the feeling felt, the conditions under which it is felt, and a self-disclosing statement that explains why the person has that feeling: I feel _____ when someone _____, because _____. For example: "I feel angry, betrayed, and mistrustful when someone steals from my purse at work, because I am poor and need the money, and because I want to feel safe and trusting with my co-workers. I feel supported, cared about, and appreciated when someone tells me that I am doing good work, because I want to succeed, and because sometimes I don't know when I'm doing well, and I never did well in school before."

But remember that interns can and should use examples that are not job-related. Repeat the "Having a Conversation" exercise from Week 4 again, but encourage them to incorporate "I" statements. Tour the room and actively prompt some of them. This is an opportunity for interns to practice making these statements, without being in the high-pressure setting of actually resolving a crisis. Thus they will be better prepared for those situations when they do arise. Remember to include on-site instructors as participants.

During the debriefing of this activity, return to the problem-solving process taught last week, and show how "I" statements can help people identify problems, both on and off the job. Take another real-life example from the group if one is volunteered. Close by showing how an "I" statement can communicate a problem clearly to another person without antagonizing that person, and how it is a powerful alternative to blame, resentment, or repression. In future lessons, this may be tied to social skills training in relationships with superiors and co-workers, but that is not essential today.

Interpersonal Growth: Ordering Job Duties

Have interns practice "Ordering Job Duties" (see Week 3).

Week 6

LESSONS IN	
|X| Job Keeping	|X| Personal Growth
|X| Job	|X| Interpersonal Growth
|X| Job Search	|X| Timely Topics

Job: Basic Clerical

See Week 3. Remind interns that they will be moving on to new tasks in the next week. Encourage them to try for a personal best in accuracy and speed. At the end of the session, give each intern a piece of paper with the skill that has been achieved so far, written out in the form in which it would be found on a résumé.

Personal Growth: Exchanging Positives; Having a Conversation

Have the group sit in a circle. Each intern must go around the room and tell another person something he or she likes about that person. Avoid being the first model, as interns may not generate and search for real feelings, and may simply mimic yours. However, you can go third or fourth to keep the pace going. When all the interns have participated to the best of their ability, let the group sit for a long moment with the good feelings that have been generated. Explain how these good feelings of praise and positiveness can be repeated in other areas of their life, including the job. Have the interns think of things they like about the people they work with, and assign them the task of delivering that praise in the coming week. Make sure that the on-site instructors prompt the interns to complete this assignment.

If there is time, prolong the good feelings by repeating the "Having a Conversation" lesson (see "Personal Growth," Week 4).

Interpersonal Growth: Ordering Job Duties

Have interns practice "Ordering Job Duties" (see Week 3).

Job Search: Job Interview Questions

Rationale

Allow the interns to discuss the importance of knowing how to conduct a job search. When they have articulated and reached a consensus on a desire to do so, offer them the services of the program. Present the interns with the Counselor–Job Seekers' Agreement (see Appendix 3.3). Read and review it, and have each intern who wants to work sign it.

Warmup/Review

Develop an intern-generated list of job search skills necessary to find a job. Write the responses on the board. Possible responses are interview skills, résumés, job applications, and job leads.

Presentation

Ask how many interns have gone on job interviews, how it felt, and what helped the most. What areas of improvement did they notice? Have they improved since their first interview, and if so how? What advice would they have for other interns? Have the interns practice answering possible questions (see Appendix 3.4 for suggestions) to learn what the interviewer is looking for.

Guided Practice

Have the interns break up into two groups. Group 1 generates a list of possible interview questions, while group 2 generates an interview rating sheet. Both activities are shared with the class. The teacher will later type up the intern-produced work. Or use the Interview Rating Sheet (Appendix 3.5) and have both groups generate questions, exchanges, and answers.

Life-Skill Competency Application

Interns will use the rating sheet and interview questions they generated to practice interviews in Week 10.

Job Search: Brainstorming for a Resume

Take the sheet of paper handed out in the Job Skills session, and have the interns review their work experiences from as far back as possible. Have them write out more of their skills (supervise young children, assist carpenter, perform janitorial duties, file records, etc.), learning the style and translating volunteer, summer job, and school work-study experience into a respectable history of things they can do. Make sure that this document is saved as it will be used to generate their résumés in Week 9.

Job-Keeping Skills: Following Directions

Take examples from the group showing instances when they have needed to follow directions on the job. Poll the on-site instructors for examples of both excellent behaviors and problems. If an intern with a problem following directions is comfortable enough discussing it, use the problem-solving process (See ''Personal Growth,'' Week 4) to perhaps come up with a solution, such as asking for help when needed, asking for modeled instructions, or asking for repeated instructions. Remind the interns that they will be doing a lot more work in this area, and that it is an important job-keeping skill.

Use the DGF lesson in the same format as in previous weeks (for example, Week 5).

Timely Topics: Tolerance and Terminations

Illustrate the continuum from school to work and a successful postsecondary life. CLP *can* be one possible route, for those who make it. Those who are terminated (list the reasons why one might be terminated: attendance, disruption, dishonesty, poor effort, poor performance) may still succeed through the other paths. The role of CLP is to be more tolerant than an employer in a typical job situation might be, but more demanding than school; we reserve the right to return any intern to school who is not succeeding by our standards, just as an employer has the right to fire an employee.

Introduce the positive role the Department of Rehabilitation can play and identify their services, including the CLP transition specialist. Say that getting a case opened is the next round of necessary paperwork that we are going to cover, and remind them that it is also going to further test this skill.

Before dismissing the interns, have them recite their name, job title, and at least three job duties. On-site instructors can prompt them to recite duties on the job during the coming week.

Week 7

LESSONS IN	
|X| Job Keeping	|X| Personal Growth
|X| Job	|X| Interpersonal Growth
|X| Job Search	|X| Timely Topics

Job: Intermediate Clerical

All interns should move to a new activity. Exceptions might include someone who is making very good progress in a specific skill like typing and wishes to continue working at it. New skills such as taking telephone messages can be introduced. Most interns will move from cash registering to calculator work and vice versa. On-site instructors should be working very hard to help interns with the transition and to get them involved in the new activity. Also, on-site instructors should have transferred on-the-job skills to the classroom. They should report on any job skills in which they have observed interns having learning difficulties, or additional skills that would increase interns' employability. Address these whenever possible.

Personal Growth: Asking Open and Feeling Questions

Tell interns that today they will learn ways in which they can improve their ability to make friends by asking good questions. Do the lesson from PCT (Varenhorst, 1980, pp. 7–11) on asking open and feeling questions. In this exercise, interns learn appropriate ways to ask personal questions that stimulate full conversation. The point of the exercise is to break students free of monosyllabic responses to questions, and to let them know how it feels to be truly interested in someone else's favorite topic, or to have several people interested in theirs.

A second lesson for this day is on active listening. Do the lesson from PCT (Varenhorst, 1980, pp. 12–16). This is an activity where students pair off; alternately, each member engages in active listening while the other shares something personal and positive.

Timely Topics: Social Skills—Why Have a Workshop on Them?

Talk about why social skills on the job—getting along with others—is so important. Tell the story of past terminations as well as the success stories, such as the story of one graduate who was poorly matched to a job at a very large business office, but whose social skills were so good that the employer found and redesigned a job that she could do. ''A decision to hire is a decision to like.'' Refer back to the CLP Pyramid. At this point, the interns should be attending regularly. Now that the interns are all going to work, are their co-workers happy to see them?

Job Keeping: Be Helpful and Friendly to Everyone at Work

Warmup/Review

Discuss what being friendly and helpful means, and why it's important.

Presentation

Do the DGF lesson and assign parts to interns.

Guided Practice

Lead a discussion based on the questions at the end of the lesson.

Life-Skill Competency Application

During the coming week, have the on-site instructors give nonjudgmental feedback to the interns based on the points of this lesson.

Interpersonal Growth: First Session and Overall Session Format

Lead a discussion in which interns articulate and own the need for having and learning social skills.

Introduce the concept of social skills and the concepts of learning and teaching using the basketball analogy in Goldstein's *Skillstreaming the Adolescent* (1980, pp. 141–160). When an intern has taught the basketball skill and the group can repeat the process (show, try, discuss, practice), demonstrate how it will be used by teaching ''Ordering Job Duties'' (see skill sheet, Appendix 2.12). This skill integrates a rote task that interns have been practicing and know from the past several weeks. Now they can put it into the social skills training format and experience mastery of the skill—enabling them to grasp the process—almost immediately. The process includes instructor modeling; letting an intern try it, with other interns rating the performance; having a quick discussion and using nonjudgmental feedback (introduce this concept—it will be taught with detail in the ''Personal Growth'' strand); and allowing the intern additional practice in it. Videotaping equipment can be used if it is available, both to record performances and to show taped demonstrations of social skills being performed.

The session format can be outlined as follows:

1. Introductions:
   a. Name something you like doing in your spare time.
   b. Name something you like doing at work.
2. Overview:
   a. Purpose of the group—learning to get along, dealing with people, dealing with feelings, handling stressful situations, being liked so that you will get hired, feeling comfortable in situations.
   b. Examples—asking for help, starting a conversation, accepting negative feedback, ordering job duties.

   c. Procedures of learning—show, try, discuss, practice.
   d. Steps—listing the steps in shooting a basketball.
3. Rules: The group is confidential, be on time, don't be afraid to perform.
4. First and subsequent sessions—overview of skill:
   a. Define the skill (trainer and interns).
   b. Give its rationale.
   c. Give examples where the skill would be used.
   d. Distribute skill sheets (Appendix 2.12).
5. Present videotaped models.
6. Give and get feedback on the models.
7. Present live trainer models—give and get feedback.
8. Organize trainee role playing:
   a. The volunteer chooses a coactor who is most like the actual person in the role-played situation.
   b. Set the stage with a lot of verbal detail of the situation. Where is it? Are you standing or sitting? What is the time of day? What is the emotional atmosphere?
   c. Develop a script. What will you say for step a? What will the coactor say? Ask the same questions for step b.
   d. Develop contingencies—what will you do if . . . ?
   e. Give a pep talk and begin.
9. Perform trainee role playing:
   a. Place one trainer at the chalkboard.
   b. Ask one trainer to prompt.
   c. Interrupt if necessary.
10. Feedback:
    a. The main actor should wait until all comments have been heard.
    b. Ask for the coactor's reactions.
    c. Ask how well the steps were followed.
    d. Ask the main actor: How do you feel about your performance?
11. Practice:
    a. Repeat until the script is mastered.
    b. Expand feedback to adjunctive components following mastery.
    c. View the videotape before final feedback.
12. Homework:
    a. Ask the main actor how, when, where, and with whom the skill could be practiced.
    b. Trainees who didn't role-play can still do the homework.
    c. Remind the trainees that they will be probed for skills on the job site.

Job Search: How to Conduct a Job Search

Show the entire group how to use a job search contact sheet (see Appendix 3.6) to help organize their efforts. Send two previously chosen interns out on a supported job search. They are actually dismissed from class, and they will "pound the pavement" with an on-site instructor accompanying them. The on-site instructor encourages them to walk into businesses, role-plays with them, and prompts the responses necessary to track job leads.

If they have not dressed well enough, send out two interns who are better dressed. In other words, show that interns will lose out on opportunities if they do not prepare for them. The rest of the class, intrigued by the dismissal of two of their peers, will immediately engage in active preparations for their job search.

Basic Skill Objectives

Interns will look for jobs through cold-calling, walk-ins, employment agencies, school programs, and the Department of Rehabilitation.

Warmup/Review

Use an intern-generated list of job search skills necessary to find a job. Put the responses on the board; include interview skills, résumés, job applications, and job leads.

Presentation

Brainstorm ways people find jobs and write them on the board, defining terms as they come up: want ads, school, family and friends, walk-ins, cold calls, employment agencies. On a clean piece of paper, have the interns write the names, addresses, and phone numbers of their personal contacts who would be good for both job leads *and* as references.

Ask each intern the number of jobs obtained through the various methods and make a tally of them. Draw attention to the fact that school programs will probably top the list, but that the interns won't have school programs after they graduate. The next most successful area is family and friends. Make the point that these resources will remain after graduation, and that they are the easiest and most reliable method. Then rank order the rest. Ask the interns why they think the resources are in that order.

Guided Practice

Have interns role-play walk-ins. Who will they ask to speak to? (The manager or the person in charge of hiring) Will they leave anything? (Yes, a résumé or job application or both) Will they call back? (Yes,

approximately every 3 weeks to remind the employer that they are still interested) Where will they go? (Many places, especially places likely to hire at that time of the year)

Role-play cold calls. Who will they ask for? (The manager) What will they say? (Their name and the purpose of the call) What if there are no jobs available? (Ask the manager for other leads) Will they take notes? (Yes, on the job search contact sheet shown in Appendix 3.6) Show the interns how to use a job search contact sheet to help organize their efforts.

Life-Skill Competency Application

Have the two interns who are the best dressed and best prepared conduct their own job search. Have them go out with support and supervision from an on-site instructor, do walk-ins and pick up applications, practice cold calls, and talk to family and friends. Have them report back every week, and praise their efforts heavily. Have them get two copies of applications, and praise them just for getting the applications. In later trips, set the goal of getting an interview. Emphasize follow-up. Pick two others to be excused for a job search the next week, and tell them to dress appropriately (the on-site instructor should provide additional prompts). If they don't, send a better-dressed intern in their place for that day. In other words, they will lose the opportunity if they do not prepare for it.

Job Search: Learning How to Do a Job Interview

Large-Group Activity

Have interns make a poster listing all the things they should do in a good interview, such as talking about their experiences related to the job they're interviewing for. Lead a large-group discussion in each class before breaking into groups, using the following topics:

1. Have the interns practice answering possible interview questions. Focus on one problem each intern has. Have the interns practice turning the negative trait into a positive trait (e.g., I'm slow, but accurate).

2. Ask the interns to list "good hobbies": team sports, reading novels versus comic books.

3. Have the interns ask the interviewer questions, for example, about company benefits. Show the film *What Are Company Benefits?* (1977).

4. Have the interns state why they want the job and why the company should hire them.

Warmup/Review

Elicit an intern-generated list of job search skills necessary to finding a job. Put their responses on the board. Responses might include interview skills, résumés, job applications, and job leads.

Presentation

Review on an overhead projector the intern- and teacher-generated Interview Rating Sheet (or use Appendix 3.5). Have a group discussion of the different areas the interviewee will be rated on.

Guided Practice

Have the interns view a brief part of a former intern's interview and rate it using the rating sheet.

Life-Skill Competency Application

Have interns form triads to interview and rate each other. Demonstrate the skill of nonjudgmental observation. This will be directly addressed in Week 8. In the latter part of the semester have a guest employer interview the interns.

Have the interns watch other interns' interviews. Have the interns note strengths and weaknesses. Heighten their awareness of language: voice tone, amplitude, clarity, sentence structure.

Week 8

```
                 LESSONS IN
 |X| Job Keeping    |X| Personal Growth
 |X| Job            |X| Interpersonal Growth
 |X| Job Search     |X| Timely Topics
```

Job: Intermediate Clerical

See Week 7. Have the interns stay with the new activity begun last week.

Personal Growth: Making Nonjudgmental Observations

Review last week's lessons in asking open and feeling questions and in active listening. Today the interns will learn how to make nonjudgmental but helpful observations. This will help them to develop questioning and listening skills and to help each other in social skills training. They will also be getting more out of life in general by becoming able to make good nonjudgmental observations and to communicate them effectively. In this lesson from PCT (Varenhorst, 1980, pp. 17–21), a third person is added to the pair to observe the interactions of the listener and the speaker, and to give feedback that objectively mirrors but does not judge. Use the items from the PCT appendix (Varenhorst, 1980, pp. 80–81) on active listening and observations.

Timely Topics: Working with Vocational Rehabilitation

Give time to the transition specialist or a staff person from the Department of Rehabilitation to address or conduct general medical exams, psychological testing, paperwork, job club, and so on.

Job Keeping: Don't Talk to Friends While Working

Do the DGF lesson.

Warmup/Review

Discuss why ''don't talk to friends while working'' may or may not be a good rule of thumb on the job.

Presentation

Do the DGF lesson and assign parts to the interns.

Guided Practice

Lead a discussion based on the questions at the end of the lesson.

Life-Skill Competency Application

Have on-site instructors or supervising employees give nonjudgmental feedback to the interns based on the points of this lesson during the coming week.

Interpersonal Growth: Ordering Job Duties

Continue practicing ''Ordering Job Duties.'' Everyone should get through it and should be able to master it, but do take enough time to give repeated practice to those interns who need it. This should complete learning and mastery of this skill, as well as orientation to the social skills training format. Tell the interns that they will be probed on the job by staff and visitors on this skill—remind on-site instructors to probe it daily—and that it is also a useful skill that will be integrated into their job interview skills.

Job Search: The Personal Data Sheet

Life-Skill Objective

At the end of this lesson, interns will be able to explain how a Personal Data Sheet can be used to assist in completing job applications.

Warmup/Review

Interns generate a list of job search skills that are necessary to find a job. The teacher writes their responses on the board. Possible responses include interview skills, résumés, job applications, and job leads.

Presentation

Break into small groups of four to five. Pass out two "completed" job applications, both from the same person. One has obvious misspellings, incomplete answers, obvious wrong dates, poor choices of personal references, and poor reasons for quitting a job. The other has no misspellings, complete answers, every box completed, professional language, and accurate dates. Have the interns compare the two applications and ask one person from each group to point out errors in the first application to the class. Discuss the tools necessary to complete a good application. Possible responses include a dictionary, phone book, friend, personal records, or a "cheat sheet" or Personal Data Sheet (see Appendixes 3.7 and 3.9).

Guided Practice

Brainstorm possible work experiences that would help build a job history. Interns then complete Personal Data Sheets in small groups. Provide a dictionary, telephone books, and teacher assistance.

Life-Skill Competency Application

Have interns bring in blank job applications or pass out different blank applications. They should use their Personal Data Sheet to complete them. If there are questions on the new application that aren't covered on the data sheet, have the interns add the information to the back of their sheets. Personal Data Sheets are to be taken to every job search. Review the interview questions generated by the group 2 weeks ago. Ask if any of the job seekers have been asked any of these questions. What were their answers?

Send a different two interns (previously chosen) out on a supported job search.

Week 9

LESSONS IN	
|X| Job Keeping	|X| Personal Growth
|X| Job	|X| Interpersonal Growth
|X| Job Search	|X| Timely Topics

Job: Intermediate Clerical

See Week 7.

Job Keeping: Keep Yourself Busy

Do the DGF lesson.

Warmup/Review

Role-play an employer who has one opening and two candidates who appear to be equally qualified. The employer can afford to hire them both for a 2-week probation period, but doesn't tell them that one of them will be retained and the other let go. Then role-play one candidate who does everything she is asked to do and finishes her assigned tasks, but then lights up a cigarette and takes a break. Contrast this role play to that of a second candidate who finishes his tasks and then goes to look for more work to do, or assists co-workers. Ask the class who they would hire if they were the employer.

Address this topic in lecture form as one of the realities of the workplace, lightly touching on, but not ignoring, the necessity to *appear* busy at times—especially when facing the public. Emphasize the situations where one can stay busy and not just look busy; however, the importance of the latter must be discussed.

Presentation

Do the DGF lesson, assigning parts to interns.

Guided Practice

Lead a discussion based on the discussion questions at the end of the lesson.

Life-Skill Competency Application

Have the on-site instructors give nonjudgmental feedback to interns based on the parts of this lesson during the coming week.

Personal Growth: Crocodile Creek

Do the value-oriented exercise "Abigail, John, Sinbad, Ivan, and Slug." In *The Laundry Works* (Cole & Heilman, 1979) this is called "Crocodile Creek" (see Appendix 3.8); it appeared originally in *Values Clarification* (Simon, Howe, & Kirschenbaum, 1972).

Timely Topics: Beginning the Job Search

Talk about the determination it takes to conduct a successful job search. Set up expectations that an intern won't "hit" on a good job opportunity until the 20th lead, and that is the number to beat. Review the best sources and techniques of job search, and the point of the program: Interns will be released from the program, but still receive their credits, if they find a suitable and approved job and agree to intermittent monitoring by CLP staff. Finally, discuss the similarities between a job search and dating: doing things to impress the other person, letting them know that you are sincerely interested, psyching yourself up for some rejections before the right person comes along.

Job Search: Complete a Personal Resume

Introduce vocabulary such as *résumé, objective, references*, and a list of action verbs (*file, type, clean, organize, supervise, sweep, prepare, cut, chop, cook, deliver, distribute, coordinate*).

Warmup/Review

Use the intern-generated list of job search skills necessary to find a job. Put these responses on the board again. Some possible responses are interview skills, résumés, job applications, and job leads.

Presentation

Show the interns two résumés on the overhead projector (see Appendix 3.9); one is obviously poorly completed. Have the interns identify which résumé is neater, is easier to read, and has the most important information.

Guided Practice

Discuss good general work objectives, references, other (job-related) interests or responsibilities, and work experience. Take a few examples of interns' work experience and "punch them up" with assistance from the class, using the list of action verbs and information from their Personal Data Sheets.

Life-Skill Competency Application

Have the interns write their own résumé using a model supplied by the instructor (see Appendix 3.9) and the various sheets on which they have brainstormed their contacts (for references), values (for interests and hobbies), skills (job duties), and so on. Pair up the most competent interns and provide individualized instruction for those who need the most help.

Final résumés are to be prepared by on-site instructors, kept on disk, and forwarded to the transition specialist.

Send two different interns (previously chosen) out on a supported job search.

Interpersonal Growth: Asking for Help or Instructions

Warmup/Review

What do we do once we get the job in order to survive on the job? The teacher asks the interns who taught them their job and who is their supervisor; the interns must name at least two people. Present the rationale for learning this skill. Ask for any stories from the job site where this skill might have come in handy, and invite discussion of some problems the interns might have had using the skill. Briefly go through the problem-solving process to get some ideas and a sense of what the skill is.

Presentation

Read this case study aloud:

> Reggie's boss rushed in and gave him a job to do. The boss explained the job very quickly. There were many things to be done. Reggie didn't have any note paper to take notes so he tried to listen very carefully as the boss talked, but the boss was in a hurry and talked very fast. Before the boss ran off she asked Reggie, "Do you understand?" Reggie said he thought he did. Reggie started to do the job but he couldn't remember which letter went in the envelope and which was put into the folder. He thought about it for some time, but still wasn't quite sure. The boss was very busy and not always friendly. Should he disturb her or should he just do what he thought was best?
>
> Choose "bother" or "not bother."

With "bother," Reggie's boss thanks him for stopping to ask more questions. She apologizes for not taking more time to explain the job and says she's never too busy to answer questions.

With ''not bother,'' the boss comes back to pick up the work and realizes that it's all been done wrong. She needs the work in 5 minutes for an important meeting. She has to correct the work herself and will be late for the meeting. She looks at Reggie and says, ''I wish you had asked me if you had a question. It would have taken me much less time to answer your question than to fix your mistake.''

Guided Practice

Have interns role play asking for instruction and giving instructions. Introduce the rating sheet (Appendix 2.12) on a transparency. Interns can observe and give feedback after the role play, and interns in the role rate themselves. Have interns use co-workers' names and real job situations first, and performers of the skill should self-evaluate last, after all other feedback has been offered.

Life-Skill Competency Application

Group interns into threes. Have them role-play asking for instructions and giving instructions. One person can observe and give feedback to the other two. The other two can also give feedback. Rotate so each person gets an opportunity to play each role. Have the interns take co-workers' names and use real job situations. The interns should rate themselves in their role of instruction giver or taker.

Week 10

```
              LESSONS IN
|X| Job Keeping   |X| Personal Growth
|X| Job           |X| Interpersonal Growth
|X| Job Search    |X| Timely Topics
```

Job: Intermediate Clerical

See Week 7.

Job Keeping: Following Directions and Making an Extra Effort

Ask for incidents from the job sites when knowing how to follow instructions has been important. The on-site instructors may have more information than the interns. Take care to present incidents accurately,

neither humiliating the interns nor glossing over any examples where they need to improve this skill. Give a *Personal Tests Industry–Oral Directions Test* (Langmuir, 1954) or any other assessment that measures instruction-following ability. Watch carefully for test anxiety; reassure interns that the test is not being graded and will only be used to help them improve performance on the job and to help find them appropriate placements.

Read aloud the following true case study and discuss it. Why was Debbie recognized by the boss for outstanding performance, while Joan was overlooked? Why did the boss like Debbie? Did the boss dislike Joan? Was Joan a good worker? Did Joan deserve the recognition? Was Debbie a good worker? Have any of you seen this happen?

> The setting is a very busy dress store two days before Christmas. Debbie, a popular salesperson, friendly with the boss and everyone else, was scheduled to work. She called in about an hour before she was due for work to say she was sick and couldn't come in. The manager called other salespeople, but everybody was busy with last-minute Christmas shopping and it looked as if nobody would be able to cover. Then the boss called Joan. Joan was a nice, quiet worker who did her job well. She was reluctant to go to work that day because she too had planned to do her last-minute Christmas shopping, but the boss really needed her and she was always willing to help. Joan went to work that day and about 4 hours later Debbie walked in with her arms full of shopping bags. Debbie greeted the boss and all the other workers. She was friendly and very happy that she was able to get so much shopping done. She admitted she wasn't really sick and joked with the boss, while Joan quietly kept working. After the Christmas season the boss had a staff meeting to thank everybody for working so hard and making the Christmas sales event so good. The boss wanted to call attention to one person in particular who had worked very hard. Joan sat up, straightened her dress, and got ready to accept the recognition that was due her, although she was a little embarrassed because she was a shy person. Joan was speechless when the boss called out Debbie's name. Everyone was very happy for Debbie; she was very popular. Of course, Joan never said anything to the boss about it, because she was a quiet person.

Personal Growth: Decision Agent

Do the Decision Agent PCT exercise (Varenhorst, 1980, pp. 32–37). This unique exercise simulates the feeling of gaining or losing control over decisions in life, and is thus extremely practical and useful for youth in transition. You may also want to use other exercises (see also Gibbs, 1987; Clark, 1979; Simon, Howe, & Kirschenbaum, 1972) that compel students to rank values and provide opportunities for them to debrief the experience, learning to value and to understand that each individual's value system is unique.

Timely Topics: Reevaluating Career Objectives

Have interns reevaluate their career objectives based on what they have learned from the Decision Agent exercise. Discuss what might look best on the résumé as a career objective and also encourage them to develop some longer-term goals.

Job Search: Baseline Job Interviews

Conduct baseline job interviews. Give everyone similar questions to answer and provide light praise rather than criticism or instruction. Take a lot of notes, however, on their performance. Instruction will begin at the next session. Since there is no feedback during baseline, it is possible to get through the entire group today.

Warmup/Review

Use the intern-generated list of job search skills necessary to find a job. The interns' responses are on the board. Possible responses include interview skills, résumés, job applications, and job leads.

Presentation

Ask how many interns have gone on job interviews, how it felt, what helped the most, what areas are in need of improvement, what areas have improved since the first interview, and how much they have improved.

Guided Practice

Have the interns (no more than six) review the list of intern- and teacher-generated interview questions. Practice and discuss good answers to the interview questions.

Life-Skill Competency Application

Have the interns practice interviews. Act as the interviewer to get a baseline of the interns' areas of weakness. Videotape the session if possible and discuss the results (good and bad) with the interns.

Send a different two interns who have been previously chosen out on a supported job search.

Interpersonal Growth: Asking for Help or Instructions

Practice "Asking for Help or Instructions" from Week 9. Encourage on-site instructors to find ways to prompt the interns and have the interns practice this skill appropriately on the job. Take reports from those interns who have done this.

Week 11

LESSONS IN	
|X| Job Keeping	|X| Personal Growth
|X| Job	|X| Interpersonal Growth
|X| Job Search	|X| Timely Topics

Job: Intermediate Clerical

See Week 7.

Job Keeping: Give Good Service

Have a discussion of what good service is about. Listen to stories from the job site and use the problem-solving process when possible. This topic will be addressed in great detail in social skills training (SST) sessions to come.

Warmup/Review

Discuss the advantages of being able to give good service.

Presentation

Do the DGF lesson.

Guided Practice

Have a discussion based on the questions at the end of the session.

Life-Skill Competency Application

Have the on-site instructors give nonjudgmental feedback during the week based on the points of the lesson.

Personal Growth: Values Ranking

Do a Values Ranking exercise if you did not do one with the Decision Agent exercise of the previous week (PCT, pp. 32–37).

This is the final Personal Growth activity before the end of the semester. Review with the interns how they have made discoveries about themselves, how they have then begun to develop more sensitivity to others, and finally, how some values are growing out of these activities. Remind them that these processes are always going on and that they can continue to use these tools in their personal relationships with their family, their peers, other interns, their on-site instructors, their transition specialist, and even their employers. The ''nuts and bolts'' of maintaining relationships with others and working on sensitivity will be carried on in the ''Interpersonal Growth'' segment of the seminar. In fact, that area will now be much more intensive. But the opportunities to speak honestly and make friends through the ''Personal Growth'' activities should continue to be offered and should be integrated into the hard work of making a successful transition from school to adult life.

Timely Topics: Past Interns' Anecdotes

Give the interns a more realistic sense of their future by telling them the outcomes of past interns. Make sure that success stories are described, and try to illuminate what the key to each person's success was: dependability, good social skills, determination, and so on. Give examples of past interns who have not done as well and explain why: friends visiting on the job, poor attendance, poor interview skills, dishonesty, and so on.

Job Search: Mock Interviews

Begin mock job interviews in earnest, modeling the format after the SST sessions and integrating that script into a job interview. Give some modeling of a particular feature that is to be emphasized—today, the recitation of job duties. Give the interns opportunities to practice and to give each other nonjudgmental feedback.

Warmup/Review

Use the intern-generated list of the job search skills necessary to find a job. Put the responses on the board again. Some possible responses include interview skills, résumés, job applications, and job leads.

Presentation

Ask how many interns have gone on job interviews, how it felt, what helped them the most, what areas of improvement they noticed, whether they improved since their first interview, and if so, how.

Guided Practice

Have interns (no more than six) review the list of intern- and teacher-generated interview questions. Have them practice and discuss good answers to the interview questions.

Life-Skill Competency Application

Have the interns practice interviews. Act as the interviewer. Videotape the session (if possible) and discuss the results (good and bad) with the interns.

Send a different two interns who have been previously chosen out on a supported job search.

Interpersonal Growth: Having a Conversation

Basic Skill Objective

Identify socially appropriate and inappropriate things to talk about on the job site: weekends versus pay or things of a personal nature; inappropriate people to talk to casually, such as the boss; and inappropriate times to talk and ways of talking, for example, too softly.

The interns should have a good feel for this from the PCT exercises early in the semester. Now we will see how they do with a more behavioral approach. But it is critical to teach that the process of making nonjudgmental observations in this format is the same process that was used in the observation exercises of Week 8.

Warmup/Review

Repeat the exercise from Week 6 in which interns deliver positive statements to each other.

Presentation

Use an overhead transparency to guide the interns through the rating form ''Starting a Conversation'' (Appendix 2.12). Discuss the meaning of the different areas, for example, complimentary comments. Discuss possible topics of conversation, taboo topics, and when and who to talk to. Have a few interns role-play having a conversation and have them rate themselves. Other interns may also participate in the rating.

Guided Practice

Have interns pair off using a count-off system. Practice having a conversation for approximately 10 minutes. Get back in a whole group and discuss how the conversations went, using the rating sheet.

Life-Skill Competency Application

Have the interns select a person at work whom they would like to know better. If necessary, role-play the conversation with the interns. Select a topic of conversation. Have the interns report back to the teacher what the conversation was about and rate themselves.

Week 12

```
                    LESSONS IN
  |X| Job Keeping     | | Personal Growth
  |X| Job             |X| Interpersonal Growth
  |X| Job Search      |X| Timely Topics
```

Job: Intermediate Clerical

See Week 7.

Job Keeping: Leave Your Personal Problems at Home

Give examples of past interns who have hurt their status on the job by not observing this rule. Show sensitivity to personal problems, and use the problem-solving process to generate ideas about how interns can deal with situations in which personal problems seem likely to overwhelm a job situation.

Warmup/Review

Discuss the importance of leaving your blues at home. What are the consequences of failing to do this?

Presentation

Do the DGF lesson.

Guided Practice

Have a discussion based on the questions at the end of the session.

Life-Skill Competency Application

Have the on-site instructors give nonjudgmental feedback during the week based on the points of the lesson.

Timely Topics: Capitalism 101

Explain that we live in a society with a capitalist economy, and describe the basic forces of supply, demand, and profit that so dramatically affect the lives of the interns. Explain that they will not retain employment unless their employer makes more money than their wages plus benefits when they are at work. Explain what may or may not be regrettable about this situation and give them other options, such as starting their own business. Use the problem-solving process to have the interns generate ideas about other ways to go about making a living, so that they understand the range and limitations of their options. Discuss how the economy determines the types of jobs that are available.

Interpersonal Growth: Giving Negative Feedback

Warmup/Review

Ask the interns if they have ever had a fight with the boss or problems on the job. Discuss the situation. Introduce the idea of negative feedback and explain its necessity and how to minimize its antagonistic aspects (nobody *likes* to get negative feedback, even when they appreciate it) without sacrificing the value of being direct. Discuss the idea that it can be very valuable and explain that it can come from a sense of caring about someone and about how he or she is performing—it does not necessarily come from a dislike of someone else. Explain that on the job, if another person really wanted them to do poorly, they probably would not give negative feedback that would help them.

Generate situations for role playing and practice the skill. Encourage the interns to use real situations they have faced during the semester. Take the time to get a deep sense of the situation, and walk the interns through the script even more carefully than usual. The script should be well rehearsed, so that the actors can bring some real anger to their role playing and practice confronting it. Using the rating sheets, have observers watch for the following features of a good performance: *Listen* to the person giving the feedback, *apologize* if you were in the wrong, *understand* what is behind the anger if you feel you are not in the wrong, *ask* for suggestions so that the situation does not recur, *ask* if it is okay to tell your side of the story, and *accept* the power differential if it is your boss who is giving the feedback.

Presentation

Role-play two different approaches to giving and accepting negative feedback. Make a videotape that enacts scenarios of a negative feedback situation with varying levels of competence, or purchase published tapes such as ASSET (Hazel, Schumaker, Sherman, & Sheldon-Wildgen, 1981). Ask the interns how they felt viewing each of the situations. Ask them to identify the positive steps that helped calm the situation.

Guided Practice

Have the interns view a transparency of the steps to giving and accepting negative feedback (Appendix 2.12). Refer back to the video to show how these steps are used. Generate situations for role playing.

Life-Skill Competency Application

Have the interns pair off in threes and give them a situation or have them give you a real-life situation in which they can practice giving and accepting negative feedback. One person observes and the other two take roles, rotating three times so each person has an opportunity in each role. The interns must rate themselves before the observer gives his or her feedback.

Job Search: Mock Interviews

Continue with mock interviews. Have the interns report on how their job searches are proceeding. Collect data.

Send two different interns who have been previously chosen out on a supported job search.

Make sure that résumé writing is included as part of this lesson if interns have not yet completed theirs (see Week 9).

Week 13

LESSONS IN		
|X| Job Keeping			Personal Growth
|X| Job	|X| Interpersonal Growth
|X| Job Search	|X| Timely Topics

Job: Site-Related Tasks

Those interns benefiting most from calculator, cash register, and computer work can and should continue. Other interns who have had specific tasks from the work site identified and transferred to the seminar setting can work on these tasks. Examples include taking telephone messages, receptionist procedures, filing, processing forms, data entry, preparing recipes, counting and reporting inventory, and learning the

local geography. All tasks worked on during this period should be specific to the internship job or to a potential placement. Some interns may work on job search skills such as filling out applications or may look into college options. This is a good time for a third visit by the transition specialist, who starts assessing the postsecondary needs and begins deeper relationships with those interns who are likely to need the most intensive services beyond graduation.

Job Keeping: Get Along with Others

Warmup/Review

Have the interns talk about why it is important to get along with others.

Presentation

Do the DGF lesson, assigning interns to read the parts in the script.

Guided Practice

Do the "Deep Think," "Decision Time," and "Discussion" activities at the end of the lesson. Allow the interns to take the discussion in a direction of their choosing.

Life-Skill Competency Application

During the coming week, have the on-site instructors give the interns feedback on how they are getting along with others, referring back to the points of the lesson as agreed-upon standards. Note that this lesson should tie in well with the Interpersonal Growth lesson for this week.

Job Search: Mock Interviews

See Week 12. Remind the interns to use their job contact sheets. They can bring them in to work and meet with their on-site instructors to plan strategies.

A discussion of career objectives is part of today's emphasis (see Timely Topics as well). The interns need a realistic picture of what the career options are and what they may hope to achieve. They need to hear that many of us do not figure out what we want to do until at least the age of 30, but that it is therefore all the more crucial to have some career goal set before that time, so the early postsecondary years are not wasted. If they invest in a job or education, when a serious career goal emerges or is set, they will have the money or education necessary to pursue it. If they discover what they really want to do when they are 30, and have spent the last 10 or more years "hanging out" and waiting for it, then the odds will be seriously stacked against them. Compare this to the situation of the person who has earned a college degree, or at least saved some money to buy the training time; consider the person who has developed a résumé of skills that provides entry into the field he or she has finally decided to enter.

Talk now about what kind of career goal will look best on the résumé of a recent high school graduate who may be looking for an entry-level position, looking to grow with a company, looking for experience, looking to combine a college education with a stable employment situation, and so on.

The group should complete the first round of mock job interviews today and begin the second. Serious dialogue and feedback hones their interviewing skills. This is a core activity, and one that many graduates have appreciated most from the workshop.

Interpersonal Growth: Giving Negative Feedback

See Week 12, and continue working on "Giving Negative Feedback." To learn this skill effectively, only two to five interns are likely to get through a role play on any given day.

Timely Topics: Job Search Strategies

This is a good time to discuss job search techniques, and in a fashion that highlights the "consulting" mode in which the program and the seminar now operate. That is, this lecture covers some useful tips that will help interns be successful in their job searches; we will assist to the extent that interns ask for assistance, but the burden has shifted to them, and they need to make the decision to use these kindly tips. Give the interns the following speech:

> A good résumé can put you on the offensive in a job interview, even (and especially) a walk-in interview, because you control the flow of information, unlike an interview or job application. Make your résumé a powerful and persuasive presentation of your strengths, keep it up to date and sharp-looking, and always have several copies handy.
>
> Don't forget that the CLP is a high-class job. When they ask you about your most recent job or work experience, this is it, and it is with a reputable company. Refer to CLP as both a training experience, an education, *and* a job.
>
> The mock interviews are not a joke, nor are they busywork. You will see, as soon as you have your first real job interview, that you will be glad you had a chance to practice here. Many of our past interns have told us this. If you do a real interview and have a problem, bring it back to the seminar and share it with us; we can work on it.

Most people get jobs through a self-family-friend network. You too are probably going to have to start with the people you know who are in a field that interests you. And just because you know them doesn't mean that you should stop trying to impress them and "sell" them on your reliability as a good employee.

If you are going to have to walk in "cold," have a strategy: be well groomed, go at a slack business hour, avoid Mondays and Fridays, get the names of the people who hire and of receptionists, get business cards, get two copies of the application, have your résumé and Personal Data Sheet (Appendix 3.7) ready, find out when to call back, and so on. And don't forget to call back.

Though some people do enjoy them, fast-food jobs are generally the pits. There is no getting around that. But it is employment, and it can serve to be a decent "bottom rung" on a ladder to a better and better-paying job. Some of you may have management potential.

Keep a Job Search Contact Sheet (see Appendix 3.6) with employers' names, when to call back, phone numbers, addresses, and so on. Do not count on your memory.

Consider the advantages of "crab-walking" your way up the career ladder with two part-time jobs, or of balancing a job with part-time school. If your first job is not the job you want, you are going to have to have other irons in the fire.

Don't give up, and don't be afraid to let us help you.

Week 14

LESSONS IN	
|X| Job Keeping			Personal Growth
|X| Job	|X| Interpersonal Growth
|X| Job Search	|X| Timely Topics

Job: Site-Related Tasks

See Week 13.

Job Keeping: Take Pride in Your Work

Warmup/Review

Have the interns talk about why it is important to take pride in their work, both for the sake of the employer and for self-esteem and self-respect.

Presentation

Do the DGF lesson, assigning interns to read the parts in the script.

Guided Practice

Do the "Deep Think," "Decision Time," and "Discussion" activities at the end of the lesson. Allow the interns to take the discussion in a direction of their choosing.

Life-Skill Competency Application

During the coming week, the interns should give feedback to the on-site instructors on whether they are taking pride in their work, referring back to the points of the lesson. Do the on-site instructors sense that this pride is sincere? If so, they should help the interns rehearse articulating this pride and receiving the good feelings of being praised for accomplishing it.

Job Search: Mock Interviews

See Week 13.

To help develop the interns' résumés and job interview skills, discuss the importance of interests and hobbies. They can be brought up (though not emphasized) in interviews, and can sometimes provide the edge in getting a job (for example, when an interest or hobby coincides with that of the interviewer). Also, they can help a person be more socially integrated on the job.

Interpersonal Growth: Giving Negative Feedback

See Week 13.

Timely Topics: Waiting for the Job You Want

As a continuation of last week's theme, repeat the main points, this time using a hypothetical example of a youth who is not going to take a "lousy fast-food job" at minimum wage, but is going to wait for the higher-paying and challenging job that suits him. Then present role plays of this person competing for that job, when it does come around, with a peer who *was* working in a fast-food job while the other was waiting. Who's going to get the job? Praise the youth who sets high goals, but develop the concept of using strategy and reaching that goal in steps. It is critical that the interns find some productive activity in work or school, and preferably both, that will, over time, empower them to get the job they want.

Week 15

LESSONS IN	
|X| Job Keeping			Personal Growth
|X| Job	|X| Interpersonal Growth
|X| Job Search	|X| Timely Topics

Job: Site-Related Tasks

See Week 13.

Job Keeping: Don't Talk Back to Your Boss

Warmup/Review

Have the interns talk about why it is important not to argue with the boss.

Presentation

Do the DGF lesson, assigning interns to read the parts in the script.

Guided Practice

Do the "Deep Think," "Decision Time," and "Discussion" activities at the end of the lesson. Make sure that the interns can take the discussion in a direction of their choosing.

Life-Skill Competency Application

See if the interns can recall instances when they could have argued or did argue with their supervisors. Have them play out and discuss the consequences of different routes they could have taken. Present situations in which they might want to argue with the boss, and let them articulate what would be likely to happen. During the coming week, see if the on-site instructors can identify scenarios on the job, and point them out to the interns to heighten their social awareness of these incidents and of opportunities to avoid trouble.

Job Search: Mock Interviews

See Weeks 12 and 13. The second round of mock interviews should be completed today, and the third round begun. Let interns know that actual employers will be used as a "final exam" on interview skills. Have interns who have been going out on job searches report to the group on their successes and frustrations. Reinforce the importance of persistence and the certainty of employment if the interns do persist.

Praise highly, and allow the group to praise, any intern who has already gotten an interview and/or job.

Interpersonal Growth: Accepting Negative Feedback

Present this lesson as the converse to the one interns have been learning over the last 3 weeks, giving negative feedback. Now that they have learned to be cool in a situation when they are angry, they can take on the reciprocal skill of being cool when someone else is angry.

As a model, use the same videotapes and the rating sheets found in Appendix 2.12.

Review the principles of social skills training. Ask why it is important to learn this. Demonstrate the skill. Let someone try it. Discuss it with nonjudgmental feedback. Provide opportunities to practice it.

Timely Topics: Realities of the Work World

Review Clark's eight realities of the work world (Clark, 1979; Clark & Kolstoe, 1990) paraphrased here:

1. Work is still the unstated but real card of citizenship and self-respect in our society (regardless of constitutional rights); guilt, anxiety, and worthlessness are felt by the unemployed.

2. Work often requires mobility and adaptation to another place:
   a. Travel training.
   b. Social standards of a workplace: dress, behavior, and so on.

3. Paid work is largely impersonal:
   a. Qualities associated with play, recreation, and love are not to be expected on the job.
   b. This may turn off an intern initially, but will avert a later failure.

4. Work has rewards:
   a. Money.
   b. Saving money (volunteer, do-it-yourself).
   c. Being of service.
   d. Opportunity to pursue interests and abilities.
   e. Ability to meet and interact with people.
   f. Avoidance of boredom.
   g. Increase in self-respect and esteem.

5. Work is bound by time:
   a. On-task behavior is required.
   b. Set times for breaks, eating, cleaning up, and so on.

6. Work is seldom performed in complete isolation or independence. One must be able to sustain critical relationships:
   a. Worker/supervisor.
   b. Worker/worker.
   c. Worker/consumer.
   d. Worker/subordinate.

7. Settings rarely exist in isolation:
   a. They are interdependent (e.g., manufacturer, wholesaler, distributor, retailer).
   b. Interns can learn the importance of all work groups.

8. Not everyone who wants to work can obtain work nor can everyone who obtains work be employed in the work of their choice (and jobs will change over one's life span):
   a. This is presented as a general fact (not just for people with disabilities).
   b. Job dissatisfaction is the rule, not the exception.
   c. Career education is a way to confront and cope with job dissatisfaction.

Week 16

LESSONS IN	
| | Job Keeping	| | Personal Growth
|X| Job	|X| Interpersonal Growth
|X| Job Search	|X| Timely Topics

Job: Site-Related Tasks

See Week 13.

Job Search: Mock Interviews

See Weeks 12 and 13. Interns should be well into the third round of mock interviews. For next week, all will have an appointment with a cooperating employer who has agreed to come in and do some mock interviews. Try to use more than one employer to give the interns a choice of field, and to avoid taking undue advantage of their goodwill. Interns should interview with a stranger. The cooperating employer should have one of our forms (Appendix 3.5), or another way to give written feedback to the interviewee.

Review and discuss various job searches, giving support and praise for those who have been putting time into it, and providing assistance to those who are working on applications or who request more mock interview practice.

Interpersonal Growth: Accepting Negative Feedback

See Week 15.

Timely Topics: What Is Postsecondary Life Like?

Have all instructional staff relate stories of their first jobs after high school, the progression of their careers, and the progression of the careers of friends and family members whose paths have been particularly interesting. Interns should be able to gain a sense in the stories of both success and failure. It is hoped that they can develop a means of applying this information to themselves as their lives continue beyond high school. Other appropriate topics include moving out from their family home and setting up an independent living situation, going to college, self-monitoring recreation and leisure pursuits, and parenting and raising a family.

If possible, this is a good session in which to bring in a graduate of the program who has done particularly well and who can articulate features of her or his career path beyond high school.

Week 17

```
             LESSONS IN
|  | Job Keeping   |  | Personal Growth
|X| Job           |X| Interpersonal Growth
|X| Job Search    |X| Timely Topics
```

Job: Continuing Development

At this point, the interns have derived the maximum benefit from the time offered during the seminar. Today, this period should be devoted to a strategy for continuing the development of the skills they have been practicing and the resources they will use: community college, tutorials, self-teaching, or any other adult service provider that can offer them more opportunities to make their skill more marketable. Interns should make relevant inquiries (letters, phone calls, etc.). Every intern should write out a strategy.

Job Search: "Real" Mock Interviews

Posttest

The interns interview with an actual guest employer representing the career the intern is interested in. The interviews are videotaped and the employer, fellow group members, and teacher rate the intern's final performance.

Other interns are out on prearranged mock interviews with real employers at their place of business. Sometimes these interviews can turn into real jobs. This is the preferred "final exam"; having interns go to employers is both more convenient to the employer and more like an actual job interview.

Interpersonal Growth: Accepting Negative Feedback

See Week 15.

Timely Topics: Open Forum

Review the purpose of the program—improved postsecondary opportunities, not pleasing the teacher or getting a good grade—and offer to review anything that is requested. If possible, let the interns lead their own group discussion on a topic of their choosing. Encourage them to function as a support group, exchange phone numbers, pass on job tips, and stay in touch beyond the semester. The workshop has formed and honed relationships based upon postsecondary success, and thus continuation of those relationships should extend that purpose beyond the life of the workshop.

Week 18

```
             LESSONS IN
|X| Job Keeping   |  | Personal Growth
|  | Job           |  | Interpersonal Growth
|  | Job Search    |X| Timely Topics
```

Job Keeping: Using an Appointment Calendar

Warmup/Review

Ask the interns to articulate why a person might want to keep an appointment calendar. What is it used for? After they have given their rationale, add the following if necessary.

Explain to the interns that the appointment calendar is a powerful tool for maintaining a job and developing a career. For maintaining a job, the calendar is a way to help remember appointments (doctor, social security, lawyer, etc.), and when work must be missed for such an appointment, the calendar can help the person remember to notify the employer. For career development, the calendar is a place to keep track of appointments with career counselors, rehabilitation caseworkers, college counselors, and so on. We have already learned that being on time and making appointments is crucial. These calendars can help us do that, and in a world that is so complex, and becoming more so, being able to keep a calendar like this one is essential. Calendars are easily obtained from companies that use them for promotional purposes.

Presentation/Guided Practice

Have the interns:

- Put their name and phone numbers in the appointment calendars

- Find their birthday and mark it

- Find the birthdays of two other interns and mark them

- Mark the day they graduate from high school

- Put in any appointments that they have coming up in the near future

- Call or meet with the transition specialist and make an appointment to see him or her before their graduation; mark off times to call and check in with the transition specialist, starting 2 weeks after graduation and continuing every 6 weeks thereafter, until the end of the year

- Set aside and mark three times in the next 2 weeks when they will either explore college (calling and making an appointment with a counselor) or engage in a job search (trying to make a job interview appointment over the phone or setting aside the time to do walking or phone searches)

- Arrange right now a day and time during which they will meet with their on-site instructor the next week for coffee and to review the use of the calendar (this can be during break time on the job)

- Pick a date by which they will reach a goal (get into college, get a job paying ''x'' dollars), and mark that date

Life-Skill Competency Application

During the coming week, interns who cannot complete the above practice in class should make the necessary appointments and show the completed work (the calendar itself) to the on-site instructor, who can then help out those who are having any problems with it. If it is the last day of the program, the appointment calendars can be checked during the date made with the on-site instructors, or by the transition specialist.

Timely Topics: Making Choices

1. Discuss the basic tenets of evolution, that creatures came out of the ocean and that, in various ways, choices were made for them by their ability to cope with the environment. Their adaptability, which enabled them to survive, turned them into different creatures, from reptiles to rodents to mammals to birds.

Distinguish between the external nature of choices that are made for us and the fact that we, human beings, make choices on a more sophisticated level than other beings. We may be born into difficult situations, or have to live around risks (like drugs or violence), but we can still make a choice. That is how we are different. The way we are the same as other animals is that once the choice is made, that is part of what we become.

2. Emphasize that the interns are in the best program of its kind. There are two reasons that it is the best. The first and most important is that we are all sitting down together and saying that, yes, it is the best one. We are making that choice. The reason so many CLP interns succeed is that they make that choice. They simply affirm that they are going to hold a job, go to college, and so on.

3. The other reason is that the staff are here. We can tell when someone really is choosing to succeed, and we are available when they are. Draw an analogy to the very wealthy person who has a staff that lines up to serve his needs in sequence, such as a maid and butler who dress, groom, and prepare him for his day. The CLP concept is similar, in that first the referring counselor, then the on-site instructor, help the choosing intern along, each of them under the direction of a supervising teacher. Finally, the transition specialist does the final brushing off of the intern who is dressed in the coat and tails of enablement. When the interns really make the choice, we are there.

4. Though our staff is in fact there to serve the interns, it is not by way of giving out jobs, money, or even skills. We give them the arsenal—social skills, assistance in navigating adult services, knowledge of what they will need to succeed on a job, on-the-job support—for the struggle to come. When the choice is made and the journey begun, there are still no guarantees. Each intern must face the struggle alone, and each will need to be a pioneer, a warrior, and a hero.

Closing Rituals

The transition specialists should attend today's workshop. They can bring guest speakers, particularly enablers from the community colleges.

Lecture the interns on what the emphasis of the program has been, and leave them with a message, not on jobs, but on literacy. Explain that it is through literacy, once they have established themselves economically, that true growth and empowerment will come. To demonstrate the power of being able to write, have them all write comments giving feedback on the program thus far. Make it very clear that these comments will be used to revise the workshop and community classroom for the next cohort of interns.

Thus, their ability to write and express themselves is, in this case, powerful.

Explain that the program is not over, that it never ends. They have merely completed the first phase. Explain also that the CLP staff are available but will leave them alone if that is their desire; we do want to know how they are doing at least twice a year, but utilization of services is optional.

Have certificates of completion made out for each intern, and have a graduation ceremony, where the interns are officially "passed off" from the community classroom staff to the transition specialist staff. As they receive their certificates, they should recite their name, job title, and job duties. The last person to congratulate them should be the transition specialist, who can also set up their first appointments.

Appendix 3.1
List of Feelings

HAPPY
gay
convivial
festive
contented
complacent
satisfied
serene
comfortable
peaceful
tranquil
joyous
ecstatic
rapturous
transported
enthusiastic
inspired
glad
beatific
pleased
blissful
cheerful
genial
cheery
sunny
blithe
high-spirited
lighthearted
buoyant
debonair
bright
free and easy
airy
saucy
jaunty
sprightly
lively
spirited
animated
vivacious
brisk
sparkling
merry
mirthful
hilarious
exhilarated
jovial
jolly
jocular
playful
gleeful
frisky

elated
exultant
jubilant

SAD
sorrowful
downcast
dejected
unhappy
woeful
woebegone
depressed
disconsolate
melancholy
gloomy
cheerless
somber
dismal
heavy-hearted
joyless
spiritless
dismal
dark
clouded
frowning
lugubrious
funereal
mournful
dreadful
dreary
flat
dull
oppressed
downhearted
in the dumps
sullen
mumpish
moping
moody
glum
sulky
discontented
out of sorts
ill at ease
low-spirited
low
discouraged
disheartened
despondent
crestfallen

ANGRY
resentful

irritated
enraged
furious
annoyed
inflamed
provoked
piqued
incensed
infuriated
offended
sullen
wrought up
worked up
indignant
irate
wrathful
cross
sulky
bitter
virulent
acrimonious
boiling
fuming
in a stew
up in arms
in a huff

HURT
injured
offended
grieved
distressed
in pain
suffering
afflicted
worried
aching
crushed
victimized
heartbroken
hapless
in despair
agonized
tortured
dolorous
piteous
woeful
rueful
mournful
sad
pathetic
tragic

AFRAID
fearful
frightened
in fear
timid
timorous
chicken
nervous
diffident
fainthearted
tremulous
shaky
apprehensive
fidgety
restful
aghast
terrified
panicked
hysterical
yellow
alarmed
shocked
horrified
insecure
anxious
worried
misgiving
doubtful
suspicious
hesitant
irresolute
awed
dismayed
scared
trembling
quaking
cowardly
threatened
menaced
appalled
petrified

INTERESTED
concerned
affected
fascinated
engrossed
intrigued
absorbed
excited
curious
inquisitive

inquiring
nosy
snoopy

FEARLESS
encouraged
courageous
confident
secure
reassured
bold
brave
daring
gallant
heroic
self-reliant
spirited
resolute
stout-hearted
enterprising
hardy
determined
audacious
dauntless
certain

DOUBTFUL
unbelieving
skeptical
distrustful
suspicious
dubious
uncertain
questioning
wavering
hesitant
perplexed
indecisive
misgiving

EAGER
keen
earnest
intent
zealous
ardent
agog
avid
anxious
enthusiastic
desirous
fervent
hot-headed
fervid

Appendix 3.2
The Paper Chase: One Big Step on the Career Ladder

NA	= You don't need this.
✔	= It's done!
	= You still need to get this in to get paid.

	Copy of Valid ID	School Application Form	Applicant Survey Form	Copy of Social Security Card	Work Permit (if Under 18)	Proof of Negative TB Test	W4 Form	X Form	A5 Form	Z Form (Tax and Deductions)	I-9 Form (Employment Eligibility Verification)

Career
Ladder
Program

Appendix 3.3
Counselor–Job Seekers' Agreement

This agreement is not a legally binding document. Its purpose is to provide a complete understanding by the counselor and the job seeker as to what they can expect of each other and to assure each of them that they have a sincere commitment and intention to carry out their responsibilities. The agreement will be read aloud and questions about any part of it should be discussed.

Duties of the Counselor. The principal duty of the counselor is to help you obtain a job. All of these services are free. You pay nothing.

The specific services of the counselor are:

1. To provide necessary photocopying service of letters of recommendation, applications, résumés, and other job-seeking material
2. To provide a telephone for your use
3. To provide typing service if necessary for your résumé and job-seeking letters
4. To provide you with job interview practice and information on how to answer common questions
5. To provide you with the specific statements you should make on the telephone when asking about a job and to arrange practice and discussion of these calls
6. To help you write a résumé of your job qualifications and make copies of it
7. To answer all questions you have on how to improve your job-finding chances
8. To write to other agencies, if you desire, to inform them of your job-seeking efforts

Duties of the Job Seeker. The principal duty of the job seeker is to carry out the counselor's instructions quickly and completely and to consider the job search as a full-time job.

The specific duties of the job seeker are:

1. To attend the meetings each day and to be on time
2. To call beforehand if you absolutely cannot attend a meeting so the leader can give you any new job leads that have come up
3. To attend all scheduled interviews on time, and to fill out the after-interview checklist immediately after the interview
4. To be honest with the leader so he can know how to help you solve any special problems
5. To keep a lookout for job leads that may be useful to other clients just as they are for you
6. To continue attending sessions until a job offer is completely definite

As a counselor, I hereby agree to do everything possible to provide the services listed above.

_____   _____
On-Site Instructor   CLP Supervisor

As a job seeker, I hereby agree to do everything possible to perform the activities listed above.

_____
CLP Intern/Job Seeker

Career
Ladder
Program

Appendix 3.4
Typical Job Interview Questions

Tell me about yourself.

What kinds of experience do you have?

Why do you want to work here?

Why should we hire you?

Tell me some of your strengths.

Tell me some of your weaknesses.

What makes a good boss?

What would you like to be doing one year from now?

What about five years from now?

What hobbies do you have?

What was the worst and best part of your last job?

Why did you quit your last job?

Do you have any questions for us?

Appendix 3.5
Interview Rating Sheet

Date: _____

Excellent 3
Good 2
Okay 1
Needs Improvement 0

The Interviewee:

Was convincing   □

Was polite and friendly   □

Looked sharp   □

Used good English   □

Had the right kind of experience   □

Asked good questions   □

Was interested in staying with the company   □

Made a good overall impression   □

Rating:
Excellent 18–24
Good 10–17
Okay 7–9
Needs Improvement 0–6

Person interviewed: _____

Rated by: _____

Appendix 3.6
Job Search Contact Sheet

Company	Address	Phone Number	Date	Contact Person	Callback Date

Appendix 3.7
CLP Personal Data Sheet

First	Middle	Last	

Street	City	State	Zip Code

Phone Number: **Date of Birth:**   **SSN:**

Can you type? ____ wpm   Can you take dictation? ____ wpm   Office machines you can operate:

Have you ever been convicted of a crime? If the answer is ''yes'' give date, offense, and penalty of conviction   Yes [ ]   No [ ]

Driver's License Number: Circle highest grade completed: 5   6   7   8   9   10   11   12

Name of High School: _____   Receive Diploma? _____

City and State: _____

List college, business, trade, correspondence, or other courses below: Name and location of school	Dates: From	To
1.		
2.		

Employment Record: Begin with most recent employment			
Job 1 *Employment Dates* From: Mo: Yr:	*Employer's Name, Address, and Phone Number*		
To: Mo: Yr:			
Total Time	Supervisor		

Occupation and Description of Job Duties	Salary	Reason for Leaving

Job 2 *Employment Dates* From: Mo: Yr:	*Employer's Name, Address, and Phone Number*
To: Mo: Yr:	
Total Time	Supervisor

Occupation and Description of Job Duties	Salary	Reason for Leaving

Career
Ladder
Program

Job 3 *Employment Dates* From: Mo: Yr:	*Employer's Name, Address, and Phone Number*
To: Mo: Yr:	
Total Time	Supervisor

Occupation and Description of Job Duties	Salary	Reason for Leaving

Special Job Skills, Activities, Special Training, Experiences, etc.

Personal References Name	Address and Phone Number	Position and Years Known

Additional Information

Career
Ladder
Program

Appendix 3.8
Crocodile Creek

Rationale: This activity is designed to develop awareness of personal values and the fact that values differ from person to person. Further, it is designed to promote acceptance of difference as being neither right nor wrong in itself, just different.

Materials: The "Crocodile Creek" graphic or one similar is vital for keeping track of the characters and for voting. The story is too complex to be effectively remembered by most people (adults included). The leader will probably need a chalkboard or some other large surface to keep a tally of opinions. Group members have always been very interested in seeing how the group as a whole voted.

Activity: Pass out graphic, then read the story to the group. From there, follow procedures under "Questions."

Crocodile Creek

Once upon a moment there was a girl by the name of Abigail who was very much in love with a boy named Abner. Now, Abigail lived on the other side of the river from Abner and in order for her to meet with him she would have to cross the bridge.

One morning on her way to see Abner to give him a present that she had spent all of her hard-earned money on and carefully wrapped, she found that the bridge had fallen down during a storm and she could not get across. She was desperate.

While Abigail sat by the water's edge and sobbed pitifully, Sinbad came rowing down the river in his rowboat. "What's the matter, Abigail?" called out Sinbad, and she proceeded to tell him of her problem. She then asked him if he would row her across the river in his boat. "Why of course," said Sinbad, "but you will have to give me something to make it worth my while. You will have to make love (give that beautiful present) to me." "Why, I can't do that!" said Abigail. "Then I won't take you across!" said Sinbad.

Abigail was so distraught, but just then she saw Ivan, the lumberjack, and told him of her problem and of the proposition made by Sinbad. "I'm sorry, I can't help you. I don't want to get involved," said Ivan and he walked away.

Abigail walked back to the river thinking that she might never see her boyfriend, Abner, again. She then decided that she loved Abner so much that she would have to sacrifice in order to see him and said yes to Sinbad. After Sinbad got what he wanted, he rowed her across the river and said goodbye. Abigail ran to Abner, fell into his arms, gave him a hug and tearfully told her story. When she was done, Abner screamed at her, "How could you do such a thing?" and angrily pushed her away from him while saying that he didn't ever want to see her again. "But I did it for you, because I love you!" cried Abigail. "Get out!" screamed Abner.

As Abigail tearfully walked along the river, feeling lonely and rejected, she ran into her old friend Slug. She told him the whole story and that Abner threw her out. Slug said, "Why, he can't do that to you! We'll see about this!" and angrily stormed down the path towards Abner's house. He knocked down the door and grabbed Abner, yelling at him, "You ungrateful slob. You have broken poor Abigail's heart." And he proceeded to punch and kick Abner senseless. All the while Abigail was standing in the doorway and was just smiling.

Question: Under each name put the number which describes how you think about each of the people (the teacher may have to summarize names and roles) using this scale:

1	2	3	4	5
Worst Person	Bad	Not so Bad	Kind of All Right	Best Person

Have the kids raise their hands when you ask, ''Who picked Abigail for the worst?'' Then go on down the scale, tallying the scores for each character. Have each person respond to why they made their choice. Point out the similarities of choice (value/morals) as well as the differences. Point out that differences make us unique and that they can also bring about problems with respect to understanding between two people. Because each person's values are unique and different, there is no way of telling who is right or who is wrong. In respecting our differences, everyone becomes right and no one becomes wrong. Point out, also, how we as human beings tend to choose our friends according to how our values match up (how similar they are) and this makes us comfortable. Note, also, that those who don't have our same values also choose friends whose values match. Neither is right, and neither is wrong. Both become right for themselves; and if we accept that we are different and that's OK, then both become right for everyone.

Source: From *Values Clarification, Alligator River* (pp. 290–294) by B. Cole and J. Heilman, 1979, New York: A & W Publishers, Inc.

Appendix 3.9
Sample Résumés

Résumé of
May Lincoln
1138-F Gateview Ave., T.I.
San Francisco, CA 94130
(415) 555-5055

OBJECTIVE: To secure a full-time entry-level clerical position

EDUCATION:
1981–1985   Galileo High School, date of graduation: January, 1985

1985   Employment Skills Workshop, Career Ladder Program (CLP)

EXPERIENCE:
1985   Career Ladder Program (CLP): File, type, collate, prepare mailings, deliver documents and receive customers for the Personnel Department at California State Auto Association, San Francisco.

1984   Tutor and assist disabled students at Galileo High School in reading and functional skills (calculator, shopping).

1984   Skateland: give out skates, patrol and monitor skating floor, sweep floors, clean snack bars, train new employees in above skills.

1982–1983   Direct traffic, give information at Candlestick Park.
Provide child care, care for family members with illness and back injury, houseclean, cook.

RELATED ACTIVITIES/HOBBIES:
Music, dancing, bicycling, singing, baseball, football, and basketball.

REFERENCES:

John Hodges
Sr. Personnel Specialist/Recruitment
California State Automobile Association
150 Van deKamp Avenue
San Francisco, CA 94102-5279
(415) 555-2190

Shepherd Siegel
CLP Coordinator
San Francisco State University
San Francisco, CA 94132
(415) 555-1161

James Portman
Galileo High School
1150 Francisco St.
San Francisco, CA 94104
(415) 555-3150

Bill Dogget
2835 Merced Ave.
San Francisco, CA 94133
(415) 555-8674

Age: 18 Yrs.
Birthdate: 11-17-67
Birthplace: S.F. CA
Social Security #: 677-98-4575

PRESENT SCHOOL: Francis Scott Key Learning Center
1350 43rd Avenue
San Francisco, Ca 94122   Grade: 12

WORK EXPERIENCE:

DECEMBER 11–21, 1985   Serra Shops
Colman State Book Store
1876 Lincoln Ave.
S.F., CA 94132
(415) 555-4678 Marcia

Summer '85
Mayor's Summer Employment Program
Audobon School - Child Care
350 Clay
S.F., CA 94115 Evelyn

Summer 84 Bill's For Sales
3450 Evans Avenue
S.F., CA
431-6843
Jack and Jonny Ross

Summer 83 S.F. YMCA %
Ingleside Branch
4576 Bookman St.
S.F. CA
555-7890   Michael

Summer 82: Polenti Bates Youth Center
1235 Walker St.
S.F., CA 94133
555-1436 David Washington

REFERENCES: Lana Hessman - Teacher
F.S.K.L.C.
1350 43rd Avenue
San Francisco, Ca 94122

Bonnie Porter
Vocational Training Center
1325 13th Avenue
S.F. CA 94133
555-7989

Career
Ladder
Program

Postsecondary Services for Youths in Transition

Matt Robert and Shepherd Siegel ■

What Are Transition Services?

A simple and reasonable definition of transition services might be "facilitation of the adjustment from high school to adult life," and by adult life we mean employment, independent living, postsecondary education, leisure pursuits, social life, and exercise of citizenship. While CLP at one time or another became involved in all of these aspects, the work focused on employment, independent living, and postsecondary education and training. When the myriad issues that must be addressed to most effectively enable this transition are closely examined, simple definitions fall short of describing the range and intensity of experiences young people encounter. But there are definable approaches that can begin to deal with the day-to-day problems of managing youths' transitions, from the tangible to the intangible, the bureaucratic to the interpersonal. And these approaches can be adapted to most school programs, often utilizing existing resources.

This chapter will outline some practices that have been developed in CLP, starting from a very general structural-philosophical outline of what an effective transition program should look like, and proceeding to ways of working with individual students with specific problems. Once this structure and its philo-

sophical underpinnings are in place, the methods described can be more auspiciously implemented. We hope to more clearly illustrate the dynamic between these youths' lives and a flexible and responsive service approach. At this point, the transition specialist is a crucial player in the empowerment of youths and the facilitation of their transitions.

The CLP transition specialists were funded by a model demonstration grant from the Office of Special Education and Rehabilitative Services. Though the transition specialist's mission clearly aligns with that of Vocational Rehabilitation, it is a role that goes beyond what the rehabilitation counselor usually provides, and the transition specialist works with a smaller caseload. However, communities can find ways to fund such positions through grants, partnerships, and special dispensations; these are discussed in chapter 6.

The key premise that underlies this discussion is that effective services and self-directed change in the lives of youths can occur within the context of a trusting relationship between the transition specialist and a youth. Planned, systematic, and data-based approaches (such as self-monitoring, charting, and role-playing rehearsals) can and will enhance the effectiveness of the change, but no change will occur if the provider and consumer are not offered the

The authors wish to gratefully acknowledge the contributions of Michele Waxman, Mark Johnson, Suzanne Shaw, Desiree French, Igen Chan, Mary Magee, and S. Kofi Avoke, who played a major role in the development of transition specialist services.

opportunity to develop trust and a sincere relationship. This, in essence, helps to create and meliorate the community in which they both interact.

Features of an Effective Transition Program

The outline begins with a description of some of the aspects of a transition-oriented service system that is poised to respond to a broader-than-usual set of behaviors from the youths served. This description traces a tenable path from an emotional and philosophical commitment to youths to a more systematic description of the services that evolve from that commitment. A team that was begun by the founders of the program was expanded, and first one, then another new professional—transition specialist—was assigned to a group of about a hundred youths who had graduated from the CLP community classroom program (see chapter 2). The team was not required to work within the constraints of any particular system. They were simply instructed to do whatever was necessary to assist the graduates in developing their careers. This section describes the first principles that emerged.

Team Building

It became obvious early on that effective services required interconnectedness among the staff, along with clear definitions of roles and responsibilities in the transition process. Though the community classroom staff and the transition specialist staff had to work to avoid extraneous or wasteful meeting time, regular contact between them was essential. Since both staffs are involved in planning transitions, communication even before the intern graduated helped to avoid duplication of efforts or working at cross-purposes. The transition specialist staff was briefed by the community classroom staff, the most current experts on the interns' situations. That staff was also able to assist greatly in getting interns to their first appointments with Vocational Rehabilitation, and so on. This team-building approach is consistent with models of curriculum-based vocational assessment articulated by Stodden and Ianacone (1981), Stodden and Boone (1987), and Irvin (1988), and facilitates a smooth handoff.

Smooth Handoff

Though this chapter emphasizes an approach that reduces and avoids "handoffs" from one system to another, the CLP model does require this one handoff from the school-based to the postsecondary staff. To compensate, extra efforts are made to personalize this process and neutralize intern or graduate inhibitions about working with a new community-based professional. When this is done correctly, the transition specialist is already viewed as part of the team, and by the time the intern leaves high school (and becomes a CLP graduate), the transition specialist has built a rapport, has a personal history with the graduate, and has some knowledge of the situation the graduate is facing. This initial service delivery overlap encourages further coordination.

Coordination of Postsecondary Service Delivery

Once the intern has graduated and developed a pattern of contact with the transition specialist (though continuing relationships with the school-based staff are encouraged), the transition specialist acts as the graduate's "personal manager." The transition specialist is a generalist who is an expert at understanding and assessing the availability and quality of other community services, agencies, and employers who might be able to serve the graduate's postsecondary needs. By acting as a case manager or facilitator-liaison between the various agencies, the transition specialist can help to prevent mixups and misuse of services. This is a broader and more longitudinal replication of the team-building approach initiated in the school-based and handoff phase and is one form of ongoing support.

Ongoing Support

Though all staff work to make their services unnecessary, it is only through consistent follow-up and continuous *availability* of services—a case is never closed—that efficient prevention of vocational failure or degeneration can be achieved. The majority of youths served in the community classroom are empowered to develop their careers, but CLP's ability to predict who will need services is not perfect. There are many who would subsist without CLP services but who have been able to earn more money, get more postsecondary education and training, and work at more challenging jobs because the ongoing support offered by the transition specialist team helps the graduate develop plans and goals.

Long-Range Planning and Goal Setting

Many of the youths we serve experience a "floundering period" (Wilson, 1987) after high school graduation that can last anywhere from 1 month to 5 years. Often this means a phase of unproductive, illegitimate, or ungrounded activity. The most important aspect of this period is that it does taper off, and the transition specialist can make the best of this time period by maintaining a relationship so that the CLP is the first point of contact when the graduate does feel ready to go to work or back to school. Also, patterns that emerge in the ether of the floundering period can be reworked or redirected into the vocational or educational potential of the graduate. By at least meeting with the transition specialist on a regular basis, the graduate can develop the ability to plan and set goals. When the youth is ready to act, the transition specialist may be critical in ''greasing the wheels'' to help the youth build and maintain this momentum, enabling the youth to avert or remove obstacles and consequently move more smoothly in the direction of independence and self-determination.

The next section further elaborates and details the services defined above. They are described here by way of introduction, and to demonstrate the dynamic allowed by the flexibility of a model demonstration project. The most important feature of the initial staff behaviors was that in place of a commitment to a particular theory or methodology, CLP staff tried to listen carefully to what was going on in the lives of CLP graduates and to maintain a commitment and dedication to finding out what would help them to succeed, not limiting the scope of what the staff would try to provide. For example, ongoing support is an elemental manifestation of this type of commitment in social services. But rather than simply expecting this to occur, we now believe that it is a valid programmatic component that can be analyzed, systematized, and learned by newcomers to the position, avoiding our trials and errors and taking advantage of the participant observations of our graduates. The first principles outlined above are responses to some of the things CLP graduates have taught us.

They experience floundering periods. A lack of vocational development can only partially be explained by a clinically assessable disability or special need. Likewise, socioeconomic status, ethnocultural orientations, family problems, and so forth are relevant and sometimes critical factors that can impede their careers. By all means these factors must be considered, respected, and addressed. But there are even more contributing pressures that may appear to be only obliquely related or totally independent. Being young is almost always a primary factor, and it conspires with the other factors to create formidable barriers to success.

For example, graduates can manifest these characteristics: They want to be on their own and do it themselves; they don't want to be associated with anything that might connect them to their special education background; they lack motivation, and there is simply no clear explanation for this; they are unrealistic in their immediate aspirations; they really don't know what they want, so they bounce around from job to job or program to program; they have serious and inhibiting fears of failure or success, so they bounce around from job to job or program to program; and they exhibit the behaviors characteristic of ''learned helplessness,'' having learned them in school or from their family, and function consistently in a helpless fashion.

Continuous exposure to these qualities inspired the CLP staff to develop a service delivery approach based upon team building, smooth handoff, coordination of postsecondary service delivery, ongoing support, and long-range planning and goal setting. The next section describes these services in more detail.

Articulation of Transition Services

Initial Team Building and the Handoff Phase

We envision a society where community is effectively created through a deinstitutionalization process. Though this is not going to happen all at once, best efforts to integrate marginalized youth into the workplace both prevent their further institutionalization by the justice, welfare, or mental health systems and create a momentum within the mainstream to accommodate their differences. In other words, we see the successful transition from school to work as one part of a larger movement to create more enduringly committed and caring relationships among all people who attend school and who go to work.

This document proposes a step in that direction. Our proposal is practical and feasible within the current service delivery model, and it necessarily retains some of the model's protocol. For example, though we have worked to personalize transition services and create ongoing relationships with youths in transition, there is currently no way to avoid having some handoff from one part of the program to another. Fortunately, it has been reduced to one handoff, from the school-based to the postsecondary staff.

This section will describe how that handoff phase—where the majority of at-risk youths ''fall through the cracks''—can be more effectively and more humanely implemented. The first step for the transition specialist is to make contact and begin to form a relationship *before* the exiting youth graduates from high school. There are a number of times and places in which the transition specialist can do this. As described in chapter 2, the family meeting provides an excellent opportunity for the participating families to get a sense of the entire team, including the transition specialist. For those interns who are expected to graduate early, or who are planning an immediate entry into the workforce or college, the transition specialist will develop contacts with their family during the semester, assisting in the necessary paperwork, counseling, problem solving, and so forth. In cases where program funding is driven by a case services agreement—where there is statistical monitoring of the number of successful case closures—this early contact is critical to getting the youth "into plan," so that work performed by the transition specialist is properly credited. A reformed system might reimburse other types of services to youths who would not otherwise avail themselves of Vocational Rehabilitation services.

Many of the interns will not experience a smooth transition into postsecondary life. Contact and acquaintance with them can begin with the family meeting and develop during the training semester. The transition specialist can visit the sites where the interns are working. This develops familiarity; the intern views the transition specialist as part of the team and becomes more comfortable with him or her. This later proves to be crucial, as many exiting youths are averse to going into clinical settings such as the Vocational Rehabilitation office and exposing themselves to their procedures. Desensitization and the knowledge that they have an ally in that system is critical. Also, by seeing the intern in a work setting, the transition specialist can begin informal assessment of the social and work skills of the intern, can suggest what might be viable fields to pursue that are consistent with the intern's vocational interest and ability, and can anticipate some of the barriers to a satisfactory employment experience.

These goals of desensitization and team identification are further achieved when transition specialists attend some of the Employment Skills Workshop sessions (see chapter 3). The transition specialists can introduce in a workshop format what rehabilitation services are, what transition specialist services are, and how they can help. The specialness of the CLP is emphasized, and any replication of this project should make that point as well. When interns are promised ongoing service beyond graduation, they do not really believe it, probably because 13 years of public education with at least 13 different teachers has taught them differently. Thus this message is crucial, and the ongoing commitment must be verbally reinforced throughout the semester and demonstrated immediately afterward. This long-term commitment

can often take over 2 years of contact before it is appreciated and understood by the youth.

This early contact with interns also serves a procedural function and can greatly upgrade the efficiency of the shift from school to postsecondary services. The paperwork that initiates the opening of a case with Vocational Rehabilitation can be completed. The first appointments with the rehabilitation counselor can be made and coordinated with the school-based program (community classroom teacher, school counselor, family, etc.). And contact with other agencies relevant to the adult life of the individual (community colleges, child care services, job training programs) can be initiated with the knowledge and aid of the transition specialist and thus better coordinated.

Finally, the first contacts with the interns serve to introduce the concept of transition planning and begin to give substance to that concept. For example, the transition specialist may attend an Individualized Education Plan or Individualized Transition Plan meeting. Expectations of the parents, the interns, and various professionals can be explored and compared. Contrasting expectations will frequently be uncovered. The possibility of beginning a postsecondary activity, either work or training or education, can be explored. And the assessment process, begun in the first contacts, can be developed by exploring the ecosystem of the youth (Hobbs, 1982). Since the services and the service delivery posture are geared toward success and emphasis of all the factors that will engender success, this is also a critical opportunity for the transition specialist to identify the stressors in the intern's life and to make adjustments and preparations for events that may impede or hinder such success. When these do occur, the transition specialist's role is expanded, from one that merely facilitates paperwork processing and access to postsecondary opportunities to one that calls for closer involvement in the life situation of the graduating intern. The transition specialist must draw from a wide-ranging palette of transition services designed to empower the youth to overcome whatever obstacles have emerged. These services are described in the next section.

Transition Services

The transition specialist must be an eclectic animal, one who can generalize from a broad base of experience and expertise and be able to respond appropriately to all the different players involved in the graduate's life as well as to the various situational exigencies that may arise. A representative (though not exhaustive) list of different hats a transition specialist could wear at any particular point in the course of this endeavor might include:

Job coach	Interagency liaison
Job developer	Advocate
Academic tutor	Ombudsman
Career manager	Peer counselor
College counselor	Therapist
Rehabilitation counselor	Support group facilitator
Social worker	Social benefactor
Financial consultant	Sounding board
Assistant manager	Researcher

And there may be still other titles the transition specialist might have to assume, as the individual need arises.

To successfully respond to the varying agendas of all the different players—parents, teachers, counselors, administrators, rehabilitation counselors, employers, and so on—a transition specialist has to be able to change hats easily and make compromises when it is in the best interest of the intern or graduate. The situations in which the transition specialist brings these talents to bear could range from just helping the graduate get through a hard day at work to developing a long-term career plan.

The following is a sample list of the transition services CLP transition specialists employ, accompanied by some additional explication of the individual categories. A summary of these transition services is found in Appendix 4.1, and Appendix 4.2 shows a self-tracking chart that allows transition specialists to record the frequency with which they deliver each service. Later sections will further discuss the organization of the transition specialist's time.

Follow-Up Contact

Routine quarterly follow-up to see how former interns are doing (this contact may be more or less frequent depending on individual circumstances), what their employment status is, if they are in school or are planning to be, and if they feel they could benefit from CLP services.

Also, the staff obtains permission to visit the job site and contact the present employer (when appropriate), co-workers, or other significant support people in the graduate's social network (for more sensitive monitoring and as an intervention-oriented assessment).

Even though it may not seem like it at times, regular follow-up is probably the most effective tool the transition specialist can use to make the job easier. In the CLP, it was found that follow-up every three to four months is most effective for the simple reason that people in urban areas and in this population move frequently and their phone numbers change

often. If contact is not maintained with some discipline, people get lost. Maintaining contact has the following beneficial residual effects as well:

1. Graduates will eventually learn the transition specialist's number so that even if they get lost they are more likely to recontact the transition specialist in the future.

2. Graduates who are out of touch but who are friends of graduates who are in contact will reconnect with the transition specialist.

3. Other beneficial activities and products of maintaining follow-up contact can be very powerful in initiating and building a group consciousness among the graduates, for example, newsletters that say what other successful graduates are doing or networks of peer support groups. This can make the graduating students see the actual value in staying in touch through the experience of their friends.

4. The persistence of the transition specialist will usually be perceived not as a nuisance but as a commitment and can help to build trust.

5. By regularly checking in with graduates, the transition specialist can better monitor progress and ferret out problems the graduates may be having, make suggestions, or intervene before a problem is unremediable.

6. Invaluable qualitative and quantitative research data as well as documentation for the accountability of a program can be collected.

7. Access to more information and convergent patterns of ability and interest can help develop a long-range career plan for graduates.

8. Graduates learn to use the transition specialist, an expert they can call upon to develop their network of resources, thus facilitating their progress to independence and richer, more productive lives.

Rehabilitation Casework

Facilitating referrals; case openings and closures; reopenings; rehabilitation services; postemployment services; case management and program planning with Vocational Rehabilitation; and consultation, coordination, and communication with the rehabilitation counselor about all CLP clients with active or inactive cases.

Facilitating referrals and case openings may sound simple but it can be one of the most difficult experiences a graduate (and a graduate's transition specialist) experiences. Some graduates have a hard time making appointments and getting to them promptly, and some just have a hard time with a particular type of appointment. One can hardly blame them. In order to get their case opened they again have to assent to undergoing evaluation, testing, *and* a medical exam—three of the most uncomfortable experiences anyone ever has to go through in life. This is especially stressful for these youths, considering that as special education students, many have already had to endure much more of this type of intrusion than any "average" person, child or adult, ever does. So their resistance is entirely understandable and is often indomitable. The most common perception among youths is that Vocational Rehabilitation is for drug addicts and ex-convicts.

In trying to facilitate the referral process, some things that have helped are (a) desensitizing interns to rehabilitation by discussing what Vocational Rehabilitation is and listening to what their perceptions of it are, (b) telling about its history and who it helps (anyone who might experience significant obstacles to successful employment), and (c) explaining why the graduates are different from Vocational Rehabilitation's usual clientele (for one thing, they are as yet unfledged in their participation in the adult world and in their emergent career development). Also, we "sell" the rationale and potential benefits of getting a case opened, particularly the financial aspects. It is much easier to get the cases opened while youths are still in school. Appointments can more easily be coordinated with parents and counselors this way. When feasible, students can be sent en masse to their testing and medical exams. Groups of 3 are usually the most manageable, although some clinics will actually go out and examine students at their school site and can see as many as 20 in a day.

The follow-along of the transition specialist also allows Vocational Rehabilitation to serve former clients who have again become in need of further services, and to provide the rehabilitation counselor with evidence to justify it. The counselors are held strictly accountable and must provide the rationale and justification for any plans they make or costs they incur. So coordination and consultation in assessment, program planning, and management are crucial. The transition specialist is negotiating a middle ground where agency protocol is met and pertinent information is brought together. Thus more effective action can be taken and appropriate services provided to the graduate. In this way transition specialists and rehabilitation counselors are very complementary and do not work at cross-purposes. Transition specialists should in most cases be like the right arm of the rehabilitation counselors, providing more comprehensive service in the aspects of case management that the rehabilitation counselors would like to be able to provide but cannot due to constraints placed on their time by large active caseloads. Many of these graduates need that extra time in order to succeed.

Postsecondary Education or Training

Counseling, referral, liaison, and tutoring services for CLP graduates who would like to go to college or participate in an occupational training program, youth employment program, or similar activity.

This is fairly straightforward, but it is another area that needs to be closely monitored by the transition specialist. Many of the graduates plan to go to school, usually to the local city college, which is open to everyone with or without a high school diploma. They do not often realize, however, that colleges are not like high school, and that they are expected to be able to manage the bureaucracy and organizational pitfalls of these institutions essentially on their own. Many young people go in unaware of special services such as career counseling, tutoring, and classroom or curriculum accommodations. Typically, they take inappropriate classes and are allowed to flunk out after a few semesters. The transition specialists help to better coordinate this process, setting up and going to appointments with students when necessary, and sometimes even tutoring them if they need more than they are getting at their school. They help graduates to make the switch from one institution to another if they are in over their head and would do better in another setting. They also can help set up a limited-enrollment situation in more than one institution if that is appropriate (e.g., between different community college campuses) or, if desired, they can help the graduates manage their schedule to work part-time and go to school.

The transition specialist also coordinates with the community college district, Regional Occupation Program, and other agencies that provide training in specific occupations or skills. Different programs come and go, their scheduling and other requirements may change, and some may be more appropriate than others for certain graduates. For this reason, it is crucial for the transition specialist to make contacts, go out and visit sites, follow up with teachers and counselors, and sometimes even attend classes to see what the programs are like and what may be demanded of the graduate, and to help the graduates understand what to expect. The best efforts of the CLP transition specialists resulted in almost twice as many of the CLP graduates enrolling in postsecondary training and college, but over half of them failed to pass their classes (Siegel, Robert, Waxman, & Gaylord-Ross, 1992). Clearly, there is a need for increased services to special needs youths if they are to attend these institutions.

On-the-Job Training

Job training and coaching, task analysis, accommodations, and mediations for CLP graduates to aid in the develop-

ment of specific job skills. Also coaching in job retention skills such as attendance and appearance.

As in the supported employment model, transition specialists learn the job and go out to the work site to help train the graduate or reinforce training. Also, transition specialists may use this time to observe the graduate briefly at different periods during the work day to make an on-the-job assessment, to troubleshoot extant or potential problems, or to see if additional training or reinforcement may be indicated. They then can provide accommodations, suggestions for adapting the job, checklists for the graduates to monitor themselves, and so on. In a general sense, the transition specialists attempt to further reinforce the skills taught in the Employment Skills Workshop and help the graduates to generalize and apply them effectively to their own work situation.

Counseling

Counseling and problem solving with graduates on personal, employment, and education or training issues as they directly affect and pertain to their career concerns.

Transition specialists probably do more of this than any other task; their services extend from crisis interventions to periodic pep talks. Therefore it is crucial for them to have some demonstrated background or ability in counseling. For some graduates, this may be the only service the transition specialists provide. Many graduates are either doing adequately on the job or may be in a situation where it might not be advantageous for the transition specialists to spend time with them on the job—for example, if it might draw unnecessary negative attention to them. The graduates are also adults and have rights, especially the right of privacy (more than they do in the school-based part of the program), and should be encouraged to have their rights respected.

Often, other issues in the graduates' life that may have been only briefly addressed in the workshop, if at all, will present themselves significantly, prominently, and progressively in the ongoing relationship. A crucial role of transition specialists as counselors develops in discovering these issues in the graduates' life. They may have seemed peripheral before but are now directly affecting the graduates' job performance or job readiness. For example, a student exhibiting chronic avoidance behaviors may be doing so not because of a learning disability, but because of more pervasive issues caused by being the adult child of an alcoholic. Until the primary issues affecting the graduate are addressed, she or he will continue to fail on the job regardless of what the transition specialist does to try to prevent it. Once a trusting relationship is built between the transition specialist and the graduate, the transition specialist can help the graduate to address these personal issues

and make referrals to other service providers when appropriate. Ironically, it is often the case that transition specialists do more good for the graduates by letting them lose a job and then exploiting that life situation to get the graduates to address their root problems and see that they need help. In some cases, this might be the most significant thing transition specialists will do in a graduate's "career" development.

Independent Living Skills

Counseling in basic skills that are not necessarily directly related to job retention, but to enhancing the quality of life—for example, issues regarding fiscal matters (like income taxes), finding an apartment, or getting a driver's license.

The level at which the transition specialist works on independent living skills varies dramatically across this population. For example, transition specialist activities in CLP have ranged from working with one graduate on doing household chores and using the public transit system, to consulting with another on how to start his own business, to helping yet another arrange for child care.

Resource Referral

When appropriate, referring graduates to other service providers and community agencies that could potentially enhance their individual transition capabilities.

This, obviously, will be a direct consequence of counseling. Particularly in urban areas, there may be a great number of community-based resources, but they are typically very diffuse and decentralized, and this limits their accessibility to graduates. It is essential for the transition specialist to get to know the resources in the community that work well with young people, and to develop trusting and cooperative-minded contacts to whom he or she is comfortable making referrals. There is no better way to burn your own credibility with a graduate than to make a bad, blind referral. The transition specialist can get to know referral sources by going out and visiting them. If it is necessary to make a referral with minimal background knowledge, the transition specialist should make sure the graduate understands this beforehand and returns with feedback on what the person or organization is like. In this context, the graduate not only is being served, but has joined the service delivery team and has taken on more responsibility, expanding the CLP team's knowledge of other agencies.

Social Skills Training

Problem solving, role playing, behavioral modeling, self-monitoring, and other techniques to help graduates work through on-the-job and/or interpersonal problems and to help them better acclimate to the particular social environment at work or in other situations.

Social skills training may be used as an effective adjunct to counseling to work through on-the-job problems. The skills can range from something as basic as learning how to say hello in the morning to learning the best way to advocate for oneself in asking for a raise. Young people in need of social skills training should be provided with and should themselves provide a rationale for why social skills are important. In many workplaces, the graduates are thrust into social environments that either are entirely new and foreign to them, are extremely diverse (and rife with intercultural clashes), or contain other employees who are much more deficient in their social and interactional abilities than the graduates. The graduates may perceive the situation differently from their co-workers or boss, and although it may seem awkward or distasteful to them, social skills are part of a game they must play if they want to reap the benefits of keeping their particular job. In this way, social skills training can be used as a tool to help graduates learn to set and rank priorities and to put them into perspective.

In some situations the transition specialist has to work with a graduate on what might be more appropriately termed metasocial skills. This involves the graduate's perception, evaluative capacity, and strategy development in more complex social environments with multiple players or problematic personalities. The need for this training will usually be triggered by some on-the-job interpersonal problem the transition specialist observes or the graduate shares. The transition specialist and graduate then get together and, based on their knowledge of different personalities at the job, past experiences, and the general tenor of the workplace, they troubleshoot potential problem situations and work on ways to negotiate them.

This training is similar to the training interns receive in the Employment Skills Workshop (see chapter 3), but usually with a narrower focus—either more situationally specific to the graduate's workplace or tailored to a specific social skill area where a graduate is in need.

Some of the techniques commonly used, such as role playing, are much easier for the transition specialists to implement since the graduates have already been inured to them in the Employment Skills Workshop and now view them as valuable and viable learning tools.

Ecosystematic Intervention

A more global intervention technique where a number of key players in the graduate's social network (such as co-workers, supervisors, relatives, counselors, teachers, and friends) are enlisted in some way to assist in the manipulation of parameters that have been collectively identified as areas in need of remediation, and to provide support and bolster the intern's capability to maneuver in a difficult or crisis situation toward an ultimately positive result.

What does ecosystematic intervention mean? In this technique the transition specialist is trying to mediate the general discord between the graduate and the environment she or he is immersed in. The focus is not on the graduate as the locus of the discord but on the interaction of all the people involved, without whose participation no problem would exist. The transition specialist's job is to uncover all the factors in the graduate's relationships to these other people that are keyed to the problem behaviors. The transition specialist must then be the conduit for communication, brainstorming possible solutions among the parties to try to mitigate the dissonance or resorting to more covert methods of manipulating the environment. For example, a young man may have the basic skills to perform the simple filing job he has been hired for, but he cannot manage it without constant supervision. An arrangement with the employer and co-workers that accommodates his needs and reduces discord may enable him to keep his job. Another worker may have her vocational development impeded by overprotective parents; counseling them to let go of their child and to develop other interests of their own may enable the young person to work. Other examples of ecosystematic intervention are cited elsewhere (Hobbs, 1982; Siegel, 1988; Siegel, Avoke, Paul, Robert, & Gaylord-Ross, 1991).

Job Search

Counseling, support, supported job search, help with applications or exams, maintaining résumés, interview skills, job leads, job development, and placement.

This follows what was taught in the Employment Skills Workshop. The main problem for the transition specialist is assessing each graduate's capability for securing a job. What are the graduates looking for? Do they need more experience in order to get the job they are applying for? Is there another job that would be easier for them to get that would be a step up the ladder to where they want to be headed? Or do they need to have more training? The transition specialist should never lose sight of the main objective of the program, which is for the graduates to be independent. So if graduates are capable of managing their own job search, the transition specialist should do no more than is needed to get them headed in the right direction, then monitor their progress and reevaluate. A "supported job search," on the other hand, might mean accompanying a graduate for moral support when he or she is applying for a job.

It may mean developing some leads and letting the graduate pursue them alone. It could mean a combination of any number of things related to the job search process depending on the individual needs of the graduate. The important thing is never to do things for the graduates that they can do for themselves. Just convincing a graduate of that can be the main element of a supported job search. How much help a particular person really needs will often be a judgment call and may involve a certain degree of trial and error. But keep in mind that the transition specialist is supposed to be sanding the rungs of the ladder so that the graduates can get a little better grip, not boosting them up every step of the way.

As an ongoing service, the transition specialists always keep the graduates' résumés on disk and update them as needed; help with filling out applications when necessary; prepare graduates for interviews (often with role playing and mock interviews); and assist in the pursuit of specialized positions or positions with certain companies or governmental agencies. Such training always focuses on helping the graduates know ahead of time what to expect.

Pregraduation Contact

Providing any transition services to interns before they have graduated from CLP.

Beginning transition specialist services before graduation is indicated in a few instances, as when mild retardation necessitates extra training time for a youth to prepare for postsecondary life; when a youth who ''graduates'' from the community classroom early by finding a better job still needs some support; or when a teen parent or other youth more urgently needs adult services in order to develop employability or a college or postsecondary training plan.

Transition Planning

Working with school-based teachers, counselors, Vocational Rehabilitation personnel, parents, interns, and others to start developing or implementing Individualized Transition Plans (ITPs) for pregraduates and recent graduates.

This is an important way to get more specificity, realistic goals, and a sense of accountability for what will happen when the student leaves high school. A full discussion of this matter is not within the scope of this book, but suffice it to say that present methods of determining what will happen to graduates upon exiting high school and how they can be prepared are vague and woefully inadequate by almost everyone's standards. All the agencies that can be identified and that may play a key role in graduates' postsecondary experience should be represented at these meetings, and the students should be able to

designate someone to represent their interests and advocate for them if they wish.

The transition specialists accomplish this now as best they can by informally coordinating with the student, parents, counselors, and other agency professionals who may be involved. Many school districts, however, are implementing ITP meetings for secondary students and setting the stage for greatly improved interagency articulation. To make these activities more tangible, Appendix 4.3 offers samples of the types of activities a transition specialist might engage in over the course of a week.

Interagency Articulation

In recent years, whenever people from human service agencies got together to talk about their problems or how they could do things better, the term ''interagency coordination'' inevitably came up, usually with respect to the relationship between agencies with similar or complementary concerns. The phrase had a ring of hope, of a group identity, of collaboration, collective consciousness, and strength. After a few attempts at coordination, however, the subject would begin to cause furrowed brows and an ''I've heard it before'' look. One would have thought it was a dirty word. Why does this happen, especially in an era of human services budget cutting, where it is practically a fiscal necessity?

There are a number of reasons. An underlying conflict, which is smoothed over and only partially reconciled by this chapter's discussion, is the difference between the value systems that drive education and rehabilitation (DeStefano and Snauwaert, 1989). Furthermore, most hardened veterans of public service are inured to a life of transient funding, understaffing, high turnover, daily emergencies, statistical requirements, and even competition with other agencies that address the same issues. They know that anyone proposing to undertake such an endeavor is either just naive or paying lip service in a moment of sublime inspiration and courage that will soon fade. The main reason it never seems to work is that it simply takes too much time and energy—time and energy that most people with full-time jobs don't have. And to really make a breakthrough takes a persistent effort. It doesn't just mean calling someone on the phone once; it means going out to an agency, meeting the personnel, seeing the program, sharing information—and then maintaining ongoing contact in some way. It means *articulation*, not just coordination. You have to be able to see and touch what is there before you can organize or coordinate it.

The reason CLP has had success in the interagency relationships between the model demonstration project, the school district, and Vocational Rehabilitation is that even from its informal beginnings, it was based on articulation. The transition specialists were housed at Vocational Rehabilitation with a desk and phone near the office of the counselor who worked with CLP. They were able to sit down and discuss cases with the counselor as needed because they were right there in the office. Reaching counselors by phone can sometimes take days and there were always necessary minor communications and details to work out. The transition specialists were able to learn from employees in the office and had access to materials, so they could learn about, understand, and respect the agency's procedural and administrative requirements. They could thus make appropriate referrals and recommendations for their clients without stepping on anybody's toes. And they were also able to educate Vocational Rehabilitation about the graduates, the school district, and other community agencies, and to provide an enriched form of assessment and a less diffuse form of direct service delivery. This reduced, rather than increased, the number of interagency miscommunications likely to occur between the schools and Vocational Rehabilitation. Because of the clarity of the CLP mission and the sublimation of the grant's priorities, the transition specialists could put the youths first and enable the cooperating agencies to serve them better as well. *Coordination* ceased to be a vacuous term because it was tangibly working to everyone's benefit.

But this took a lot of time, energy, mistakes, and troubleshooting, and it continues to require a special effort. People must make a commitment to do it, set up a manageable itinerary that meets with everyone's satisfaction, and stick to it. Then, when problems, inconsistencies, or incompatibilities come up, the agencies can collaborate to overcome them, rather than dismissively using them as fodder to denounce the relationship as being unmanageable.

Some of the issues that can impede a successful interagency relationship, and that must be confronted, circumvented, reformed, or otherwise dealt with, are described below. Each community and each interagency relationship must try to come to terms with these issues in its own fashion. Advocates of legislative reform and systems change can take note and plan for procedural changes that will nourish collaborative relationships. But success in these relationships usually derives from an intense personal commitment at the local level that cannot be legislated.

Conflicting Value Systems and Procedures

The employers' concerns are many, but the most decisive one is profit. The school district and Voca-

tional Rehabilitation have some common concerns, but also many that are in conflict. For example, schools operate as an entitlement program (and special education on a zero-reject principle) and are mandated to enroll and enable all citizens of school age. Vocational Rehabilitation is not an entitlement program and is only supposed to serve those who are determined to be eligible. One of these eligibility criteria is the likelihood that clients will benefit from services and retain employment. By staying informed and sensitive to reciprocal needs, inherent conflicts such as these can be eased if not resolved. These system differences are the most burdensome for the exiting youths.

Partial Solutions

CLP staff have been advocating that assessments be streamlined, so that the final educational assessment of a special education student can be equivalent to the assessments that will open a rehabilitation case or that will obtain special services at a community college. Unfortunately, the systems differ in their qualifying criteria and use different tests to determine eligibility. If lists of special education students are provided to Vocational Rehabilitation several years before graduation, numbers can be projected by Vocational Rehabilitation and staff funding allocated accordingly. The path of contact between the schools and the rehabilitation staff should be a well-known, school-based staff, and the rehabilitation-based staff should know who to contact in the schools as well. School counselors and teachers need to know exactly who does qualify for rehabilitation services and should be able to describe those services accurately to their students.

Interagency agreements are one way to formalize a working relationship and to give the people on the front line a green light to devise solutions and fashion the system more sensitively to the needs of the youths. Ideally, such an agreement softens the bureaucratic mold and makes it more responsive to exiting students' needs. The responsibility shifts more heavily from the system to the people involved in service delivery. In this instance, the system's demands for successful case closures become a subset of superior and more comprehensive service delivery. If model services are being provided, then the successful case closures will follow naturally.

Strategic Advocacy

The beneficiaries of any advocacy are always the youths being served. This context requires careful scrutiny of assessments or procedures that may be preventing the youths from getting what they want. For example, some agencies that would serve a particular youth might well reject him or her because of an unwritten ''creaming'' policy that only serves the most ready clients. The transition specialist may be able to effectively intercede. An employer or rehabilitation professional may not consider a particular youth for a job because of assessment data that may not be accurate or that do not reflect the possible enhancement of the youth's ability through a job accommodation or other transition specialist services. The transition specialist, through participant-observer[1] relationships with youths, may be able to present evidence that is contrary to test results and get a youth into a program.

Other situations that have called for strategic thinking and advocacy by the transition specialist include those that call for protection of confidentiality, regulation of information to employers or other programs, and openness to the likelihood that a particular youth is ''disabled'' only in a school setting. Two examples that called for strategic advocacy follow.

A young man working in a fast-food franchise performed so well that the employer wanted to promote him to a managerial position. However, he had to take a reading test soon after the promotion, and when he failed it, he was terminated. When the skills tested do not pertain to the job requirements, such testing can be considered an act of discrimination.

Another young man held an entry-level job as a mover, lifting and loading furniture. He held the job for over a year, but then sought a job with the post office. However, he could qualify for the post office job only through a ''Schedule A'' placement that permitted him to bypass the civil service exam. He could not qualify for ''Schedule A'' unless he had his rehabilitation case reopened. Since he was working full-time and demonstrated no apparent vocational handicap, there was no way to legitimately reopen the case. If he wanted to try for the post office job, he might have to consider quitting his present job just to qualify. These examples represent systematic constraints that limit youths served by Vocational Rehabilitation to entry-level positions and prevent them from developing a career ladder, though there are conditions that qualify for reestablishing eligibility for Vocational Rehabilitation services: unemployment, underemployment, or job retention services.

In these cases, as well as others, the advocacy is called *strategic* because it has to be a well-planned, diplomatic process of bringing information together to arrive at solutions that are in the graduate's best interest. It is important for transition specialists to avoid adversarial postures that burn their bridges or bridges for their current and future clients. However, no Vocational Rehabilitation services were easily available to the two graduates described above.

Clearly, this discussion only scratches the surface in describing the conflicts and potential conflicts in the service delivery system. Rather than providing a lengthy handbook on how to manipulate the system to provide optimum service, this section only describes a few of the major conflicts and solutions in order to set the stage for what we believe to be a sensible reform of that system. In the next section, we propose a new model, inspired by the work of transition specialists. It calls for changes that would free a well-trained and dedicated corps of transition specialists to develop a new state of the art in social service delivery.

Next Stages for Social Service Delivery

In a market economy, the provider offers a product or service and must spend less than the customer in order to remain in business and make a profit. Through advertising, the provider tries to heighten the temptation to buy that product or use that service by promising virtually anything. In most cases, the provider will cut off service as soon as possible after the money has changed hands. The only reason to provide service beyond the sale is to keep the customer coming back—to develop a regular business relationship for repeat business or to provide guarantees that encourage sales.

This model does not isomorphically transfer to social services, but unfortunately, that has been the conventional approach. The goal of current social services is to serve inexpensively, but ideally to avoid repeat business, which is costly to the government. In rehabilitation services, the 60-day case closure is the most salient example of this—there is no incentive for the provider to offer service beyond the documentation of a successful case closure. But the high school diploma or pass-off to other adult agencies provide similar examples of the disorganized, decentralized, inappropriate, and irresponsible ways our systems ignore youths with special needs. Furthermore, well-meaning professionals are prevented and

---

[1]Participant-observation is defined by Edgerton (1967) as ''learning about the problems of [individuals] by observing and participating in the lives of such persons and by permitting them to present their own lives in their own words . . . participant-observation [includes] trips to recreational areas, grocery shopping, shopping excursions in department stores, sight-seeing drives, social visits in their homes, invitations to restaurants, participation in housework, financial planning, parties, and visits to the homes of friends and relatives'' (pp. 16–17).

even discouraged from delivering quality service because of the market-based quota systems imposed on their roles. In the long run, such market-oriented policies are more costly because they do not last long enough to truly empower people to take care of themselves. Good social service professionals are on the run because the constraints of their quotas prevent them from developing quality relationships with the people they serve, and they quickly burn out because they are prevented from sharing in whatever successes occur; they are compelled by their job descriptions to continually deal with the situations in which services are not working. In other words, the social service deliverer, in the current system, can be characterized as someone who is putting out fires rather than tending blossoms.

Good social service professionals operating in an improved systems environment will be less likely to leave their jobs for the private sector and private pursuits when the naturally occurring rewards of empowering disenfranchised individuals are allowed to be felt. A new model is called for that can deliver on its promises accountably and inexpensively, but that is based on authentic and ongoing human relationships, not a commodity exchange, and is not driven by a quota-oriented fiscal policy. One solution that will ultimately bring value and reward to social service occupations is what we are calling the *cohort service delivery model*.

The Cohort Service Delivery Model

The concept of cohort service delivery is simple, and it is one we believe has potential for improving social services, ultimately reducing the costs of and need for "safety net" programs like Aid to Families with Dependent Children and shelters for the homeless; in a best-case scenario, this model improves the quality of life for "clients" and all the people involved with them.

First, we would like to describe the current mode of service delivery (and the typical consumer-merchant relationship) as one based on an "in-out box" paradigm. Concern for the condition and outcomes of a consumer is time-limited. This means that services are delivered as long as the case is "open": The criteria for closing the case have not yet been met, and the likelihood of meeting those criteria is high (in the same way that the merchant delivers services or goods as long as the likelihood of payment is high). Though they operate with varying degrees of efficiency and success, all examples of business or service delivery are driven by the same economic system. In the case of social services, the criteria for closing a case are based on some approximation that is thought to indicate an improved quality of life (e.g., high

school proficiency exam, 60 or more consecutive days of stable employment, earnings beyond a certain level). In some contexts, such as specific skills training, medical treatment, or certain specific accommodations, this arrangement is efficient and allows a professional to serve a large number of people with some effectiveness. However, in the instances of at-risk youths leaving the public school system, or certain other at-risk populations seeking to enter or reenter mainstream society, such an approach simply will not work.

As is often the case, individuals with the most severe disabilities have led the way by inspiring professionals to develop state-of-the-art services that would later have implications for other special needs groups. Developers of supported employment for people with profound and multiple disabilities were the first to realize that some of their clients would need lifelong support in order to retain jobs. Given a philosophical commitment to the social and labor contributions of such individuals, there was no turning back. If part of one provider's job was to continue to facilitate accommodations for an individual, then so be it. Economic arguments (which can be made) aside, it was the right thing to do. In fact, this can be viewed as only a slightly unconventional extension of the existing interdependence of jobs in the work world.

The CLP took its cue from this model. Although the students with so-called mild disabilities we served appeared "normal," they presented a complex and infinitely varying array of problems and explanations for vocational failure. In short, they demonstrated a need, if not for continuous services, then for continuously *available* services. Measures of success were not easily quantified, and the problems inhibiting vocational adjustment fell beyond the domains of a conventional "in-out box" service deliverer's job description.

We have discovered, through our ongoing contact with and availability to the CLP graduates, a new way of conceptualizing social service delivery. In place of the "in-out box" service delivery system, we propose the "cohort" approach.

In a cohort service delivery system, a transition specialist or other social service professional is designated to a semifinite number of youths who come under a particular descriptor, for example, every student to leave school A's resource specialist programs over a 6-year period, or every youth released from institution B over a 1-year period, or every teen parent who is served by community agency C over a 2-year period, depending upon what an optimal maximum load is.

It is the transition specialist's job to maintain a minimum of three contacts per year with all members of the assigned cohort, and to make services available as needs arise. As far as we know now, the commitment should be ongoing, but it is possible that the need for services will taper off for many over a period of time, say 5 years. Without risking a return to an "in-out box" approach, a transition specialist could gradually take on new graduates over time.

What, then, is the function of the transition specialist beyond contact? The array of possible services is described in the "Articulation of Transition Services" section above, but we wish to emphasize here that the function is often that of a generalist, and it is certainly appropriate for a transition specialist to make a referral to another organization or agency that has high-quality and appropriate services. However, as the graduates' "personal manager," the transition specialist still has the obligation to see that the referred services are appropriate, of high quality, delivered, and consumed, and that they realistically fit into the career plans of the graduates. So no matter how many agencies or programs a youth interacts with, the transition specialist who first was designated to that youth remains the primary responsible party. Ethically, we believe that this is the most responsible way to deliver services. Practically, we believe it to be more efficient and compassionate to offer an at-risk youth the expertise and guidance of someone whose job it is to know what services, jobs, educational opportunities, and other activities are available in the community and who can provide appropriate counseling. We call the practical operations of delivering this style of service *continuous cyclical triage*; it develops logically from an initial commitment to ongoing support, which is described in the next section.

Ongoing Support

As mentioned before, in ongoing support a case is never closed; the window of service delivery for a particular client through the CLP is always open. The Department of Rehabilitation has seen this as an area of need and a place where their programs can combine with the model demonstration project, mutually benefiting from identifying and filling these gaps in service delivery. The Department of Rehabilitation cannot currently provide this kind of service—its funding is driven at the federal level by the number of people served successfully and those numbers are generated by opening and subsequently closing cases. A person's vocational rehabilitation plan may go on for many months, sometimes years, but once that person is successfully on the job, the case can be closed after 60 days. It can be argued that it is always possible to go back and get a case reopened if need be. However, in some cases the client may no longer be eligible. Clients also cannot go back to get help

with a career change just because they are unhappy with their job. Such a request must be justified by their having problems on the job as a result of their disability. An overriding problem with this population is that, for various reasons, the majority of the time they do not go back and have their cases reopened. It has been our experience in CLP that if the transition specialist is in touch with graduates and prompts them to do so, they will come in and reopen their cases when appropriate. This also is part of ongoing support—not just being available, but prompting graduates to avail themselves of services.

Given a cohort service delivery model, how can an agency possibly provide continuous availability of service at any given time to a group that increases every semester, with only one or two transition specialists? The answer is that it can't, at least not in the sense that a staff can work with everyone continuously from the moment they graduate. Some graduates will be more self-sufficient, some will have nothing to do with the agency, some will move, some will become parents, some will remain in school for awhile, some will be satisfied to retain the jobs they secured right out of high school, and the rest should need only periodic support if the community classroom training and Employment Skills Workshop have been implemented effectively. The problems of ongoing support are those of resource management, the primary resource being the transition specialist's time, and of developing reasonable methods of managing the allocation of this time among all the graduates. It is also important to remember that follow-up contact actually makes the transition specialist's job easier in this respect. When follow-up is maintained through the "floundering" period, it has the short-term effect of keeping the graduate on track, avoiding or remediating problems as they come up. This can actually free up the transition specialist's time (for example, helping a graduate stay on a job through ongoing support will be more time- and cost-effective than having to help develop a new job every time the graduate loses one). It also has the long-term effect of helping the graduates develop and maintain some direction in their life that will carry them beyond the floundering period. By avoiding involvement with other social service agencies later in life, they will be less of a drain on public resources. Most graduates who have less than severe impairments should be skilled and independent enough to negotiate their own career development by the time they are 23 or 24.

Continuous Cyclical Triage

The following is a method developed in CLP to effectively manage the cohort of graduates and the allocation of the transition specialist's time in relation to it. First, we borrowed some terminology, the notion of triage, which is generally associated with emergency medicine. The word *triage* means, very simply, to sort or cull. For example, in the medical model, the doctor or nurse performing triage in a busy emergency room has to determine who is in the greatest medical need and, consequently, in what order the patients should be seen by the physician on duty. One person may have a minor problem and could go home and see his or her personal doctor the following day. Another might have a potentially life-threatening head injury, while yet another is experiencing a heart attack and requires immediate attention. In a M.A.S.H. unit, the person in charge of triage might have a much graver responsibility over patients' lives. If a particularly large group of wounded came in that taxed the unit to its capacity, it might become necessary for the triage personnel to determine not only who was in the greatest medical need, but who of the most critically wounded had the most reasonable expectation of surviving surgery. In relating the above examples analogically, it is crucial for transition specialists to be able to make such determinations intelligently in their own version of triage—that is, (a) who is in the greatest need of services, and (b) of those in need, who seems to command the greatest expectation of success if the transition specialists intervene. If the transition specialists are overwhelmed by the service need at any particular time, they might have to add the additional criterion of temporarily limiting their service only to those who are actually availing themselves of it. A transition specialist can't go out trying to drum up business if she or he is already over-extended, especially if graduates are not following through on their appointments. Other reasons for prioritizing graduates might be to deal with people who have outstanding cases with Vocational Rehabilitation, or those who have most recently graduated.

Typically, other human services agencies in this domain do not have a version of triage that corresponds to the medical model described above. Once eligibility has been determined, services are rendered. If there are not enough "slots," the remaining people go on a waiting list, regardless of their relative need.

Another thing that makes both this and the medical model different from the one used in CLP is that if providers and their administrators (who are actually policy makers) are not committed to follow-up, monitoring, or ongoing support, triage is only an expediency of the in-out service model. Eligibility or need is determined (that's triage); treatment, training, or other services are delivered; and the person goes back out on the street. In many job training pro-

grams, a clock starts ticking the moment people begin, and if they don't "get it" by the end of the period prescribed by the program, they are out of luck. For those with learning and other mild disabilities, for example, this is particularly problematic because they typically do need more time or repetitions before they understand a procedure or concept.

Since CLP employs a model that incorporates ongoing support, triage is conceived of quite differently. It becomes more dynamic in relation to time and the changing status of graduates. It also becomes an indispensable tool to help transition specialists allocate resources. There is never any set number of active service delivery "slots" at a given time as there must be in time-limited programs.

In CLP, the first step in the triage process was to establish three somewhat gross categories to assign to graduates. We used numerical designations of 1, 2, and 3 to represent each graduate's status in terms of potential need and consequently the level of labor-intensiveness this would indicate to the transition specialist. This taxonomy was done with the realization that it was imperfect and not a substitute for more comprehensive assessment measures, that many graduates might fall into gray areas, and that certainly many would change status over time.

Those designated as 1s were considered relatively competent, highly motivated graduates, who continually exhibited good job responsibility behaviors. Services they might require were predicted to be minimal (this was not always the case) and would include things such as maintaining résumés, providing job leads, assisting and advising in career changes and postsecondary education, certifying for special programs, and counseling. The 1s were graduates who would probably do fine on their own and could conduct their own job search. We could assist them in enhancing their career potential, upgrading their abilities, and so forth. Though their needs for survival were not dire, we believe that in many of these cases we played a significant role in enabling them to climb the career ladder into better-paying and more challenging jobs.

Those designated as 2s usually had problems that held them back a little more. Whether it was social-behavioral competence on the job or a problem with task-related competence, they needed more guidance and support. These youths were also motivated, but might need remediation in certain areas.

Those designated as 3s usually had some fairly intractable problems. They were severely limited in either their job skills, social skills, or job responsibility skills; they lacked motivation; or they demonstrated various combinations of these things. They could range from highly functioning young people with some underlying emotional and behavioral problems to youths with mild retardation who perhaps should have been eligible for supported employment services through the regional centers, but who were denied. People from this group often represented a significant time investment on the part of the transition specialist.

A further distinction that can be useful in this regard is determining the level of short-term need and long-term need. The above-mentioned categories would typically be used to characterize the level of long-term need, taking into account such issues as degree of self-sufficiency and severity of disability. The short-term level of need might address the temporal exigency of a particular service (e.g., referral to mental health services, application assistance, or certification of other paperwork needed for a special program). This could be illustrated by analogy to the coding system used in the dispatch of emergency vehicles. Code 1 usually means to stack the call, indicating that it is not an emergency; Code 2 means that the call is an emergency and should be attended to as quickly as possible; Code 3 indicates that it is a life-threatening emergency requiring immediate response and all due haste; and Code 4 means that the situation is under control and no further assistance is necessary. For perspicuity and simplicity's sake, in CLP's model these categories were reduced to three, indicating an increasing level of need from lowest to highest. So a graduate would receive a two-digit designation, the first denoting short-term level of need (what level of service will be immediately delivered) and the second denoting the graduate's long-term need level (what is our assessment in the overall situation). This assists in accounting for a 3 who may be refusing service for the time being (32); a 1 who has a great job lead but needs her résumé updated immediately and is unable to do it alone (13); or a graduate who is in jail—a serious situation—but about whom the staff can do nothing until his release date is closer (31).

Regular staffings were held on a biweekly basis where these determinations would be debated and assigned. The cohort was divided up to evenly distribute the time constraints of the different categories as well as to make sure that graduates were matched with the transition specialist who was most appropriate to their situation for more specific qualitative reasons. For example, the transition specialist might be of the same sex, linguistic background, or ethnicity as the graduate, or might have a background of dealing effectively with a particular graduate in the past. These concerns were incorporated into the triage process.

At each staffing, the transition specialists bring a simple CLP Job Placement Record (see Appendix 4.4) to expedite the meeting and to effectively brief the other members of the team on the current status of different graduates. Using the staffing to briefly acquaint all team members with the current history of each graduate serves several purposes: It encourages joint brainstorming and problem solving; it alerts team members and managers if a particular transition specialist is becoming overwhelmed; and it allows the transition specialists to coordinate their efforts. If one transition specialist is having a particularly difficult time working with a graduate or having interpersonal differences, or if it is just mutually determined that another transition specialist might be a better match, the staffing facilitates the exchange of responsibility. A form referred to as the Quick Progress/Planning and Assessment Sheet (see Appendix 4.5) consists of a list of all the graduates in the cohort and has columns for follow-up (if it is needed and by when), transition specialist (who is the responsible party), and priority (is this person a priority for follow-up or some other need), with an additional column for comments to briefly state what the graduate is doing or may require in the way of transition services.

Unfortunately, until ongoing follow-up is more widely practiced, transition specialists will have caseloads that are too large to continually manage. They must again invoke the concept of triage and sort their group according to the criteria described above, and they must learn to "cluster" groups of graduates according to their individual circumstances. The transition specialists want to make sure that the graduates most in need are served as well as the largest number of graduates possible. So there should be an evaluation of different areas of need for the graduates, what their triage designation is, and how much time they will require; a schedule should be organized (usually week by week) to accommodate their plans. Geographic proximity of different job placements can play into this determination and should also be considered (as it is for community classroom site selection for interns). In order to keep the whole project manageable, it is crucial to have regular staffings to facilitate the triage process at periodic (cyclic) intervals and on an ongoing or continuous basis, so the team is always apprised of the status of the cohort and able to respond. Hence the term *continuous cyclical triage*—triage performed at regular, periodic intervals on an ongoing or continuous basis—is appropriate. It may sound redundant, but we have found this intensified attention paid to the semifinite cohort to be effective.

The whole idea of providing ongoing support and continuous availability of service for an indeterminate number of graduates can be conceptually overwhelming. That is why it is helpful here to use a metaphor to illustrate how a team might go about the logistics of managing such a project.

Picture a module of input jacks like the switchboard a typical telephone operator might have. Assume that this is a cohort of graduates, one input jack for each person.

Each transition specialist has a certain number of phone jacks that can be used at any given time, labeled "1," "2," or "3," corresponding to the triage category designation discussed previously. In effect, these labeled jacks represent the amount of time a transition specialist will be able to devote to graduates at a particular moment. So each transition specialist will have perhaps two to four 3s, twice as many 2s, and a substantial number of 1s that could be operable at any given time.

The triage process determines how these units of service delivery time, or "jacks," will be allocated. Since there are only a certain number of jacks of different designations that may be operable for any transition specialist at a given moment, the entire cohort is not really being served all at once, but rather in manageable "clusters" of graduates. A cluster might significantly change in a period of a month, or even a week, but there will always be essentially the same number of jacks or allocations of the transition specialist's time per graduate. These relatively discrete and stable units of time will just be used by different graduates. This is why the triage process is so important in managing time. It is necessary to determine which graduates are going to be put on hold for the time being, however cold that may sound. These will generally be the graduates at either end of the triage spectrum. They may be the high-functioning 1s, who are very capable of conducting their own job search with minimal suggestions and direction on the part of the transition specialist or who may want to make a change although they already have a job that is stable. Or they may be the intractable 3s who are not ready for a job, refuse to make appointments, and generally are in a state where they are just a drain on the program and the transition specialist's time.

There has to be some reasonable expectation of success in order to make the time commitment a 3 usually demands. Again, this is not to say that these 3s, who are probably the most at-risk youths in the program, should be abandoned. One of the luxuries of having ongoing support and follow-up is that the transition specialist can stay in contact with them and come back to them when they are in a position to be more receptive to the transition specialist's efforts. This also gives the youths time to see that the program's commitment is real and that someone really has been calling to check on them and see how they are doing, as was promised when they were in high school. If the program is working well, there will be many periods where the transition specialist's time will free up enough to work with this group, or to

spend more time with the more self-sufficient graduates. The other graduates who typically will be put on hold are those who do not want to associate with the program, at least for the time being, the single parents with infant children, and people who are unreachable (which means that reasonable efforts to track them down have been unsuccessful). But the crucial qualitative difference between the cohort model and conventional social service delivery is that no one is ever forgotten or completely neglected by the system. The transition specialist's job has that feature built into it.

When a new group of interns graduates, enlarging the cohort, a new module is added on to the right side of the "switchboard," becoming part of the extant cohort accumulated from previous semesters. So what you should see, if the triage process is working well, is clusters of jacks moving up and down, but progressively to the right (give or take a few stragglers moving or remaining back with some of the older graduates). There should be enough jacks in each transition specialist's patchboard so that a patch cord can be stretched back to a student from an older group who has a renewed interest or need for services.

Once the number of cohorts reaches the point where it is not feasible or physically possible for the transition specialist to reach patch cords back and forth, that transition specialist (or transition specialist team) has essentially reached the capacity of graduates that can be accommodated, and either the existing team must be expanded or new teams must be generated to be able to continue to serve all the existing groups effectively. It is time to begin a new cohort.

Management Issues

Staff Self-Management

The question of how many transition specialists are necessary to make a cohort service delivery system like CLP run effectively is difficult to answer. It depends on a number of things, including the characteristics of the cohort, the apparent permanence of their success, idiosyncrasies of the geographic area (major industries, services available, public transit, etc.), and other intangibles such as the actual capability and commitment of a particular transition specialist to manage a particular caseload. However, there are certain aspects of the position that should remain relevant across situations, cities, and school districts.

As the cohort approach developed, a new transition specialist was hired. After a solid year in which only one served the cohort, it became obvious that two transition specialists could serve 100 graduates better than one could serve 50. One important reason is that this allows the two sexes to be represented, which can make it much easier to deal with certain subjects that might be harder to broach for someone of the opposite sex, such as birth control, parenthood, or hygiene and grooming issues. Another advantage is that clients are exposed to a positive role model of the same sex. Many graduates come from backgrounds where they may never have had a positive role model of the same sex the entire time they were developing, growing up, becoming socialized, and being educated. A similar argument can be made for having a transition team that doesn't just respect the ethnocultural backgrounds of the graduates being served, but adequately reflects it.

Two well-matched transition specialists bring different strengths and weaknesses to the work and can thus develop complementary styles that enable them to respond more effectively to a broader range of circumstances. Everyone has stylistic differences, individual biases, talents, preferred counseling strategies, and so on. If one transition specialist's style is more suited to a certain graduate for some reason, it might be the crucial factor that engenders the graduate's acceptance of the transition specialist and consequently his or her ultimate success. For example, one transition specialist may be very good at getting to know the student, building rapport, and identifying very personal stressors that may be affecting the student's success, but may have a hard time developing a plan based on this information and getting the graduate to stick to it. Conversely, that transition specialist's partner may be highly skilled at the needed intervention skill and is able to work with the other transition specialist to provide more sensitive and comprehensive service.

This diversity in personalities combined with frequent staffings easily allows the transition specialists to cover for each other in the event of scheduling conflicts; to switch assignment of a graduate from one transition specialist to the other if it seems that they may be a better match; or to effectively combine efforts to co-counsel one graduate. This last approach can have the effect of fostering the feeling of a team effort, especially for the graduate. It also serves to minimize the typical institutional, client–service-provider dichotomy that presents its own problems when working with this population.

It is also an advantage for the transition specialists just to have another staff person involved in similar activities with similar concerns. We think that this is especially important considering the implicit demands of the job and the fact that the job takes the transition specialist into the field much of the time. This job is almost entirely performed in isolation from other staff. The transition specialists are out facing a challenging and exclusionary mainstream by themselves. It is important for them to have someone with whom they can share experiences, brainstorm, and develop support systems. Otherwise, they will be much more prone to burnout.

Time Management

Another crucial area that must be addressed when implementing the role of transition specialist is that of time management. Considering the demands placed on the transition specialists by the various "as-needed" services they provide, combined with the programmatic component of ongoing commitment, their hands are more than full. They have to get the business of managing their time down to an art. Otherwise, the demands of the job will take on a life of their own, gain control, and dictate the allocation of time. The transition specialists could easily crash and burn in the process.

One method that is helpful is to use the clustering approach, working with groups of graduates as described above. This idea can be generalized to help organize time by clustering not only the graduates, but the requisite, ancillary activities their success may hinge upon, such as follow-up, job development, outreach, and interagency articulation. But even with the most masterful organizational skills, the crucial factor in the transition specialist's scheduling technique is flexibility. A person who needs the structure of a 9-to-5 workday will have a hard time as a transition specialist. A number of activities have to be accomplished that make working at odd hours necessary. Many graduates are unreachable during the day because they are working or out of the house; many have jobs on the weekend or strange shifts. It is also important for the program itself to have a mechanism for dealing with the fluctuating hours a transition specialist may have to keep and an effective way of accommodating them. Issues such as the mode of pay (salaried, hourly) and compensation for overtime need to be addressed. An alternative scheduling mode such as flextime or some version of compensatory time may be indicated. The necessary flexibility of transition specialists in accommodating other people's schedules should be reflected in the program's personnel and payroll management in order to protect the interests of the transition specialists as well as their accountability.

Another issue that must be considered in managing time for the transition specialist is travel time.

Transition specialists are always on the move and may spend up to 2 hours a day getting from place to place, not including their travel time to and from the office. This can be very costly, especially in a city like San Francisco. Because of the efficient mass transit systems available in the San Francisco Bay Area (and a parking situation with odds akin to the state lottery), CLP transition specialists rely almost exclusively on public transportation. Using this mode of transportation has advantages. For example, the whole problem of parking, traffic, car maintenance, and keeping track of these costs is obviated by simply buying monthly transportation passes. It also forces the transition specialists to become familiar with the public transportation system so they can give directions to graduates or instruct them in its use. Another potentially catastrophic problem this circumvents is the issue of liability if the transition specialists were to drive a graduate in their personal vehicle and an accident occurred. Another potential benefit that may not seem as compelling is that it forces the transition specialists to be more organized in arranging visits for the day; it also allows travel time to be used for reading, paperwork, or other incidentals relevant to the job, instead of attending to driving.

Finally, to illustrate more graphically the way transition specialists distribute their time, a typical week is described (see Appendix 4.6). The hours shown are longer than a normal 40-hour work week because it is a composite week, intended to describe a range of activities and the variation of hours. However, it should be noted that sometimes a transition specialist may have to put in a 10- or 12-hour day if the need arises, and, as mentioned before, arrangements need to be made to adequately compensate for this situation.

Job Development

A number of excellent materials on job development already exist, and so the process will not be explicated beyond what is offered in chapter 5. We particularly like Bissonnette and Pimentel (1984) and the *Work-Ability Job Development Manual* (California State Department of Education, 1986). In chapter 2, the process of teaching interns to conduct their own job search is explained, and relevant lesson plans are described in chapter 3. Youths must be taught to do their own job searches in every possible instance. However, there is still a place and a need for the transition specialist to develop jobs as well.

In the process of following up on a graduate, the transition specialist can be a catalyst for re-creating the community that takes care of its own (this is more common in rural than urban areas) and can parlay

one successful placement into others. There have been several instances where a second or third graduate was added to a particular employer's workforce, or where a graduate who left a job for school or a better job was replaced by another, more recent graduate.

Clearly, rushing or pressuring a graduate into a job without considering the quality of the match is a very poor way to develop jobs, and research (Siegel & Gaylord-Ross, 1991) as well as experience has taught us this. Quota systems encourage this kind of expediency, and in many cases, a 60-day placement can be obtained, but a poor job match is ultimately destructive to the youth, the credibility of the job developer, the employer, and the authentic servicing of career growth.

There is also the fine art of knowing how to disclose information about a candidate that honestly informs the employer about the youth's strengths and limitations, but does not compromise that youth or predispose the employer against her or him. We recommend the development of nonjudgmental behavioral descriptions and relevant data that can help an employer to anticipate the special needs of a new employee, and that can enable the transition specialist to negotiate the support services that will help to engineer a success.

Sometimes a person may be an excellent transition specialist in every area except job development, or may be new to an area and lacking in contacts, or may be severely time-constrained due to the intensity of other duties, especially that of enabling job retention for those already hired. A consultant from the business world may be a necessary new member of the team who can develop training and job placements that the transition specialist team fills (see chapter 5). This can create a new interdependency and need for articulation among the team, as the transition specialist must deliver on promises made by the job developer. In this revision of the model, the job developer makes the cold calls, knocks on doors, and performs other activities that might eat up the transition specialist's primary direct service time with graduates. A well-connected business consultant can save the program staff many hours when they are trying to break into a big corporation by his or her ability to contact an executive at a high enough level to open that company's doors.

Finally, an essential aspect of job development and initial placement is the ability of the job developer or transition specialist to sell and deliver to the employer the tax credits and/or training stipends (targeted jobs tax credits offered through the Employment Development Department and on-the-job training agreements sponsored by the Private Industry Council). To effectively build a network, the work site must be assessed and a good match made. The intensity of initial service must be likewise assessed, and the commitment made. Finally, the promise of ongoing support and regular contact with the employer must be delivered as well.

Documentation

Another important task for the transition specialist is that of record keeping and documentation. There are a number of reasons for this requirement and different ways it can be accomplished. Since the concept of the transition specialist is fairly new and innovative, documentation can provide invaluable information to others who want to replicate this role, or for troubleshooting within the program to help increase the efficacy of the transition specialist and revise the job description. It also can help an overwhelmed transition specialist to see ways to be more time-efficient. It is an important advocacy tool that can justify the position or revisions in the position, it provides accountability, and it aids in research efforts.

Probably the easiest and most effective way to document efforts is by keeping a daily journal. This journal doesn't have to be extremely detailed. It should essentially be a list of the day's activities, with brief descriptions of all contacts, interactions, or services provided to graduates or interns.

The journal can be useful in a number of ways, one of the more important being to help the accountability of the transition specialist. Since transition specialists are out on their own most of the time, they can be protected by a journal that documents dates and services. The journal can also be used to justify certain activities or the amount of time spent on them if the need arises.

The journal can also be a valuable tool for following individual graduates, charting their progress and problems, and discerning patterns in their emergent career development, and it can provide evidence the transition specialist may need in order to advocate for a graduate. For example, a rehabilitation counselor may feel that a certain type of job is not indicated for a graduate because of the graduate's test scores, but the transition specialist may be able to provide compelling observational evidence to the contrary, and thus help the counselor to justify the graduate's plan. In addition, the journal can be used as a general way of keeping track of the graduates; it is possible to go back and glean the journal, discovering information that was not previously recognized as being important, and supplying this information at a later time (e.g., for particular research concerns, or for graduates who need their résumés updated).

The journal can be a valuable adjunct to more formal data collection or research projects, especially because it can be implemented right away. It also can provide useful information in the development of other instruments as the program progresses and different patterns or variables begin to emerge. The importance of the research component of a program cannot be overemphasized, because in many cases, it is what drives the funding and refunding of special programs.

Research makes a program more objectively valuable and determines its potential for replicability. What are the variables involved? Can a program that works in San Francisco work in other areas as well? The journal, other instruments, and accompanying research can help to make this clearer and to identify the salient issues. Clearly, this book is only a first step, and those who attempt to replicate CLP will improve upon the suggestions made here.

Follow-Up

A rich, multifaceted information base is a by-product of the ongoing support component of the program—its follow-up. Regular follow-up is important not just to offer service, chart success, and prove results, but also to maintain contact and to avoid losing people. CLP has reevaluated and modified its content and methods of follow-up a number of times. The most recent version was developed according to the following criteria:

1. It is convenient and minimally time-intensive for the program staff.

2. It is convenient and minimally disruptive to the graduate.

3. The database compares to those of others conducting similar studies.

4. It has simple data coding and storage for maximum flexibility and manipulability.

5. Most importantly, it confirms the verisimilitude of the main treatise of the program: career ladders.

Are we really helping these students to climb a career ladder? CLP's most recent follow-up data are being compared with the national survey of youth with disabilities being conducted by the Stanford Research Institute. This survey, the National Longitudinal Transition Study, will attempt to chart movement up and down the career ladder as well as career satisfaction levels (Siegel, Avoke, Paul, Robert, & Gaylord-Ross, 1991; Siegel, Robert, Waxman, & Gaylord-Ross, 1992).

This type of rich follow-up data fulfills both the quantitative and qualitative concerns of a program like this. Combined with a journal, it is very useful for developing ethnographic or anecdotal case histories, and for demonstrating the program's process, as the following vignette does. When an interaction is established, ethnographic, interpretive information can continually corroborate the quantitative data collection and sustain a reasonably high level of social validity.

Gloria: A Case Study

The following case study illustrates some of the principles of case management described in the previous sections. Rather than describe techniques in isolation, our intention is to demonstrate theory in practice and to show how the transition specialist takes a "big picture" or ecosystematic approach to a given case. It is impossible to reduce this role to a simple formula or procedure. By telling this story we hope to capture the complexity of the different technical, bureaucratic, and human issues that must be confronted by the transition specialist, and especially to show how they all interact in the case of a particular young person.

The responses and reactions of the transition specialist demonstrate how professionals can and must respond creatively and flexibly to the problems that arise as an at-risk youth attempts to enter the workforce. Finally, we hope to illustrate the importance of keeping informed on a regular and frequent basis during the first two years of employment. The transition specialist in Gloria's story is the first author.

Gloria participated in CLP as an intern in the spring of 1986 and graduated a year before the advent of a full-time transition specialist, myself. Her community classroom experience was in a large insurance office where she performed basic office duties including photocopying, filing, and some minimal typing. The general consensus of the program's staff and employee evaluators was that she was a very good worker, was very responsible, and had good grooming habits and job-keeping skills, but one area of concern was her shyness; it was thought that this might hold her back in the future. After graduation, CLP placed Gloria in a retail store in the financial district of San Francisco that seemed like a good match for her demonstrated skills and abilities. After an initial training period of about 2 months, the employer seemed to be very happy with Gloria, so the CLP instructor's monitoring of the situation was faded out.

Gloria did well on the job. However, she did seem to have some problems that involved her level of social sophistication as it pertained to functioning in this particular environment. Her perceptions of certain on-the-job situations and her consequent behavior were often incompatible, for whatever reason, with the expectations of her supervisor. For example, Gloria's job occasionally required her to lift and move boxes around. None of this was beyond her physical capability, yet Gloria routinely enlisted the help of male co-workers in these tasks. She was oblivious to the fact that this behavior greatly annoyed her female manager, to whom it appeared that Gloria was being manipulative and shirking responsibility. Though this was a factor to be considered, it did not directly affect her employment status. She ultimately did lose the job, however, because nobody contacted her employer when Gloria was forced to go on medical leave after being hospitalized for a nervous breakdown.

About 6 months after her hospitalization, Gloria first met with me to discuss her plans and have her case reopened with the Department of Rehabilitation. She presented to me as attractive, well groomed, and cooperative, but a little shy, nervous, and somewhat withdrawn. She had been in therapy all this time and her psychiatrist now recommended that she go back to work on a limited basis. The doctor was very cooperative and gave me as much information as possible, listened to my concerns about Gloria, and addressed them as best he could. Gloria had had adverse reactions to the medication she took, which necessitated further medication to counteract the serious side effects of the primary medication. These medicines in turn had their own unpleasant, although more tolerable, side effects. The doctor had tried to reduce Gloria's dosage in the past but she had experienced a major decompensation. Because of her situation at home and her need to bolster her self-concept in recovery from her mental illness, the doctor felt it was important for her to be out of the house as much as possible doing something constructive like work or school.

Gloria concurred with this. Her situation at home was not entirely unsupportive, but she had several brothers who were "troublemakers" and she worried about them, sometimes obsessively. She and her doctor agreed that she needed to take some initiative with her own life. Since her mother and brothers were essentially supportive of her in this plan, and since her mother could not speak English, I did not involve the family directly other than introducing myself and letting them know what my role was. In other situations, family members might be consulted more intensively to encourage them as natural support systems for the young person in transition. This is especially true in situations where youths may be exceptionally at risk, or where demands may be made on them by their family, either knowingly or unknowingly, that could potentially sabotage their success on the job. But since the family was supportive of her efforts, and Gloria, though withdrawn, was very honest and forthright given a chance, I felt confident that she could report to the family any information relevant to their role that they might need to know. I might have investigated the family dynamics further to see if there were any suggestions I could make or helped in some other way that might obliquely enhance Gloria's chances for success. But after assessing the situation between the relevant players—Gloria, her doctor, her brothers, and her mother—I determined that anything further than what I was already doing might be too ambitious or invasive and therefore possibly counterproductive. At this point, the overriding priority to balance out the system was to get Gloria out of the house as much as possible by finding her a job and some kind of remedial education program. The doctor was helping Gloria deal with her family problems and seemed to be doing a good job. There was no reason to supplant, duplicate, or do anything else that would create interference between services. I had gleaned enough information to make this determination through coordinating with Gloria's existing support network to see where I could most effectively assist her.

Gloria's immediate vocational goals were to get a clerical job and enroll in remedial education to upgrade her basic skills, particularly her reading and writing. She liked the idea of working in an office atmosphere but had little clerical experience other than the routine stock work she had done at her previous job. She had no real typing or phone skills, and I wanted to avoid putting her into too challenging a setting right away. Too much pressure was the last thing she needed right now in her state of recovery. Gloria could file fairly well and perform most other basic office tasks. Her reading level was very low but workable, and she also had a problem with vocabulary and lexical access to some common English words. It was not clear whether this was due to her learning disability, her level of English proficiency, potential side effects of the medication, or a combination of all three.

I set up an interview for Gloria at a large law firm that needed another interoffice messenger. Gloria made a good impression in the interview and they decided to try her out. The personnel manager was a little concerned about her shyness, but he figured that this would take care of itself once she became comfortable with the job. Since I was confident that Gloria could accommodate all the tasks the job might require, I did little more than offer my services if

Gloria needed any help learning the job. The personnel manager himself was new, inexperienced, and a little nervous about just how he was going to perform at his new job. So I felt that the best approach at this point was one of reassurance; I thought that Gloria would do well and I could be available to take care of any problems if they came up, rather than drawing unnecessary, potentially negative attention to her. Unfortunately, giving too much background information to an employer can have this effect in some situations and actually do more harm than good.

I discussed setting up a remedial education program with Gloria and it was mutually agreed that we should hold off until we established how she was tolerating the job.

Gloria started working part-time, 5 hours a day, from 9:00 A.M. to 1:00 P.M. I checked in the first day and made sure everything was going smoothly. The mail room was very cramped and since I already knew the job, I could tell that Gloria was in good hands (she was getting one-on-one training from a person who had exactly the same job), and she seemed comfortable, so I just observed for awhile, making sure she was understanding her instruction, and then left. I checked in with Gloria that night and fairly regularly for the next 2 weeks, also checking with the supervisor the 1st day, 3rd day, and 7th day, and then once a week for the first month. There were no complaints. Everything seemed to be going well. The only ancillary service I provided for Gloria at this time was to get a voucher from the Department of Rehabilitation for shoes and pants as she didn't have enough clothes to put together appropriate outfits for an average work week.

Then one day, at about the 8th week, I was in the office with a graduate who was interviewing for another position in the firm, when Gloria's supervisor pulled me aside. He asked if there was anything particularly wrong with Gloria and I asked what he meant. He said there had been a few complaints that she had been making mistakes, delivering documents to the wrong offices. He said it wasn't serious, but because of the time constraints on attorneys it was very important that things went where they were supposed to in a timely manner. He also said that something else was wrong that he couldn't quite put his finger on. He said that he liked Gloria, that she was very nice, always appropriately dressed, on time, and so forth, but that there was something different about her. For some reason, she didn't quite fit in. I asked a few questions to see if I could elicit more helpful information to further pinpoint what the problem might be, but that was as far as I could get. She just didn't quite fit in and the supervisor was at a loss. He said that he didn't want to let her go but might have to if things didn't improve or if they got any worse. I thanked him for his honest feedback and reaffirmed that I was there to help in just this sort of situation. I asked the supervisor if I could have 1 to 2 weeks to work with Gloria and see if I could somehow remediate the situation. The supervisor happily agreed and gave me permission to come in and work with her whenever I liked.

The next hurdle was approaching Gloria, because she was in a fairly fragile emotional state. I did not want to unnecessarily frighten her or initiate any undue stress that might cause her to become ill, regress, or behave on the job in a way that might make the situation even worse. But I needed to make her aware that some changes had to happen in order for her to keep the job. The first thing I did was interview her to see if she liked the job. There would not be any sense in trying to keep her on the job if she were truly unhappy with it. This might just drag out the inevitable to nobody's benefit. But she really did like the job. She had met one or two people she liked and had conversations with, and she seemed to self-perceive that she was doing all right. She mentioned a task-related problem she was having that involved memorizing the names of the attorneys, so I offered to come in and work with her a little each day of the following week to see if I could come up with some strategies to help her with this task.

It took fewer than two visits to assess and establish what the problems were and to see that they were in no way insuperable, except for the additional element of the time factor involved. If I had not taken the supervisor's word that Gloria was doing so well and had done an on-the-job assessment sooner, she could have been working on these things for a few weeks by now. But it was academic at this point.

I started out by showing up when Gloria started work in the morning and essentially just shadowed her for a few hours, asking her questions about what she was doing to make sure she was understanding everything. If she wasn't, I encouraged her to ask questions of the appropriate employee. This also allowed me to get a reading on the general tenor of the office, to see which people might be enlisted as potential allies of Gloria and which might be potential detractors who would be best avoided. I was able to accomplish all of this in less than a week so that it appeared that I was just another employee who was being trained by Gloria. By the time any of the office workers had a chance to figure out my role, I was gone.

There were three basic areas I identified that needed attention if Gloria was to keep the job: (a) basic job skills and the accommodations and adaptations needed to enhance them, (b) things she could do to fit in better socially at the workplace, and (c) the opportunity for her to have more time to learn the job, to allow the effects of the remediation plan to take hold, and to let the social ecology of the workplace begin responding positively to her and accepting her. I set separate appointments away from the job to work with her on these things, then went back and shadowed her on the job a few more times to evaluate the effects of my training and also to cue her and reinforce certain areas if needed.

I got an excellent clue as to what was going on the moment I arrived on my first day of shadowing. Gilda, the head receptionist who had been with the company for 15 years, had her own commentary about what she thought the problem was. Gilda was one of the only people in the office who knew that Gloria came from a special program, because she had made a point of asking me a lot of questions on the occasions when I had visited the personnel manager. At that time, she had gone on and on about what a wonderful program she thought it was; she said she wished her neighbor had known about it for her son. But it was clear on this visit that she did not really have Gloria's best interests at heart. She made a point of filling me in on all the mistakes Gloria had made and said that it appeared she could not read at all for she would often stare in a confused way at the list of attorneys she used to make deliveries and at other documents. All of this was offered up in a rather petulant tone, as if I might be at fault for putting Gloria in a job she was not capable of doing. Consequently, one of my first instructions to Gloria was to give Gilda a wide berth.

The next thing I did was to inspect the list Gloria used to make deliveries. The system for the attorneys' office addresses went like this: A Post-it™ note with the attorney's initials was stuck on the document. Until someone was familiar with all the initials, a list had to be used that gave the attorney's full name next to the initials in alphabetical order, along with the name of each attorney's secretary. Some interoffice mail was to always go to the secretary and some to the attorney. So Gloria had to match the initials on the Post-it note to the initials on the list, figure out the attorneys' names (and there were some unusual ones), match them to the sign on each attorney's door (which could be on any one of three floors), and learn who all the secretaries were. There were over 100 attorneys and secretaries in the firm.

The first problem was with the list. It had been reduced so many times to fit onto a tiny 6-by-9-inch piece of paper that it was almost unreadable to me. So I had a more perspicuous version of the list blown up and color-coded according to floor. I had several sessions with Gloria on pronouncing the difficult names and came up with mnemonics to help her remember the exceptional ones. She started showing some improvement after two sessions, which was noticed by the supervisor as well as myself. I also contacted her doctor and asked if the medication she was receiving could be making this harder for her and might account for some of her apparent confusion and spaciness. He said that it easily could and that he would try to start reducing her dosage as much as he could. Gloria also responded positively to this. At this time, I also accompanied her to speak with a counselor at the community college and she enrolled in some remedial classes in basic skills, reading, vocabulary, spelling, and math. She again responded very positively. She improved measurably in a very short time, especially in vocabulary, the area where she was most noticeably deficient.

The next area to address was how to improve the way Gloria was assimilating into the social environment at work. I felt that in her case it was an especially delicate subject to broach. I wanted to present it in such a way that it did not affect the progress her success at this job was having on her self-esteem. At the same time, I needed to alert her that some changes had to be made or she would be in danger of losing the job. And the truth is, it was not Gloria's ''fault'' that she was shy; it had to do with the insensitivity built into the office environment, which can be especially unforgiving in this regard. So that is approximately how I broached the subject with Gloria—by emphasizing the fact that there was nothing wrong with her, but that this was an unusual situation that had different rules. For example, I told her that just as you might not talk and behave the same way around your mother as you do around your friends, there are certain modes of behavior that are more acceptable in the office environment outside of just showing up to work on time and doing your job.

I came up with three simple, manageable ways for Gloria to change her behavior, which could be viewed as tools to *empower* her and allow her to *play the game* of the workplace, not to change her personality because she was a bad person or didn't fit in. I included her in this experiment, telling her that if she tried a few techniques, she would be surprised by the way that people would treat her differently. What I had her do to try and effect this environmental assimilation was (a) smile and address people a little more than she was doing when she passed them in the halls or when she entered a room to make deliveries, (b) speak up a little bit when talking, and (c) move a little faster from place to place while she was working. This again was put in the context that these changes weren't actually necessary to execute her duties—she was doing fine in that regard. They would just help her to make a positive impression on the attorneys, her supervisors, and her co-workers,

using techniques that might not have been readily apparent to her.

I shadowed her a few more times to make sure that she was effecting the behaviors I had coached her in, and she was doing so quite competently. The next step was to approach the supervisor and see how he felt about her quick progress. Unfortunately, what I feared most was about to happen. Things had gone on too long without any intervention, and he was still getting complaints about Gloria and pressure to replace her. In an attempt to buy a little more time, I reminded the supervisor that there really had not been enough time for my attempts at remediation to take hold. The supervisor apologized and said that he would have to let her go but would wait a few weeks, until after the holidays, to do so, more out of respect for Gloria than anything else. A week later, I contacted him to ask him just when Gloria's last day would be because I wanted to place her into another job as soon as possible. At this point, the supervisor said that they had put the idea of terminating Gloria on hold temporarily; she seemed to be improving and there had been no complaints at all about her work since the last time he and I spoke with each other. I kept checking in until it was obvious that Gloria was succeeding. In fact, she was the best messenger in the office, second only to the person who trained her (who was also a graduate of CLP). Gloria is now completely off any medication for her psychiatric condition, has been working successfully for over a year and a half, continues to improve, and is now working with me on plans to get further training to be a medical assistant and possibly to continue on to be a Licensed Vocational Nurse.

Conclusion

Young people today face an ever-growing and daunting array of circumstances in their transition from school to adult life—a faltering economy and shrinking budgets, unemployment on the rise, a threatened, deteriorating environment, decreased educational opportunities, drugs, homelessness, and more. With this in mind, it is obvious that our youths with special needs face an even greater, seemingly insurmountable challenge. Programs like supported employment that strive to develop natural supports in the workplace can enhance the potential for vocational success. But it seems unlikely that job coaches, employers, co-workers, or even involved family members can by themselves have the resources to adequately make an impact on the myriad issues facing the majority of these youths.

The role of the transition specialist ideally takes into account the complicated, interactive sets of circumstances that affect a young person's acculturation, assimilation, and integration into the workplace and adjustment to adult life. To this purpose, the transition specialist attempts to develop a global, ecosystematic, and more humanistic profile of the youth in transition as a person developing a long-term career. The transition specialist then acts on this assessment as a counselor, case manager, and resource developer for the youth, making appropriate linkages with family, employers, school staff, and other adult service providers (see Appendix 4.1).

It is from this perspective that CLP and its participants have enjoyed significant successes. It is hoped that this role, or one with similar philosophical underpinnings, can be developed further, thus enhancing the quality of postsecondary service delivery, independence, and success of youths in transition, and dispelling the notion—changing the reality—that vocational services are pawns in a larger scheme of "tracking" individuals into entry-level jobs and leaving them there.

Appendix 4.1
Summary of Transition Services

Follow-up contact. Routine quarterly follow-up to see how former interns are doing (this contact may be more or less frequent depending on individual circumstances), what their employment status is, if they are in school or are planning to be, and if they feel they could benefit from CLP services. Also, obtaining permission to visit the job site and contact the present employer (when appropriate), co-workers, or other significant support people in the graduate's social network for more comprehensive monitoring and as an intervention-oriented assessment.

Rehabilitation casework. Facilitating referrals; case openings and closures; reopenings; rehabilitation services; postemployment services; case management and program planning with Vocational Rehabilitation; and consultation, coordination, and communication with the rehabilitation counselor about all CLP clients with active or inactive cases.

Postsecondary education or training. Counseling, referral, liaison, and tutoring services for CLP graduates who would like to go to college or participate in an occupational training program, youth employment program, or similar activity.

On-the-job training. Job training and coaching, task analysis, accommodations, and mediations for CLP graduates to aid in the development of specific job skills. Also coaching in job retention skills such as attendance and appearance.

Counseling. Counseling and problem solving with graduates on personal, employment, and education or training issues as they directly affect and pertain to their career concerns.

Independent living skills. Counseling in basic skills that are not necessarily directly related to job retention, but to enhancing the quality of life—for example, issues regarding fiscal matters (like income taxes), finding an apartment, or getting a driver's license.

Resource referral. When appropriate, referring graduates to other service providers and community agencies that could potentially enhance their individual transition capabilities.

Social skills training. Problem solving, role playing, behavioral modeling, self-monitoring, and other techniques to help graduates work through on-the-job and/or interpersonal problems and to help them better acclimate to the particular social environment at work or in other situations.

Ecosystematic intervention. A more global intervention technique where a number of key players in the graduate's social network (such as co-workers, supervisors, relatives, counselors, teachers, and friends) are enlisted in some way to assist in the manipulation of parameters that have been collectively identified as areas in need of remediation, and to provide support and bolster the intern's capability to maneuver in a difficult or crisis situation toward an ultimately positive result.

Job search. Counseling, support, supported job search, help with applications or exams, maintaining résumés, interview skills, job leads, job development, and placement.

Pregraduation contact. Providing any transition services to interns before they have graduated from CLP.

Transition planning. Working with school-based teachers, counselors, Vocational Rehabilitation personnel, parents, interns, and others to start developing or implementing Individualized Transition Plans for pregraduates and recent graduates.

Appendix 4.2
Transition Specialist Self-Tracking Chart

Month _____

	Follow-Up	Rehabilitation Casework	Postsecondary Education/Training	On-the-Job Training	Job Search	Counseling	Independent Living Skills	Resource Referral	Social Skills Training	Pregraduation Contact	Transition Planning	Ecosystematic Intervention
64.												
65.												
66.												
67.												
68.												
69.												
610.												
611.												
612.												
613.												
71.												
72.												
73.												
74.												
75.												
76.												
77.												
78.												
79.												
710.												
711.												
712.												
713.												
714.												
715.												
716.												
717.												
718.												
719.												
720.												

[a]The first digit identifies the semester of community classroom training. The second and third digits code the specific graduate.

Appendix 4.3
Activities a Transition Specialist Might Engage in over the Course of a Hypothetical Week

- Make a home visit to a family to collaboratively make and engender support for a vocational plan for the CLP graduate.

- Visit a CLP graduate on-site who is enrolled in another program, e.g., a program where he is learning how to tune up cars and replace brakes. The transition specialist would check on progress, check on the quality of the program and adequacy of the placement, and begin to make plans for what will occur after the training program ends.

- Spend solid time listening to a CLP graduate discuss family, sexual, drug, social, or other problems. This may lead to a referral or further establish the transition specialist as a trusting confidant and source of support. It may help to solve a job search or job retention problem.

- Assist a Vocational Rehabilitation counselor in the paperwork and procedures necessary to open or close the case of a CLP graduate, facilitate the delivery of a service normally funded by Vocational Rehabilitation, or advocate for the delivery of such services through the presentation of transition specialist–collected documentation to Rehabilitation.

- Conduct a supported job search, where the transition specialist will ''pound the pavement'' with one or two CLP graduates who have good but not great job search skills. The transition specialist provides the extra ''push'' it takes to find and gracefully and efficiently pursue job leads.

- Develop jobs for CLP graduates who lack job search skills but have demonstrated good job retention skills (this is done for less-than-high-functioning youths).

- Facilitate a support group of CLP graduates. This could be a heterogeneous group of newcomers to post–high school life, a mix of newcomers and veterans, or a group who share a particular circumstance, such as parenting, drug involvement, alcoholic parents, or job dissatisfaction.

- Tutor a CLP graduate in courses taken at a community college, such as a course that would go toward a youth earning a credential in early childhood education, and thus being able to climb a career ladder in the child care field.

Appendix 4.4
CLP Job Placement Record

_____

Client _____ CLP Staff _____

Position _____ VR Counselor _____

Employer _____ Supervisor _____

Address _____ Telephone _____

First Day of Work _____ Perm. __ Temp. __ Hours per Week __

Wage _____ Name of Union _____

Benefits _____

Job Duties _____

_____

_____

Remarks _____

_____

_____

30-Day Follow-Up Date:

_____

_____

_____

60-Day Follow-Up Date:

_____

_____

_____

Appendix 4.5
Quick Progress Planning and Assessment Sheet

DATE:				
NAME	F°up	TS	Pri	COMMENTS
1.				
2.				
3.				
4.				
5.				
6.				
7.				
8.				
9.				
10.				
11.				
12.				
13.				
14.				
15.				
16.				
17.				
18.				
19.				
20.				
21.				
22.				
23.				
24.				
25.				

Instructions:
- F°up (follow-up) column—necessary?, yes or no, date to follow up by, ASAP or other instructions.

- TS (transition specialist) column—Initials of TS, or other CLP staff responsible.

- Pri (priority) column—Indicate if person is a priority and/or degree of priority, e.g., (blank) = no pri; (−) = low pri; •, •+ = high. Or use numbers, like 1, 2, 3.

Career
Ladder
Program

Appendix 4.6
Transition Specialist's Composite Week

	Monday	Tuesday	Wednesday	Thursday	Friday
7AM 7:30	Job coach BD at café " "	Job coach BD at café " "	Job coach BD at café " "	Job coach BD at café " "	– OFF – " "
8:00 8:30	" " Staffing with counselor	Job development: SFO " "	Supported job search, CC, GH, CT; interview for CT	Counseling appointments, in office	DR case staffings " "
9:00 9:30	Mock interview, résumé for DS	" " " "	" " " "	" " " "	Phone calls; follow-up " "
10:00 10:30	Supported job search for CC and GH	Job development: Serramonte " "	" " " "	" " " "	Job Fair at Hilton " "
11:00 11:30	" " Check on BD and other grads downtown	" " " "	" " " "	Phone calls, follow-up with grads, employers; paperwork	" " " "
12PM 12:30	Check with City Coll on reg. status, progress	CLP staff meeting	Peer support group at pizza parlor (recent grads)	Parent meeting at CSAA " "	Lunch " "
1:00 1:30	Staffing with TS Check on LL at auto tech program	" " " "	" " " "	" " " "	Check on grads working downtown
2:00 2:30	Help BD close " "	Help BD close " "	Meet with City Coll Enabler re: student referrals	Visit Employment Skills Workshop at Transition Center	" " " "
3:00 3:30	Return phone calls " "	Office intake w/DR cnslr " "	" " Return phone calls	" " " "	Help BD close " "
4:00 4:30	Discuss voc. plan with JB's parents	Return phone calls; paperwork, etc.	" " " "	" " " "	– OFF – (COMP TIME)
5:00 5:30	Reports, letters, misc. paperwork	" " " "	– OFF – " "	– OFF – " "	" " " "
6:00 6:30	Dinner " "	Dinner " "	– OFF – " "	– OFF – " "	" " " "
7:00 8:00	Phone calls, data entry " "	Parent meeting at Transition Center	– OFF – " "	– OFF – " "	" " " "

Career
Ladder
Program

Site Development for Community Classrooms

5

CHAPTER

Gary Meyer and Shepherd Siegel ■

Introduction

The person who initiates the liaison between the school community and the employment community is the job or site developer. This individual could be a program manager, teacher, on-site instructor, or transition specialist. Any number of staff persons can play this role, but in some cases, program staff may decide that they want a position dedicated to the development of new sites. That person becomes the caretaker of the program's relationship to the business community. Certainly, all staff will have critical contacts with the employment community and can benefit from familiarity with the job developer's skills. When a staff can share the job and site developers' duties, they maximize their presence in the community through the active utilization of a broad network—everyone on the staff is pursuing his or her own contacts. Also, such a sharing of the task reduces both compartmentalization of roles and the number of people the business contacts have to know, thus making the program's service more personal. For example, if the site developer and transition specialist are the same person, the employer works only with that person. With a specialized job developer, the site has to be "turned over" to another transition specialist once it has been developed. But given that not all staff can develop all skills, a competent job developer will in many cases free other staff to train and maintain youths in jobs, and that job developer

can represent the best side of the program to the business community.

This chapter is on job-site development, but perhaps it would be better to call it "Sales 101," because the most important lesson to be learned in job development is that it is really a sales job. It is based on the simple fact that the person doing job development is trying to sell a service to an employer. In CLP, that service is a student or young adult with a learning or emotional disability, or mental retardation. The only way to break down the possible apprehension the employer might have is by the job developer showing good sales skills. *This means that job developers sell themselves first, their program second, and the student third.*

This chapter will describe the selling process, applying it to programs like CLP, and will finally put the job developer's role into the context of the CLP mission.

Selling

As in any business that sells a product or service, the best salespeople are those who have the most sincere belief in the quality of the product. In the "business" of increasing career opportunities for marginalized youth, the potential for a high order of belief and commitment is enormous. This work can never be approached as just a job. A deeper understanding of the forces that make certain youths difficult to employ, and a moral position supporting their right to citizenship and the dignity of a meaningful and legitimate career, can fuel the job developer's enthusiasm and create an engaging and convincing momentum that will make employers want to participate in the program and join the team in service to these youths. Take, for example, the job developer who truly believes in the integrity, honor, and righteousness of integrating marginalized youths into the mainstream. Even if the content of that job developer's "pitch" is solely addressed to the profit advantages, the underlying belief will still be communicated nonverbally and will create the winning atmosphere—it will sell the program.

In one form or another, we all have engaged in selling activities. Perhaps we convinced our parents to let us stay out late or borrow the family car. At that point in developing our relationships with our parents we were trying to show our trustworthiness and our responsibility, to meet the needs, desires, and requirements they had of us as their children. If we were successful in selling our talents, we got the family car. The same pertains to job development. If we understand the employers' needs, desires, and requirements, we have a better likelihood of success.

It is important for the job developer to study her or his own background and experience and then evaluate and compare it with the competition. The competition is not just another individual who is trying to do job development; it consists of all the salespeople who call on a given employer. The employer's decisions will be based on his or her perception of the job developers or transition specialists, and their ability to understand the employer's problems. Hence, dress, mannerisms, and business knowledge are important. In many cases, job developers in our programs come from an academic background, which gives them book knowledge, skills in working with youths, and a research perspective. On the other hand, they may lack the experience in business that is required for success. A good job developer should have some sales experience.

Selling Yourself

One of the first things a prospective job developer should consider is appearance. For the most part, people coming from the school community are accustomed to being able to dress in a more comfortable and relaxed manner. Yet the prospective employer is accustomed to seeing salespeople in business attire: suits and ties for men, tailored clothes for women.

If in fact we do not appear to be businesspeople in front of the employer, we start off on the wrong foot.

Many times a decision will be made in the first few seconds by the employer as to which you represent, a problem or a solution. There is an old adage that says that you can never have a second chance to make a good first impression. Hence, you should eliminate the things that can be perceived negatively. This is similar to your desire in high school to blend in, rather than being different. In this case, you again don't want to be different, so dress becomes important. For men who are job developers, the requirement is a suit, tie, and dress shirt, or perhaps a sport jacket with slacks, but always with a tie and shirt. Even if you are making a blue-collar sales call, you will find that salesmen calling on that organization generally are in a suit and tie, and saleswomen in appropriate business dress. If you are calling on a corporation that prefers that their women employees do not wear pants or jeans, certainly you would not do that. You should be dressed in a manner that reflects the policies that each corporation requires for its employees. Also, your first contacts are frequently gatekeepers. If they are Human Resources staff, and they take an interest in your program, they will be surmising what kind of impression you will make on the people *they* hope to impress within their company. You must show them that you can make a good impression for *them* in any setting.

The second most important thing that we must realize is that the corporate world is based on profit and loss. A prospective employer is often represented by the head of a corporation's personnel department. That manager's day is spent interviewing people whose sole purpose in life is to impress upon him or her how good they are. This person may be in Personnel or may be a buyer, or a salesperson, or the manager of the company, who spends the day barraged by professional salespeople who are experienced in presenting their product and their company at the highest possible level. A job developer who is hurled from the environment of the educational world into this highly competitive, highly stressful business world is going to be judged by the prospective employer, not totally on his or her program or on the credibility or worthiness of the possible employee, but overwhelmingly on the prospective employer's opinion of the person representing the program. So appearance, sales presentation, follow-up, and the thoroughness of this presentation are key.

Unfortunately, for the most part job developers do not have the experience necessary to successfully present their product, which in this case is the young student or young adult. The only possible way for job developers to be successful in presenting their product is to have sales and marketing skills. These skills begin with physical appearance and include a knowledge of their product and of the customer's needs. Salespeople also must take into account the customer's requirements, which may differ from their needs, and must present solutions to the employer in a manner that will make the employer want to do business with the organization, to employ students, to see it as a way to solve her or his own problems, and to bring profitability and credibility to her or his company.

Although major corporations have made limited attempts to help society, there is one basic rule: If you don't make money, you don't last. From the top chief executive officer of a corporation down to the smallest department head, administrators are ultimately judged by their ability to make money. When we are discussing job opportunities for students, we are at a decided disadvantage unless we can present profit benefits as the bottom-line reason for employing our people. On the other hand, if we can show middle managers (who in today's business climate are getting squeezed for more work with less people) that we can supply them with long-term working people with positive attitudes, we can ultimately increase their profits and be a solution for them rather than a problem.

One of the most common mistakes made by new salespeople is the desire to hit the home run, or make the long touchdown pass. In other words, they want to find an employer in the community who will hire all the students on a regular basis so that more time can be spent assisting them in other areas. This is like the case of the new salesperson who hopes to make a giant sale at the major corporation, fulfill the quota, and take Fridays off for the rest of the year. The simple fact is that it just doesn't happen. Successful salespeople build successful careers by building a solid foundation and rising from that foundation to the level of success that they need to fulfill their goals and desires. Hence, job developers who hope to find the perfect corporation will be very disappointed, and the students that they are responsible for will not have the opportunities they would have had if the job developers had made a more realistically planned marketing effort.

A successful marketing plan consists of many elements: some cold-calling, some new calls, and some return visits to present customers. The terminology used here is that of a business atmosphere, rather than the nomenclature used by counselors and teachers. In the business world, you have to operate like a business. One of the big advantages of cold-calling, for instance, is that when you present your ideas and thoughts and personnel to a prospective employer with whom you have had no previous contact, you have the opportunity to practice your presentation,

to know the points that you feel are most important, and to practice getting these points into the conversation. The most successful salespeople answer most of the customer's concerns and questions before those questions are actually asked. When you are able to do this, you come across as a knowledgeable, well-prepared salesperson. The only way to learn those questions is by constantly making cold calls and developing your sales presentation. In the cold-call situation, you have less to lose by making a mistake than when you are making an important sales call on a partially developed prospect, where there is much more at stake. The advantage of making calls on your existing employers, on the other hand, is that it gives you the opportunity to make sure that you are maintaining a high level of expertise and a high level of service, so that the employer will continue to want to work with you. It also gives you the opportunity to develop more jobs within the organization, and more importantly, it gives you the opportunity to find out if your contact, who meets regularly with peers and the competitors, might be able to suggest other places where you can place people.

As stated before, a salesperson may want a big order, whereas all the customer will give him is a small order that doesn't amount to much. We may want an employer to hire 10 to 12 of our students, but all he or she will consider is the possibility of one. The key is to place one of your best students, the one who is sure to be a success, into that position. Many times salespersons or job developers will prefer to say that this is not very important and that just anybody can be put in there. You now have your foot in the door. It is very important to be successful with the first placement. A satisfied customer is the easiest customer to sell to a second time. A satisfied employer is the easiest one to convince to hire additional personnel from your organization. If you develop enough "singles" and "doubles" in the early stages of your work, you are more likely to eventually score that "home run."

If you can develop a personal relationship, an authentic friendship, a manager may decide to work with your program simply because he or she likes working with you. The program must still be as excellent as you claim it to be, but the relationship may be the factor that leads the employer to the initial choice to work with you. As we tell our CLP interns, the decision to hire them (or work with them) is the decision to like them. The function of the transition specialist at one of our sites was to have coffee with the manager and listen to her complain about all her other employees, but not the CLP graduate. In this case, when a counseling role was assumed with the manager, the placement of the CLP youth was rarely the topic. Nonetheless, that youth's position with the company was protected by this additional service provided by the transition specialist. See chapter 4 for more on this topic.

Selling the Program

You have two ways of presenting yourself to an employer at the first meeting. One is as a person from the school who is trying to do something in the community and who is looking for work for the school's students, and the other is as a person who has a solution to a problem the employer has, which will benefit the corporation and increase its profit margin, while at the same time providing a community service the corporation can be proud of.

One of the most important things you can do to ensure your success is to develop a written proposal that can be presented to a prospective employer and that thoroughly explains the program you are offering. This proposal should include a history of your program, some success stories, how the program works, and the program's basic foundation. If the program has any tax advantages related to it, explain how those might work, as well as any other item you feel it is important to express to the employer. There is a twofold reason for writing all this into a formal proposal that you give to the prospective employer. First, your contact will have something to take forward to her or his supervisor for final approval, in a way that expresses your most important points to that ultimate decision maker. Second, by having a proposal that you give to the employer during the interview process, you will have a copy in front of you that ensures that you will present the most important points in the discussion. This also allows you to have consistency among all the job developers who work within the same organization; the story being told is consistent and thorough throughout the community.

Appendixes 5.1, 5.2, and 5.3 consist of a brochure, a letter of introduction, and the business proposal used by CLP to develop both community classroom sites and job placements. Here are some additional guidelines on how to sell a work experience/job placement program (with thanks to George Nocetti).

1. *Scan the market.* Do research on a few major businesses in the area. How many employees work there? What kinds of skills are they looking for? Is there a union involved? What is the product and its future in the marketplace? The Chamber of Commerce bulletin lists all the businesses, the number of employees in each, and the types of jobs they offer. Equally viable are service clubs such as Lions, Kiwanis, and Rotary. They are often more interested in giving money than service, but get names and follow up. These are the civically service-oriented places. If you are invited to speak at one of their meetings, remember that they want to be entertained. You can do that and then challenge them at the end to make some kind of contribution to the effort.

2. *Pick your times wisely.* Never contact employers on Monday morning, the day after a holiday, or right before the weekend. Avoid rush hours in eating establishments.

3. *Consider using the "walk-in" approach.* Sometimes an unannounced visit can catch the right person at the right time. "Can I see Mr. Jones for 5 minutes, please? I represent the _____ School District. Mr. Jones, my name is Louise Mann. I was just in the neighborhood following up on one of the youths in our program, and I saw your sign . . ."

4. *Don't hide limitations, but point to successes if you can.*

5. *Have a business card with your name, school district, and phone number.*

6. *Respect the receptionist.* Receptionists are often powerful people in organizations, and their favor can help you to develop contacts. If they do not feel respected, they will invariably harm the relationship.

7. *Just ask for 5 or 10 minutes.* If that is what you are granted, don't take more uninvited. You can, at the end of your time, try to get employers to talk about what their business does, and listen attentively when they do.

8. *Have a flyer or brochure that explains the objectives of the program.* If the flyer is successful in gaining some interest, a proposal such as the one in Appendix 5.3 should be prepared to follow it up and demonstrate that the program is a serious and accountable organization.

9. *Send out a follow-up letter after every visit.* This task can be made simple by using a word processor that can customize a form. Send the letter out whether or not you are initially successful. It will have a role in most of your eventual successes. Without it, initial rejections will never turn around.

10. *Continuously develop more leads.* Ask yourself which employers can benefit from the program. Some employers who cannot immediately work with you may have associates in other companies who can.

11. *Be upbeat and positive.* Emphasize the strong points of the students and the supportive services your program offers, which are like a warranty (see chapter 4). Be able to describe all the advantages, and be knowledgeable about the program's benefits (e.g., no increase in workers' compensation, minimum

wage exemptions during training, tax credits, on-the-job training contracts with the local Private Industry Council). Stress in the interview that your people will adhere to all the corporate rules and regulations that are in effect for employees within that organization. So if 100% of the males wear suits, white shirts, and ties, your students would be required to do the same. Present to your contacts, whose primary responsibility is to ensure the profitability of the corporation, the idea that your students will be a solution to their problem, contribute to their success, make them successful within the corporation, and make their department more profitable for the corporation.

12. *Ask for a tour of the business.* It is wiser and will earn you more respect if you take the tour after you have explained the program and before you make any requests.

13. *Negotiate an initial low wage with raises rather than starting at a high wage.* Without losing any self-respect, these youths need, like anyone else, to first get their foot in the door.

14. *Negotiate a scale of commitment.* If in fact employers are receiving incentives like tax breaks or subsidies to hire an at-risk youth, they must be willing to make some accommodations or take some extra training time. The agreement is a two-way street, and at this point, the job developer should not avoid articulating and negotiating what the employer must provide to help make the placement a success.

15. *Try large companies with affirmative action policies.* You may be able to find a go-getter in the company who is eager to have an exemplary program. Perhaps you have a friend who will act as a contact and introduce you, or you may know of a parent on a board or citizen's advisory council. Companies with more than 25 employees are generally an easier setting for obtaining placements. Though smaller businesses should not be disregarded, as the small business entrepreneur is a very special person, these companies usually require more skills per person, and many of your candidates may lack the necessary versatility. Unionized companies can require more time for developing a placement because union representatives must be involved in the process of bringing on youths from special populations, especially in a work experience program. In the case of both the union and management, go to the leadership for support.

16. *Try to work with the unions.* This is a long-range goal. It is difficult, slow work, but it can ultimately be rewarding.

17. *Develop a network.* A successful job developer will spend a lot of time at meetings, conferences, social gatherings, fraternal organizations, business clubs, and organizations. Because you have an opportunity to meet people socially, over lunch or dinner, or perhaps at a social function, you have the opportunity to become a friend. As one telephone company says, the most important business calls are personal. If you can develop personal relationships with individuals, more doors will open for you, making sales calls on prospective employers easier. Attend as many meetings and workshops as you can. Get involved in civic functions; they increase your opportunities to meet people. These are places to make contacts and to develop critical skills. Your sources are going to consist of cold-calling, leads from present employers, social parties, business meetings, and your personal friends. Useful departments to call on are Sales, Public Relations, and Advertising. Realize that it is all right for students to start part-time. And don't forget the possibility that their parents might be able to open doors at their place of employment to get other students hired. They may be reluctant to get their own child hired, but they may not mind getting another youth hired. A parents' committee might in fact help with job development.

18. *Work with the food industry.* Like it or not, this is the first proving ground for many new workers and a major force in the service-oriented economic direction of the United States. Fast-food establishments provide a work experience that is valuable to many youths.

19. *Develop relationships with employment agencies.* This is an unexplored potential resource. Of course, your state's Employment Development Department and the Department of Vocational Rehabilitation may already play an active role in your program. Implementation of collaborative arrangements with these agencies takes work. The work experience coordinators at your schools are good information resources who generally know the job market, and they can certify what's already going on.

20. *Develop relationships with other adult service agencies.* Often, a student or graduate can stay in your program and at the same time be a participant in another one, which might offer further subsidies of wages or other means of support. You must be alert to situations where employers exploit youths by terminating them when the benefit or subsidy expires. For more information on collaborative resources, see chapter 4.

Selling the Applicant

Many of our candidates are hired for entry-level positions. The problems most employers encounter at the entry level is that many of the workers have not been trained in job survival skills, and many do not have the patience to stay with the job very long. The result is that employers are forced to fire some people because of lack of effort. The ones the manager likes often end up quitting because they become dissatisfied with the position very quickly. The job developer should try to emphasize the job survival training that the students have completed—the community classroom experience. Of course, the proposal also should contain descriptions of some of these job survival skills so that the employer will understand that in some cases our students might require additional training. Many of them have received training in the classroom preparing for the job that other entry-level employees do not have. Hence, there is a higher likelihood of our students staying on the job for a longer period of time, which extends the period in which the employer receives benefits from employing the entry-level person. It also reduces the company's training costs and turnover.

How are our candidates solutions to employers? It is very important to repeatedly emphasize why it is profitable to employ students with learning, intellectual, sensory, emotional, and physical disabilities. We cannot rely on the corporations' responsibility to the community. We must rely instead on the economic benefits of employing our students. In any presentation it is important to try to emphasize to the prospective employer that the youth who we will be supplying is not a handicap to the operation of the business, but a solution. This person has been trained to survive in the workplace, is eager to please, and will be a benefit to the employer. He or she is the best candidate for the job.

Many large corporations are of the opinion that people coming from a program such as ours are not prepared to go directly into full-time employment. But these corporations can be convinced of the need to give students on-the-job experience and are often willing to set up community classrooms within their facilities to give students the opportunity to learn job survival skills, how to dress, and how to behave in a business environment. Ultimately they will select people from this classroom to whom they will give an employment opportunity.

Maintaining the Relationship

You will not be able to hit home runs. There is no shortcut; there is just hard work. The goal is just to get a few positive hits each week.

You can develop long-term relationships with employers as a by-product of long-term relationships with youths. When a youth is placed in a position

you have developed with an employer, the work has just begun. If you are a job developer who is now handing the care of a youth over to a transition specialist, it will be up to the transition specialist to help make that placement the greatest possible success. Even in this "pass-off" situation, there are two activities that will make your good work—developing the job placement—into quality work.

First, meet with the transition specialist who will be placing and supporting the new employee, or who perhaps is sending a few candidates to be interviewed. Share all the information about the job and the job environment. The single most important factor in making any job work is the job match, and you want to make sure that the most appropriate candidates are referred. At this point, it is best to avoid having another meeting and introducing another new face to the employer, but if you have doubts about the match or the job, you should go out to the site again, perhaps with the transition specialist, and get detailed information about the job and working conditions. An employer who sees the care with which you are approaching the placement will doubtless appreciate the service you are providing.

The second important thing is to have at least two follow-up contacts with the employer. You are calling to make sure that the youth is working out and that the support services are adequate and excellent. If the rest of your team is now doing a good job and the match was good, there is no reason why you won't start getting calls from the employer asking you to send more more candidates. This is where home runs come from: the follow-up support that makes a job developed through your organization a truly satisfying experience.

If you are the transition specialist, your role in enhancing job retention for the new employee is even more involved (see chapter 4), and your follow-up with the employer should be systematic and extensive. If there is no additional support for the new employee, the job developer's role becomes either part of a burnout cycle or part of a training program so excellent that its graduates do not need additional support. However, such candidates usually don't need job developer services, so this is not a likelihood under current arrangements.

Long-term, dependable relationships are what people, regardless of their role in life, value most. If what began as a sales call brings about long-term and dependable (and profitable) relationships with new employees, with the program's staff, and with you, the job developer, then we have begun to move beyond the dollar value of the service provided, and into the realm where community is built. The employer sees the need to employ and work with the youths you represent and reaps the human as well as monetary value that comes from bringing individuals into the economic mainstream who might otherwise live on the margins. The work you have done is not an intellectual exercise, but the creation of felt and experienced human relationships that nourish all of us.

The Big Picture

Though this chapter has taken a strong position about accommodating the business perspective, the altruistic element is not lost and has an important value and place in this work. When you are out developing new jobs, you will find that employers can be approached on the level of profitability and convenience, but that the altruistic approach has its place as well. Sometimes convenience is what employers are looking for, because as part of a larger company, they have been instructed to implement a policy of hiring people from disadvantaged groups, either as part of an affirmative action requirement or because the management has assessed the profitability of tax credits. So the employer is already convinced or directed and, in these cases, will be looking for the job service that is the most convenient and will supply the best candidates.

But what about the moral appeal? In fact, the business world is full of people who are able to run profitable businesses and retain a sense of conscience and social responsibility. Look at the type of products or the type of image the company is developing, and see if it might be consistent with the idea of hiring marginalized youth.

Large companies that aren't particularly oriented toward social responsibility often have a sizable number of workers who are alienated from their jobs. These are people who may be trapped; they make too good a wage, and have too many debts to service, to maintain a pleasurable life-style without working. Thus they feel imprisoned in a job they do not really like. They may not be the manager or personnel specialist, but they will be among the co-workers who are going to work alongside your candidates. Many of these people are looking for a way to make their job more meaningful, and they will be grateful for a chance to keep their well-paying but otherwise mundane and socially irrelevant job, and still make a contribution to improving social welfare. They get to contribute to the improvement of soci-

ety, their own job becomes more interesting because they are working directly with students with special needs, and there is little of the risk that would be involved if they quit their job in search of a more socially relevant one. You are offering that opportunity and, for many workers, you have the most valuable product on the market: meaningfulness. Never sell it short.

Some employers can be appealed to on the basis of ultimate social cost. A youth who is given an opportunity now to be integrated into the workforce is much less likely to become an expense to society later: to be disabled or poor and need welfare support or institutionalization, to become a drug abuser and need treatment or institutionalization, or to get into crime and steal goods, driving up the cost of commodities, law enforcement, and institutionalization.

The alternative is to turn this person into a taxpayer and a contributor to society, rather than an expense. This is a strong argument that combines rather effectively altruistic and economic considerations.

Finally, everyone is part of a family. Among virtually all extended families are people with disabilities. A little time with an employer will probably reveal that he or she knows or is related to someone who fits this category, and perhaps even someone who needed a special opportunity at one time.

Coping with a disability, poverty, or low skills is a serious disadvantage. To overcome it requires a struggle. No one really engages in this struggle alone or succeeds without the help of someone else. Employers may be willing to share stories of how they struggled to succeed, and with skill and insight, you can show a relationship between their personal stories and the lives of the youths you are serving.

Finally, the underlying message that is being carried in every interaction with the employment world is that we are one community. Profits cannot be made without a healthy community that buys the goods and services offered. There is really no point to making a profit if it is not part of a community life. Business as well as government and education is there to serve people, and the greater participation of marginalized youth in the world of business and employment can and must appeal to the sense of fairness that lives in us all. Giving an employer the opportunity to actively participate in this movement by hiring a youth who is at risk is truly the greatest investment an individual can make.

Appendix 5.1
Brochure

Are Your Entry-Level Employees . . . . heading for the exit?

Turnover can really be a problem.

Are Your Brand-New Employees . . . . presenting the same old problems?

Absenteeism, poor social skills, and irresponsible behavior
reduce efficiency and make life in the workplace less pleasant.

**Are You Getting the Maximum Return on Your
Investment in the Labor Force?**

Failure to take advantage of incentives
and support services can cost you money.

The Career Ladder Program is a concerted effort of the California Department of Rehabilitation, the San Francisco Unified School District, and San Francisco State University to integrate special needs youths into the work world. Services of the Career Ladder Program are provided to you **at no cost.** Our success is based on our ability to meet your needs as an employer of entry-level workers. Our commitment to quality has produced high employer satisfaction with our services, and savings of thousands of dollars. Call us today at 555-7851 for more information.

''This is a great program. They supervise their interns, and I've hired several of their graduates.''
—Carolyn George, Marriott Corporation

''There should be more programs like this.''
—Robert Tucker, State Workers' Compensation Insurance Fund

''We've saved over $5,000 by hiring CLP interns.''
—Lyle Engeldinger, California State Auto Association

Career
Ladder
Program

Appendix 5.2
Letter of Introduction

Dear Employer:

Many Bay Area employers have told us that their business has two important employment aims. First, they want to find the competent, reliable employees and match them to the right job within their organization with a minimum of "trial and error" and employee turnover. Second, they want to make economically sound personnel decisions to fill entry-level positions and, at the same time, support the development of the community in which their business operates. I am writing to you to tell you about a youth employment program that will help your business achieve these goals.

The Career Ladder Program (CLP) is an innovative collaboration between major community agencies and employers in San Francisco. It offers you, the employer, a number of benefits:

- Screening of Applicants. CLP screens applicants for potential jobs and refers only qualified individuals, avoiding undue inconvenience for the employer and unnecessarily setting up the potential employee for failure.

- Preemployment Training. CLP interns receive extensive on-the-job training in a professional work environment to develop marketable job skills in their particular areas of interest.

- Job Retention and Social Skills. In concert with their on-the-job training, interns attend weekly seminars to further develop a general repertoire of desirable work habits, as well as learning techniques to enable them to interact more cooperatively and effectively with their co-workers.

- Tax Credits/Employer Incentives. CLP can facilitate certification for tax credits under the Targeted Jobs Tax Credit (TJTC) program and other incentive programs to eligible employers.

- Ongoing Commitment. CLP makes an ongoing commitment to its clients and employers, and at no cost to them provides further on-site training, follow-up, job coaching, accommodations, mediations, and other services as the employer feels it is necessary.

The motivation of CLP is to create an opportunity that is cost-effective and beneficial to both the employer and the community at large, and one that establishes an actual two-sided commitment—a "win-win" situation for everyone involved.

I have enclosed some information describing the program in more detail. I will be calling you in a few days to set up an appointment to discuss this program, which we believe could be very beneficial to your organization. Thank you so much for your time and consideration.

Sincerely,

Mark Roberts
Transition Specialist
Career Ladder Program

Appendix 5.3
Business Proposal

To complete a business proposal, include just a few samples of materials that explain how your staff operates and delivers quality service. Phase I: Use samples of community classroom instructional materials (intern recording sheets, vocational performance records). Phase II: Use samples of postsecondary service materials (summary of transition services, Appendix 4.1; record-keeping materials).

A Proposal

made by

The Career Ladder Program

to

The ABC Corporation

for

Phase _____ Career Ladder Program Services

_____, representing CLP

_____, representing ABC

January 1, 1993

The Career Ladder Program (CLP) is a federal model demonstration program. Our purpose is to enable the successful transition from school to work or college for youths in San Francisco with special needs. It is a collaboration, begun in 1985, between the Department of Rehabilitation, the San Francisco Unified School District, San Francisco State University, and several local employers. Our success rate of approximately 90% has meant low turnover, intelligent matching of candidates to job descriptions, and an excellent return on investment to participating employers.

The core of the program is a semester-long on-the-job training program. We provide a half-day work experience for interns at a real work setting that is accommodated by the presence of an instructor from the program's staff. We call it a community classroom. Four days a week the CLP interns ''go to work'' for three hours at one of our sponsoring sites (CSAA Insurance; Marriott Food Service, Inc.; Photo and Sound Company; and the University of California Medical Center). In the beginning of the semester, they receive intensive supervision from the on-site instructors. As they demonstrate competence and independence, the instruction is gradually faded until the end of the semester, when our presence is no longer necessary on the job.

Interns are assessed in vocational and social skills and must meet objectives if they are to successfully complete the program. One day a week, they attend an Employment Skills Workshop, where they learn entry-level job skills, job-keeping skills, social skills, peer counseling techniques, and job search skills.

If an intern successfully completes the program, we make an ongoing commitment to the career development of that individual. A transition specialist follows each of the over 100 interns who have graduated CLP, providing services that range from on-the-job training and supported job searches to counseling in social skills and assistance in college enrollment. We believe in career development—a career ladder—for every CLP graduate. A participating company gains not only the production of the new employee or intern, but the services of an entire team of professionals dedicated to the success of our youths and the satisfaction of the employer.

Career
Ladder
Program

Phase I. The Community Classroom

Who are the Career Ladder Program (CLP) interns?

CLP interns are high school seniors chosen from the special education programs of the San Francisco Unified School District (SFUSD). They have motivation to work, family support, and good attendance records. Though interns have some disability, they are each "matched" to a job site where their deficit will not impede their ability to become competent workers.

What services are provided?

The SFUSD employs an instructor who is on the job site with the interns. The instructor comes to the site several days before the interns to learn the job tasks. The instructor then provides the necessary training to the interns and enables the regular supervisors to eventually take over. The educational supervision is "faded out"—our aim is to make the interns employable and competitive with the labor force at large. San Francisco State University's Vocational Special Education Program makes their staff and services available. A program coordinator provides ongoing supervision and monitoring of CLP. Transition specialists, who work out of the California Department of Rehabilitation, provide liaison to postsecondary activities such as work, college, and training.

What does CLP want from the employer?

Most importantly, we want work. Our interns need a place where they can develop and perfect the skills that will make them good employees. We have found four afternoons a week of three hours each to be effective, but other arrangements can be made. We would like to send at least two candidates for each intern position in your company, and have you make the final selection of interns based on a job interview. There should always be enough work for them to do. As they reach competency in the job tasks and work behaviors, supervision should come from the regular job-site supervisors, enabling the interns to work more independently and freeing the instructor to work with those interns in need of more training.

How much extra supervision will these interns require?

Each intern is individually assessed, and their direct supervision, provided by the on-site instructor, is adjusted according to their needs. As the interns demonstrate competence, that supervision is faded out incrementally, engineering a successful experience that acclimates the youth to the work environment and demands. Some interns require almost no extra supervision from the very first day. Others are watched and guided more gradually toward independent performance. Eventually, all work with about the same level of employer supervision that is provided to any entry-level employee with your organization.

What about liability?

The interns receive school credit and a state-supported stipend for their time on the job. They are employees of the school district and are enrolled as full-time students. They are insured against injury or liability by the SFUSD, at no cost to you.

Phase II. Postsecondary Services

What happens to the interns after their internship ends?

Interns are all about to graduate high school, and in the CLP, we seek to have them employed full-time as soon as possible. The interns attend a weekly Employment Skills Workshop where they learn job-keeping, job search, and job interview skills. Their search begins in earnest during the last half of the semester. While we hope that all our interns will have become highly desirable employees by this time, we only request that they be seriously considered by the CLP sponsors for permanent positions. CLP makes an ongoing commitment to the careers of its interns and will provide services not only to help them get their first job, but also to sustain employment.

Who are the CLP graduates?

CLP graduates have exited the San Francisco public schools and met all of the stringent training requirements of a CLP internship (see Phase I). They are trained in generic job-keeping skills and are motivated and prepared to enter the job market. Some CLP graduates have special needs: perhaps they do not read well or have a specific learning style. The CLP staff addresses these needs either by matching the graduate to a job where this difference is not relevant, by providing additional support and accommodation, or by assisting in the provision of an accommodation at the workplace.

What are the advantages of hiring CLP graduates?

The advantages are many. As shown on the Return on Investment chart for Phase II, tax credits, training costs, and accommodations can be arranged and financed. When you work directly with our transition specialists, we screen our graduates to make sure that we send you candidates who are qualified and motivated to work in the field. Our graduates all have work experience. They are acclimated to the demands of the workplace. They are eager to develop their careers and grow with a company. Finally, they are not "dropped off at your door" and forgotten. They and you will have the ongoing support of our transition specialists to ensure that the job placement is satisfactory and successful. The appendix "Summary of Transition Services" [Appendix 4.1 of this book] outlines the types of services we provide.

How do I know that this program works?

As part of the federally mandated effort to enlarge transition opportunities for special needs youths, the CLP engages in rigorous studies, evaluations, and revisions of its services. Employers, parents, and the graduates themselves provide us with the feedback we use to upgrade our services. Furthermore, part of our evaluation is to follow up on the outcomes of our graduates. The last count, made in December 1990, showed that over 92% of CLP graduates were working, were in postsecondary school, or took part in a combination of the two. Their job retention rate is excellent. Endorsements from the people we serve, media coverage, and the continued support of the main social service agencies in the area testify to the profitability and positive contribution of the CLP. When you meet with any of our staff, we will be happy to refer you to participating employers who can describe to you themselves the experience of working with us.

Phase I. Return on Investment

	Sponsor	CLP
Costs	No initial costs	On-site instructor Transition specialist Vocational instruction Minimum wage stipend
Commitments	Three hours work/day for each intern Willingness to assume supervision over an 18-week period	Initial supervision Instruction Career counseling Demand of excellence
Returns	Production Positive public service Positive public relations	Employability Integrated workforce Continuation of services

Phase II. Return on Investment

	Employer	CLP
Costs	Entry-level wage and benefits	Transition specialist Rehabilitation case services
Commitments	Whatever is offered to other entry-level employees	Ongoing support for the career development of CLP graduate
Returns	Low Turnover Already trained—cuts costs Motivated Acclimated to workplace Meets affirmative action guidelines Tax credit: 40% of wage for the first year through targeted jobs tax credit (TJTC)* Subsidy: 50% of wage for a negotiated training period through Private Industry Council/On-the-Job Training (PIC/OJT)*	Employability Integrated workforce Continuation of services

*TJTC and PIC/OJT can be arranged in sequence, but not concurrently.

Career
  Ladder
    Program

To pursue the development of your affiliation with
the Career Ladder Program, contact:

Phase I: Mary Jones   555-4999

Phase II: Mark Roberts   555-3330

Career Ladder Program: 555-7858
John Smith, Coordinator
Gerry Marks, Site Developer
Ron Golder, Project Director

A Historical Perspective of Transition: Blueprints for Systems Change

CHAPTER

Robert Gaylord-Ross, William Halloran, and Shepherd Siegel ■

Transition: The Federal Initiative

In special education, the 1970s were characterized by concerns with equal access for all students with disabilities, appropriate education conducted in the least restrictive environment, individualized educational planning, and due process assurances under the law for students and their families. Ten years later, the special education community took stock of its accomplishments since the passage of Public Law 94-142 and could point to progress in these areas and mark the achievements.

But follow-up studies conducted in the early 1980s revealed that despite this emphasis on equality, integration, and independence (seen in P.L. 94-142 and other legislation), large numbers of special education students leaving public education were entering segregated, dependent, nonproductive lives. Two-thirds of adults with disabilities were not employed, and others were served in segregated programs or no program at all. Consumers became concerned that school experiences, despite their exemplary quality, would lead to an ''aging out'' into meager adult services. These findings, along with concern on the part of parents, professionals, and policy makers, gave rise to the issues of the remainder of the 1980s: early intervention, transition from school to work, maximum participation in regular education, family networking, and follow-up/follow-along responsibilities.

These issues expanded the role and responsibility of public education to younger and older age groups. They also emphasized the importance of developing relationships between the school and elements of the community, such as families, employers, adult service agencies, and social services. Although in the seventies accountability through increased documentation and legal resources was stressed, emphasis in the eighties shifted toward assisting real-life outcomes associated with special education. Educational agencies began to identify adult adjustment goals for their students in the areas of postsecondary education, employment, and independent living; to plan educational programs and work experiences to achieve those goals; and to follow up graduates and those who left school in an effort to gauge the effectiveness of school programming.

Transition was first introduced in federal legislation in the 1984 Amendments to the Education of the Handicapped Act, P.L. 98-199. The amendments drew specific attention to the need to improve the scope and quality of transition services. The U.S. Department of Education's Office of Special Education and Rehabilitative Services defined the critical components of transition planning and put new demonstration programs into place throughout the country. These components of transition include:

1. Effective high school programs that prepare students to work and live in the community

2. A broad range of adult service programs that can meet the various support needs of individuals with disabilities in employment and community settings

3. Comprehensive and cooperative transition planning between education and community service agencies for the purpose of developing needed services for completers, those who leave school, and graduates

The CLP adapted these critical components in its conceptualization and development. The uniqueness of CLP is demonstrated in its overriding principle, which states that its services are shaped by the needs of the youths being served.

The research and demonstration efforts supported by the federal discretionary program stimulated the development of other new and unique approaches throughout the country. These programs demonstrated that public education can assist youths with a variety of disabilities and levels of impairments in making the adjustment to adult life in their communities. They set in place interagency cooperation between school and adult programs. They also provided instructional support systems to ensure that an individual with disabilities could succeed in real work settings.

Studies of program effectiveness have shown that three essential components are necessary for all levels of disability. First is the need for families of youths with disabilities to be included as partners in the development and implementation of purposeful activities that maximize independence. CLP's design and the findings of its follow-up studies support the efficacy of this feature. The family is a major facilitator of transition. Second, transition programs like CLP must be community-based, and opportunities to experience and succeed in employment and other aspects of community life must be provided. The third component, one also found in CLP, is the need for working partnerships with employers to ensure that the efforts of the schools are consistent with employers' needs. Programs that prepare youths with disabilities for employment should include measurement of employers' and employees' satisfaction. Additional strengths lie in effective and systematic coordination of agencies, organizations, and individuals from a broad array of disciplines and professional fields.

Successful demonstration efforts led to the development of policies and practices in state and local educational agencies to ensure that transition services would be made available to all youths with disabilities. CLP's adoption by the San Francisco Unified School District and by the corresponding district of the California State Department of Rehabilitation began implementation of more universal availability. These initiatives, demonstrations, and adoptions were a major factor in convincing Congress that federal law should guarantee that all students have transition services included in their educational programs. Transition services and plans for youths with disabilities are now mandated under the recently enacted Education of the Handicapped Act Amendments of 1990 (P.L. 101-476). This law was formerly known as the Education of the Handicapped Act. With the passage of P.L. 101-476, the name was changed to the Individuals with Disabilities Education Act (IDEA). This law requires that plans for transition be included in a student's Individualized Education Plan by age 16. Section 602(a) of IDEA defines transition services as:

> A coordinated set of activities for a student, designed within an outcome-oriented process, which promotes movement from school to post-school activities, including post-secondary education, vocational training, integrated employment (including supported employment), continuing and adult education, adult services, independent living, or community participation. The coordinated set of activities shall be based upon the individual student's needs, taking into account the student's preferences and interests, and shall include instruction, community experiences, the development of employment and other post-school adult living objectives, and when appropriate, acquisition of daily living skills and functional vocational evaluation. (Education of the Handicapped Act Amendments of 1990, P.L. 101-476, Section 602(a) [20 U.S.C. 1401 (a)])

Clearly, transition planning will soon become an essential component of the educational process. Recent studies and reports provide many reasons for this increased attention. For example, according to the U.S. Department of Education's Office of Special Education and Rehabilitative Services (U.S. Department of Education, 1990b), over 200,000 special education students exit our nation's schools each year. Upon leaving school, many students with disabilities and their parents have difficulty gaining access to appropriate adult services and/or postsecondary education and training programs. The *Twelfth Annual Report to Congress on the Implementation of the Education of the Handicapped Act* (U.S. Department of Education, 1990b) indicated that 47% of all students with disabilities do not graduate from high school with either a diploma or a certificate of completion. This figure is corroborated by data from the National Longitudinal Transition Study (Wagner & Shaver, 1989). This study indicated that 44% of students with disabilities failed to graduate from high school and 36% of students with disabilities dropped out of school.

Employment data for people with disabilities are similarly discouraging. While the national unemployment rate is about 5%, almost two-thirds of all Americans with disabilities between the ages of 16 and 24 are not working (Harris & Associates, 1986). These studies suggest that many factors contribute to this situation, including attitudinal, physical, and communication barriers; lack of appropriate training opportunities; and scarcity of effective transition planning and service programs.

The transition initiative developed in tandem with the notion of supported employment (Rusch, 1986; Wehman, 1981). Supported employment provides temporary or ongoing instruction at the work site to supervise, instruct, and facilitate the social and work integration of the employee with disabilities. Supported employment programs, particularly for persons with severe disabilities, have grown exponentially and proven empirically successful (Wehman, Moon, Everson, Wood, & Barcus, 1988). But there has been much less work with the ongoing vocational support of adults with learning or other mild disabilities. Most such transition programs, when they do exist, merely place the young adult in a job, and at best provide time-limited training and support. These less intensive vocational models did not generally lead to long-term substantive employment of individuals with mild disabilities. For example, a review of follow-up research (Siegel et al., 1990) indicated that anywhere from 10% to 60% of adults with learning and other *mild* disabilities remain unemployed in adulthood. There was clearly a need for more potent vocational packages to reverse these dismal statistics.

Concurrent with the federal initiative, our society has begun to change its attitudes toward people with disabilities, recognizing both the possibility and importance of their successful employment. As attitudes change and opportunities for employment broaden, schools will play an increasingly significant role in preparing our nation's youths with disabilities for adult life. Transition services will play— and should play—an integral part in helping them to address this critical period in their lives.

In addition to changes in attitudes, there are more reasons for optimism concerning the provision of transition services:

- Special educators are starting to accept responsibility for preparing youths with disabilities to live and work in the community.

- Technological advances in teaching employment skills are enabling a much broader population of youths with disabilities to enter the job market and obtain competitive employment.

- Demographic changes and population shifts are causing employers to consider youths with disabilities as a partial solution to the dwindling working-age population.

But do these changes in the educational field correspond with the current needs and trends in the workplace?

The Readiness of the Workforce

The United States has entered an economic crisis. Large trade imbalances and governmental debts have placed its economic future in jeopardy. As the country has gone into increasing debt, Americans have sold many properties and businesses to foreign investors. A number of industries, particularly the automotive, electronics, and computer industries, have become dominated by foreign competitors. Jobs have gone "offshore" to foreign countries. Certainly, a main attraction of foreign manufacturing is the cheap cost of labor, but sometimes a more important factor has been the superior quality of workmanship in foreign lands. Employers have said that they cannot find enough well-trained employees in this country. In this context, our socioeconomic occupational structure is becoming bifurcated into highly professionalized, well-paying jobs (e.g., engineers) and low-paying, limited-skill work (e.g., fast-food positions). Better-paying technical positions are becoming deskilled or vanishing offshore (Johnston, 1990; U.S. Department of Labor, 1991; William T. Grant Foundation Commission on Work, Family and Citizenship, 1988).

A number of futurists and policy makers do not feel that these downturns are irreversible. For example, highly paid workers in Sweden have successfully challenged Asian car products with their motto "work more intelligently," not "work harder." Positions have been redefined at Volvo from deadening, repetitive tasks to more creative, multiple tasks and design operations. It is becoming clearer with other examples that technical businesses can succeed in worldwide competition, but only when their workers are highly productive. Productive workers further correlate with motivated and intelligent employees. One domestic experiment that addresses such issues through worker-based management is the Toyota/General Motors (Nummi) partnership in Fremont, California.

In this analysis, it becomes clear that education has a critical role to play in preparing an educated workforce. Education will certainly consist of teaching basic academic skills in the classroom. It will also offer relevant occupational training in industry-related courses (Gaylord-Ross, Siegel, Park, & Wilson, 1988). As this book has detailed, on-the-job work experiences are invaluable in preparing and placing students into jobs. Furthermore, follow-along vocational services seem essential for maintaining high rates of employment (Siegel, Avoke, Paul, Robert, & Gaylord-Ross, 1991; Siegel, Robert, Waxman, & Gaylord-Ross, 1992).

Career Ladders

Given the economic need for well-trained workers, there is obviously some discrepancy between the workers American schools are turning out and extant personnel needs. Besides graduating (or losing) students who are often semiliterate, schools find that many of these youths lack the motivation to work. Although numerous entry-level jobs may be available, many disenfranchised youths size these up as low-paying, ''slave'' jobs that have little potential for career enhancement. In fact, these lower-paying jobs, which have substantially expanded in an increasingly service-oriented economy, have been filled largely by part-time workers such as homemakers, high school students, immigrant newcomers, and senior citizens. Their low pay, typically without benefits, cannot support a head of a household. More importantly, these entry-level positions do not often lead to career advancement. They are, in fact, dead-end slots.

An effective and responsible vocational education program needs to orient and train individuals for employment opportunities that incorporate upward mobility. The program described in this volume was crystallized around the notion of such career ladders. It was believed that CLP staff could penetrate the business community and identify positions with career ladder potential. The staff therefore sought and engaged a number of companies of substance that could understand and promulgate this vision. Students received on-the-job training in these companies, and this training often led to permanent employment. Positions typically had the potential for upward mobility in terms of job classification, salary, and benefits. In some cases, graduates were counseled to take an entry-level job with less career potential, but as a stepping-stone to a subsequent position with greater promise. (See Siegel, Robert, Waxman, & Gaylord-Ross, 1992, and Siegel, Avoke, Paul, Robert, & Gaylord-Ross, 1991, for details on CLP interns' career outcomes.) Since CLP transition specialists worked directly with the graduates, they could guide them through their career paths. Furthermore, the students were told of, or brought into contact

with, former participants in the program who were now succeeding in impressive positions. Such role modeling by competent individuals with similar backgrounds has proved to have a powerful psychological effect.

In the future, we hope to propose a model for extensive job shadowing in the middle school years that will test the effects of intensive role modeling on youths who are facing risky circumstances. In the meantime, CLP has attempted to motivate students to at least entertain the concept of being trained and placed in positions that offer enhancing career paths. As CLP's research data show, a notable proportion of participants have entered successful career paths.

Academic and Vocational Education

In the past, vocational education has often been posited as being at odds with basic academic instruction. Although we view this conflict as unfortunate and avoidable, it is useful to describe its characteristics. In its most adversarial and pejorative form, vocational education is viewed as removing lesser students from academic instruction and preparing them for unknown or outmoded positions—tracking lower-class students into lower-class jobs.

Since vocational education programs are disproportionately populated by minority students, there have been accusations that vocational education is racist in this tracking of students into low expectations and watered-down courses of study. In addition, the past decade has seen a growth in at least the demand for basic academics and excellence-in-education movement. States such as California have identified an academic core curriculum that must be addressed throughout the school day. Narrow interpretations have viewed vocational offerings as being outside the core curriculum. In some instances vocational courses have been reduced or eliminated to make way for expanded academic coursework.

A more mature view of career and vocational education can lead to its effective synthesis with academic instruction. In fact, vocational education should be defined as one instructional strategy within an array of such methods. It should certainly not define itself as a related service and assume second-class status among the curricular offerings. Considerable demands may be placed on youths in their work experiences. In fact, in our experiences we have often seen students perform academic (math, writing) tasks in a more spirited manner in work settings than in classroom contexts. Some businesses and career education programs have begun to systematically cross-reference core academic curricular competencies with competencies performed in vocational activities. Thus, the student can receive justifiable academic credit for vocational experiences. Such syntheses of academic and vocational curricula are important and must be expanded in future endeavors.

The CLP assumed a method that efficiently coordinated traditional academic and vocational coursework. A student received a balance of such work in the 11th and 12th grades. Upon leaving school, the individual conferred with the transition specialist about continuing education as well as about permanent employment. Some persons might opt for one or the other experience. A number of persons, though, prefer to work *and* continue their education, for example, at a community college. Thus, academic and vocational activities are balanced in adult life as well. Ultimately, a curricular agenda that is focused on citizenship (Siegel & Sleeter, 1991), where students learn to own, care for, and serve their communities, will resolve the false conflict between the agendas of vocational and academic education. Excellence in the education of youth for citizenship in a democracy will resolve both the academic and employment ills of our citizenry.

Federal Grants and Local Programming

The rapid growth of the CLP was primarily supported by a model transition federal grant from the U.S. Department of Education. Since the inception of the transition initiative, the federal government has funded a number of similar model programs. This secondary transition network of model programs first attempted to show that successful transition models could be implemented. Success was defined as generating effective interagency relationships that continuously serve the disabled individual from secondary to postschool living, placing the individual into permanent employment in a nonsheltered setting, and constructing a quality of life and related services that encourage the person to flourish independently in the least restrictive environment. A second goal was to have the model projects serve as ''seeds'' to germinate the growth of similar transition programs in that particular region and throughout the country. Model projects receive visitors to their sites and disseminate information at professional meetings; they publish articles and manuals like the present one. Thus, programs like CLP are intended to model exemplary practice and result in an expanding, if not statutory, implementation of the transition concept.

Model programs do not always achieve this dissemination or seeding function. Some programs, in fact, do not last beyond the life of the 3-year federal grant. That is, the external federal money dries up and local agencies do not have the fiscal wherewithal or ideological resolve to continue the program.

The CLP had a more successful experience in engaging local agency support. Historically, the program began as a high school senior work experience program. A teacher was funded by the San Francisco Unified School District and in-kind coordination was provided by San Francisco State University. The federal grant expanded staff and services to include vocational services for graduates through transition specialists. This expansion, particularly at the postschool level, was further supplemented by local funding from the California Department of Rehabilitation. In addition, CLP expanded downward through the 10th and 11th grades as the school district provided more dollars to fund community vocational instructors. The current fiscal support mechanism for CLP evolved from priorities developed by the State of California. The Department of Rehabilitation initially funded over 20 cooperative transition programs throughout the state. Successful CLP activities encouraged the selection of San Francisco as one of these sites. Thus, ongoing local funding for transition activities has been assured by state and local educational and rehabilitation agencies.

Blueprints and Hopes for the Future

The history, experience, and scenario of CLP paints an optimistic and idealistic picture for the future. The success it achieved, and the enlightened response it engendered from the local and state leadership, would certainly seem to bode well. But there were inevitable conflicts as well. Certain aspects of the program's principles—the degree of attention afforded each intern, the ongoing availability of services, the development of sustaining peer support—strained or challenged the existing system beyond the level its resources, regulations, and resolve could attain. Within a year after adopting the program, the intensity of the Employment Skills Workshop decreased, and the availability of ongoing services became greatly constrained. Clearly, for substantive innovation to gain footing in this realm requires change on more than one level.

Urie Bronfenbrenner (1979) talks about human development occurring in four different arenas. *Microsystems*—the isolated interaction between the teacher and the student—are the smallest and most closed relationships. *Mesosystems* include the multiple interactions among people who have overlapping contact with each other, much like Hobbs's (1982) ecosystems. *Exosystems* are those whose events have an impact on people, although there is no contact between the actor and the affected, such as legislative action. Finally, the *macrosystem* is the entire cultural milieu that can pervade all the other systems and create a social ambience and atmosphere conducive (or resistant) to change.

This volume has dealt primarily with micro- and mesosystematic events and has offered a model for effecting change at that level. That is, given the freedom and latitude that was afforded CLP staff through the license of a federal model demonstration project, a significant alteration in the mode of vocational services was suggested and validated. In many ways, it is a reform of vocational services parallel to that proposed by Lisbeth Schorr (1988) for pre- and perinatal services to families—the CLP is based upon the same principles of reasonably sized caseloads and opportunities for long-term relationships to develop. But for either model to precipitate any significant impact, exo- and macrosystematic change must occur subsequent or parallel to local demonstration.

With exosystematic change, even more liberal deregulatory projects must be given legal sanction in order to allow the further testing and implementation of the CLP model (or other innovative, principle-based approaches). Some reforms that would open the door for a dedicated cadre of service delivery professionals would include (a) experimental criteria for case closure and case reopening with Vocational Rehabilitation that are more meaningful than 60 successful days on the job or full unemployment, (b) a cohort approach to caseloads (see chapter 4), (c) alternative criteria to IQ testing for need and eligibility of services, and (d) reform of social security benefits (see Conley, Noble, & Elder, 1986; Elder, Conley, & Noble, 1986). It is hoped that future waves of federal initiatives will provide some of these opportunities. What is actually slated next on the federal agenda?

Social Changes Necessary to Expand and Improve Services

As we begin the 1990s we witness the legislative changes that have moved transition services from a privilege to an entitlement for youth with disabilities. CLP and numerous other exemplary demonstration projects will be providing significant direction to the field as the need for transition services becomes recognized. Development and improvement in transition programs and services can be enhanced through the identification and replication of effective practices. However, among successful efforts there are compo-

nents that can be attributed to the unique differences that exist in local areas. Often, attempts to replicate successful programs do not take this component into account. Each successful program uses the resources of its community and therefore develops a strong sense of local ownership. The more this sense of ownership is dispersed among agencies, organizations, and individuals, the greater the likelihood of commitment to the goal of ensuring that students exiting the program will become well-adjusted and suitably employed members of their communities. Thus there is an interdependency of permission and constraint that ricochets between exo- and mesosystematic progress.

The Office of Special Education and Rehabilitative Services has identified four transition issues for the 1990s: self-determination, secondary curriculum reform, public policy alignment, and anticipated service needs. Each issue is presented briefly here in an effort to assist policy makers and professionals in building an action plan for the next decade.

Self-Determination: Education's Ultimate Goal

Issues of independence, self-sufficiency, and informal decision-making capacity are emerging in rehabilitation and education literature as essential attributes for successful community integration of persons with disabilities. The ultimate goal of education is to increase each student's responsibility for managing his or her own affairs. Actualizing this goal would require a major change in our approach to educating, parenting, and planning for children and youths with disabilities. Reform aimed at self-determination would distribute the responsibility for learning and performance among teachers, parents, and students, with primary control remaining with the students.

Secondary Curriculum Reform: Completing the Initial Transition

Transition should be perceived as a "rite of passage," and a "right of passage" for all youths with disabilities leaving public school programs. If we believe it is a right, we must advocate a major change in educational practices for youths with disabilities. The goal of special education programs should be to prepare individuals with disabilities to work *and* live in their communities. This major change in focus will expand the role of education from preparing individuals for transition to making the initial placement in appropriate community settings with sufficient time for "follow-along" before school exit. The measure of effectiveness of secondary special education programs should be not only employment, but also the quality of community life experienced after exiting school.

Public Policy Alignment: Supporting Educational Efforts

The commitment to integration and the provision of transition services necessitates a redirection of our secondary special education programs to ensure that all youths with disabilities have the opportunity to become well-adjusted, suitably employed members of their communities. As our educational efforts become more focused on programming for future environments, the need for adjustments in current policy and procedures will become apparent. We have already identified three areas of policy that will need adjusting: graduation/high school completion, compliance with the Fair Labor Standards Act, and the Supplemental Security Income (SSI) program. The issues of graduation and high school completion should be aimed at continuing to engage or to reengage graduates or dropouts in responsive programs until successful transitions are completed. Utilization of community work sites as educational environments has raised a conflict between schools and the U.S. Department of Labor, which is responsible for ensuring that individuals with disabilities are not being exploited in the workplace. The Fair Labor Standards Act allows training in community work sites, but a clear understanding of when and under what conditions this can be done must be articulated. Recent changes in the SSI program include incentives that can provide needed support for individuals to live and work in the community without losing benefits prematurely. School personnel and families must acquire a working knowledge of these entitlements and how they may be applied.

Anticipated Service Needs: Waiting Lists for Adult Services

Deinstitutionalization and the mandate for free, appropriate public education have led to an implied promise of responsive community-based adult services. This implication is false! The vast majority of students with disabilities are leaving school and joining ever-expanding waiting lists with little hope of timely placements in responsive programs. Families, educators, and adult service providers must develop strategies for working together to improve this untenable situation.

These four issues build upon the ideas of equal access, independence, and integration that have been central to special education policy in the last two decades. In the nineties, however, these ideas may reach new levels of actualization as students are placed in a position to influence their own learning and its outcomes. As secondary curricula and policy acknowledge the importance of vocational and independent living competencies—*as well as* academic competencies—community networks of schools, adult service agencies, employers, families, and friends will need to communicate and advocate for efficient, integrated service provision. Leadership at all levels is necessary to address these issues. If it is provided, the 1990s could hold special significance in the history of special education and the lives of the children and youths it serves.

America 2000

On April 18, 1991, President George Bush released *America 2000: An Education Strategy* (U.S. Department of Education, 1990a). This is a bold, complex, and long-range plan to move every community in America toward the national educational goals set by the president and the governors at an education summit meeting in 1990.

In the past 15 years, students with disabilities have successfully integrated our nation's schools. However, the shortcomings in our schools that led the National Commission on Excellence in Education to declare us a ''nation at risk'' are shared by special education. Outcome and follow-up studies indicate that many individuals fail to make a successful transition to community work and adult living.

America 2000 presents a national strategy, not a federal program. It recognizes that real educational reform happens community by community, school by school, and only when people come to understand what they must do for themselves and their children and set about to do it. It states (p. 19) that by the year 2000:

1. All children in America will start school ready to learn.

2. The high school graduation rate will increase to at least 90 percent.

3. American students will leave grades four, eight, and twelve having demonstrated competency in challenging subject matter including English, mathematics, science, history, and geography; and every school in America will ensure that all students learn to use their minds well, so they may be prepared

for responsible citizenship, further learning, and productive employment in our modern economy.

4. U.S. students will be first in the world in science and mathematics achievement.

5. Every adult American will be literate and will possess the knowledge and skills necessary to compete in a global economy and exercise the rights and responsibilities of citizenship.

6. Every school in America will be free of drugs and violence and will offer a disciplined environment conducive to learning.

The CLP is aligned with the reforms that are currently under way to improve the outcomes for individuals making the transition from school to the community. The ordering principle of the CLP, services that are shaped by the needs of the youths served, must be the bottom line that holds us accountable. The contexts, services, and tools embodied in the six principles of CLP combined with the enthusiasm of its implementation present a unique formula for pursuing the reforms necessary to enable youths with disabilities to become well-adjusted, suitably employed members of our communities.

The final layer of change, then, is macrosystematic. It is a change in the way our entire society views its responsibility to the post–high school outcomes of its youth. Ultimately, the success of the service changes proposed in this volume is conditional upon that macrosystematic, culture-sized change. Quality education costs much more money than we currently spend on it, as does quality adult service. Beyond the basic needs of education, training, placement, and support lies the universal need for more authentic and meaningful relationships and lives. When this need finds its way into the mainstream and is articulated in a fashion that stimulates a culture-wide change in values, then education will no longer be labeled as either academic or vocational. Instead, it will be defined simply as a service to enable full participation in a democratic society. This service will be readily available to those who need it, and will not be squandered on those who do not. It will serve the desire for excellence that resides in all citizens and will transform work, study, social integration, and the evolution of all our institutions into tools for making meaningful, connected, and satisfying lives for all.

References

Anema, D., & Lefkowitz, W. (1990). *Don't get fired! How to keep a job.* Belmont, CA: Fearon/Janus/Quercus.

Bissonnette, D., & Pimentel, R. (1984). *Performance based placement manual: Job development techniques that work!* Northridge, CA: Milt Wright and Associates.

Bronfenbrenner, U. (1979). *The ecology of human development: Experiments by nature and design.* Cambridge, MA: Harvard University Press.

California State Department of Education. (1986). *WorkAbility job development manual.* Sacramento: California State Department of Education.

Clark, G. (1979). *Career education for the handicapped child in the elementary classroom.* Denver: Love.

Clark, G., & Kolstoe, O. P. (1990). *Career development and transition education for adolescents with disabilities.* Boston: Allyn & Bacon.

Cole, B., & Heilman, J. (1979). *The laundry works.* Sacramento, CA: Juvenile Court Schools Center, Office of the Santa Clara County Superintendent of Schools and California State Department of Education.

Conley, R. W., Noble, J. H., Jr., & Elder, J. K. (1986). Problems with the service system. In W. E. Kiernan & J. A. Stark (Eds.), *Pathways to employment for adults with developmental disabilities* (pp. 67–83). Baltimore: Paul H. Brookes Publishing.

DeStefano, L., & Snauwaert, D. (1989). *A value-critical approach to transition policy analysis.* Secondary Transition Intervention Effectiveness Institute. Champaign, IL: University of Illinois.

Edgerton, R. B. (1967). *The cloak of competence: Stigma in the lives of the retarded.* Berkeley: University of California.

Elder, J. K., Conley, R. W., & Noble, J. H., Jr. (1986). The service system. In W. E. Kiernan & J. A. Stark (Eds.), *Pathways to employment for adults with developmental disabilities* (pp. 53–66). Baltimore: Paul H. Brookes Publishing.

Entering the world of work: Your first days on the job. (1979). Bloomington, IL: McNight.

Gaylord-Ross, R., Siegel, S., Park, H., & Wilson, W. (1988). Secondary vocational training. In R. Gaylord-Ross (Ed.), *Vocational education for persons with handicaps.* Palo Alto, CA: Mayfield Publishing.

Gibbs, J. (1987). *Tribes: A process for social development and cooperative learning.* Santa Rosa, CA: Center Source Publications.

Goldstein, A. P., Sprafkin, R. P., Gershaw, N. J., & Klein, P. (1980). *Skillstreaming the adolescent.* Champaign, IL: Research.

Harris, L., & Associates. (1986). *Disabled Americans' self perceptions: Bringing disabled into the mainstream.* Study no. 854009. New York: Lou Harris and Associates.

Hazel, J. S., Schumaker, J. B., Sherman, J. A., & Sheldon-Wildgen, J. S. (1981). *ASSET: A social skills program for adolescents.* Champaign, IL: Research.

Hobbs, N. (1982). *The troubled and troubling child.* San Francisco: Jossey-Bass.

Irvin, L. (1988). Vocational assessment in school and rehabilitation programs. In R. Gaylord-Ross (Ed.), *Vocational education for persons with handicaps* (pp. 111–141). Palo Alto, CA: Mayfield.

Johnston, W. B. (1990). *Workforce 2000: Executive summary.* New York: Hudson Institute (317-545-1000).

Kelly, J. A. (1982). *Social-skills training: A practical guide for interventions.* New York: Springer.

Langmuir, C. R. (1954). *Personnel Test Industry–Oral Directions Test forms.* New York: Psychological Corporation.

Rusch, F. R. (1986). *Competitive employment issues and strategies.* Baltimore: Paul H. Brookes.

Schorr, L., with Schorr, D. (1988). *Within our reach: Breaking the cycle of disadvantage.* New York: Doubleday.

Siegel, S. (1988). The Career Ladder Program: Implementing Re-ED principles in vocational settings. *Behavioral Disorders, 14,* 1, 16–26.

Siegel, S., Avoke, S. K., Paul, P., Robert, M., & Gaylord-Ross, R. (1991). A second look at the adult lives of participants in the Career Ladder Program. *Journal of Vocational Rehabilitation, 1,* 4, 9–24.

Siegel, S., & Gaylord-Ross, R. (1991). Factors associated with job success among youths with learning disabilities. *Journal of Learning Disabilities, 24,* 1, 40–47.

Siegel, S., Park, H., Gumpel, T., Ford, J., Tappe, P., & Gaylord-Ross, R. (1990). Research in vocational special education. In R. Gaylord-Ross (Ed.), *Issues and research in special education, Vol. 1.* New York: Teachers College Press.

Siegel, S., Robert, M., Waxman, M., & Gaylord-Ross, R. (1992). A follow-along study of participants in a longitudinal transition program for youths with mild disabilities. *Exceptional Children, 58,* 4, 346–356.

Siegel, S., & Sleeter, C. E. (1991). Transforming transition: Next stages for the school-to-work transition movement. *Career Development for Exceptional Individuals, 14,* 1, 27–41.

Simon, S. B., Howe, L. W., & Kirschenbaum, H. (1972). *Values clarification: A handbook of practical strategies for teachers and students.* New York: A&W.

Stodden, R. A., & Boone, R. (1987). Assessing transition services for handicapped youth: A cooperative interagency approach. *Exceptional Children, 53,* 6, 537–545.

Stodden, R. A., & Ianacone, R. (1981). Career/vocational assessment of the special needs individual: A conceptual model. *Exceptional Children, 47,* 600–609.

U.S. Department of Education. (1990a). *America 2000: An education strategy.* Sourcebook 0S91-13. Washington, DC: U.S. Government Printing Office.

U.S. Department of Education. (1990b). *Twelfth annual report to Congress on the implementation of the Education of the Handicapped Act.* Office of Special Education & Rehabilitative Services, 0-272-000:QL3. Washington, DC: U.S. Government Printing Office.

U.S. Department of Labor. (1991). *The Secretary's Commission on Achieving Necessary Skills (SCANS).* Washington, DC: U.S. Government Printing Office.

Varenhorst, B. B. (1980). *Curriculum guide for student peer counseling training.* Palo Alto, CA: B. B. Varenhorst, 350 Grove Drive, Portola Valley, CA 94028.

Wagner, M., & Shaver, D. (1989). *Educational programs and achievements of secondary special education students: Findings from the National Longitudinal Transition Study.* Menlo Park, CA: Stanford Research Institute.

Wehman, P. (1981). *Competitive employment: New horizons for severely disabled individuals.* Baltimore: Paul H. Brookes.

Wehman, P., Moon, M. S., Everson, J. M., Wood, W., & Barcus, J. M. (1988). *Transition from school to work: New challenges for youth with severe disabilities.* Baltimore: Paul H. Brookes.

What are company benefits? (1977). [Film]. Kalamazoo, MI: Interpretive Education, a division of IE Products, Inc.

William T. Grant Foundation Commission on Work, Family and Citizenship. (1988). *The forgotten half: Pathways to success for America's youth and young families.* Washington, DC: William T. Grant Foundation Commission on Work, Family and Citizenship.

Wilson, W. J. (1987). *The truly disadvantaged.* Chicago: University of Chicago Press.